LANGUAGE, CULTURE, IDENTITY AND CITIZENSHIP IN COLLEGE CLASSROOMS AND COMMUNITIES

Language, Culture, Identity and Citizenship in College Classrooms and Communities examines what takes place in writing classrooms beyond academic analytical and argumentative writing to include forms that engage students in navigating the civic, political, social and cultural spheres they inhabit. It presents a conceptual framework for imagining how writing instructors can institute campus-wide initiatives, such as Writing Across Communities, that attempt to connect the classroom and the campus to the students' various communities of belonging, especially students who have been historically underserved.

This framework reflects an emerging perspective—writing across difference—that challenges the argument that the best writing instructors can do is develop the skills and knowledge students need to make a successful transition from their home discourses to academic discourses. Instead, the value inherent in the full repertoire of linguistic, cultural and semiotic resources students use in their varied communities of belonging needs to be acknowledged and students need to be encouraged to call on these to the fullest extent possible in the course of learning what they are being taught in the writing classroom. Pedagogically, this book provides educators with the rhetorical, discursive and literacy tools needed to implement this approach.

Juan C. Guerra is a Professor of English and Chair of the Department of American Ethnic Studies at the University of Washington, Seattle, USA.

NCTE-Routledge Research Series

Series Editors: Valerie Kinloch and Susi Long

Alsup
Teacher Identity Discourses: Negotiating Personal and Professional Spaces

Banks
Race, Rhetoric, and Technology: Searching for Higher Ground

Daniell/Mortensen
Women and Literacy: Local and Global Inquiries for a New Century

Rickford/Sweetland/Rickford/Grano
African American, Creole and Other Vernacular Englishes in Education: A Bibliographic Resource

Guerra
Language, Culture, Identity and Citizenship in College Classrooms and Communities

Haddix
Cultivating Racial and Linguistic Diversity in Literacy Teacher Education: Teachers Like Me

The NCTE-Routledge Research Series, copublished by the National Council of Teachers of English and Routledge, focuses on literacy studies in P-12 classroom and related contexts. Volumes in this series are invited publications or publications submitted in response to a call for manuscripts. They are primarily authored or co-authored works which are theoretically significant and broadly relevant to the P-12 literacy community. The series may also include occasional landmark compendiums of research.

The scope of the series includes qualitative and quantitative methodologies; a range of perspectives and approaches (e.g., sociocultural, cognitive, feminist, linguistic, pedagogical, critical, historical, anthropological); and research on diverse populations, contexts (e.g., classrooms, school systems, families, communities), and forms of literacy (e.g., print, electronic, popular media).

LANGUAGE, CULTURE, IDENTITY AND CITIZENSHIP IN COLLEGE CLASSROOMS AND COMMUNITIES

Juan C. Guerra

NEW YORK AND LONDON

National Council of Teachers of English
1111 W. Kenyon Road, Urbana, Illinois 61801-1096

A co-publication of Routledge and NCTE

First published 2016
by Routledge
711 Third Avenue, New York, NY 10017

and by Routledge
2 Park Square, Milton Park, Abingdon, Oxon OX14 4RN

Routledge is an imprint of the Taylor & Francis Group, an informa business

Library of Congress Cataloging-in-Publication Data
Guerra, Juan C., 1949–
   Language, culture, identity and citizenship in college classrooms and
communities / by Juan C. Guerra.
      pages cm
   Includes index.
   1. Language and culture—Study and teaching.   2. Sociolinguistics—
Study and teaching.   3. Academic writing—Study and teaching—Social
aspects.   4. Multicultural education.   I. Title.
   P35.G84 2016
   306.44—dc23
   2015011567

ISBN: 978-0-415-72277-3 (hbk)
ISBN: 978-0-415-72278-0 (pbk)
ISBN: 978-1-315-85808-1 (ebk)
NCTE stock number: 22780

Typeset in Bembo
by Apex CoVantage, LLC

para ti mami
for you babe
for you too mi'jo
and for all my students

CONTENTS

PREFACE

If this book has a specific beginning, it is the Literacies and Literary Representations Symposium that Michelle Hall Kells organized at Texas A&M in October 2000, titled "Posing Questions and Framing Conversations about Language and Hispanic Identities." In my keynote address at the symposium, later published as the lead essay in Kells, Balester, and Villanueva's edited collection, *Latino/a Discourses: On Language, Identity and Literacy Education* (2004), I introduced *transcultural repositioning*, a concept I had coined for an invited talk in April of that same year at the Peabody College of Education at Vanderbilt University, titled "The Practice of Transcultural Repositioning: A Possible Alternative in Education to Assimilation and Accommodation" (2000). In my view, the concept of transcultural repositioning captures the liminal qualities in the reading, writing and rhetorical practices that students in my classes invoked whenever I asked them to tackle any of the many prompts I assigned during my 15 years as a basic writing teacher at the University of Illinois at Chicago in the 1970s and 1980s, and my 3 years as Director of the Educational Opportunity Writing Program at the University of Washington at Seattle in the early 1990s (see Guerra, 1997, 2004). In a more recent publication, I describe it as the rhetorical ability many disenfranchised students have learned to enact intuitively, but one they must also learn to regulate self-reflectively if they hope to move back and forth more productively across "different languages and dialects, different social classes, different cultural and artistic forms, different ways of seeing and thinking about the increasingly fluid and hybridized world emerging all around us" (Guerra, 2007, p. 140).

About 12 years ago, Michelle—who appreciated the explanatory power reflected in the concept of transcultural repositioning and used it as a theoretical component in her own research (see Kells, 2002, 2004)—coined another term, *Writing Across Communities*, that lies at the heart of the work we have been doing together. Six years ago, in the context of what we saw as the promise of the Writing Across Communities initiative that she and her colleagues established at the University of New Mexico in 2005, Michelle and I developed a proposal for a pragmatic book that would illustrate the logic that informs the approach. Because we quickly realized that the initiative Michelle and her colleagues had developed still needed time to mature before we could extrapolate much from the research data they had collected, we decided that scholars in composition and literacy studies interested in this kind of work would profit more fully if we first developed a book-length treatment of the theoretical notions informing a Writing Across Communities approach, then followed it up with a book-length qualitative case study. After we completed our book proposal, but before we persuaded an editor to consider it for publication, Michelle decided to return to a book project she had temporarily put aside, currently titled *Vicente Ximenes and LBJ's Great Society: Twentieth-Century Mexican American Civil Rights Rhetoric* (forthcoming). Because several theoretical ideas related to our project were coming together in my own thinking, Michelle and I agreed that I should go ahead and, in a book of my own, identify the key theoretical principles that inform a Writing Across Communities approach to the teaching of reading, writing and rhetoric. This book is the result of that decision.

In the ensuing six years, I have broadened the scope of what I think it takes to establish a campus-wide approach to the teaching and learning of reading, writing and rhetoric relevant to the present moment. To begin with, I have come to see the Writing Across Communities initiative at UNM as the manifestation of an emerging perspective in the field that scholars are increasingly referring to as *writing across difference*. According to proponents of this perspective, we are no longer in a position to argue that the best we can do is to inculcate our students with the predispositions they need to make a successful transition from their home discourses to academic discourses. Instead, we need to acknowledge the value inherent in the repertoire of linguistic, cultural and semiotic resources our students use in all their communities of belonging (Kells, 2007, p. 88) and encourage them to call on these as they best see fit in the course of learning what we are teaching them in the college writing classroom. In short, our students can no longer become successful readers, writers or rhetoricians by simply figuring out how to meet traditional expectations related to the production of Standard Written American English. As Selfe (2009) so elegantly puts it,

> Young people need to know that their role as rhetorical agents is open, not artificially foreclosed by the limits of their teachers' imaginations. They need a full quiver of semiotic modes from which to select, role models who can teach them to think critically about a range of communication tools, and multiple ways of reaching their audience. They do not need teachers who insist on *one* tool or *one* way.

p. 645, emphasis in original

In response to Selfe's call to action and in line with the work that Michelle and I have been doing over the past 16 years, *Language, Culture, Identity and Citizenship in College Classrooms and Communities* presents a conceptual framework for imagining how we can institute campus-wide initiatives, such as Writing Across Communities, that attempt to connect the college classroom to the students' other communities of belonging. The book accomplishes this task by first tackling one of the biggest conundrums we currently face in the field regarding the extent to which fixity (standardization) and fluidity (difference) can be utilized simultaneously (Chapter 1) if we are going to provide all our students, but especially the disenfranchised among them, with the tools to navigate and negotiate the range of reading, writing and rhetorical challenges they encounter in college classrooms over the course of their studies and in communities beyond once they complete them. In Part I of the book, I take the four key dimensions that inform a writing across difference approach—language, culture, identity and citizenship—and discuss each in turn before Part II, which contains case studies I conducted in a single classroom and in a campus-wide program to test my theories.

After exploring the dialectical relationship between fixity and fluidity in the introductory chapter, I shift the discussion to the role that language (Chapter 2) plays in the lives of students—especially the disenfranchised among them—who are required to take writing courses in postsecondary institutions. There is arguably no issue more salient in composition and literacy studies right now, because language is at the heart of everything we do in the classroom as reading, writing and rhetoric teachers and one of the key semiotic practices our students must know how to enact productively over the course of their everyday lives. In light of recent debates about how best to respond to language difference in the writing classroom, the study of language strikes me as the ideal place to begin any conversation about how we can bring about change in our curricular and pedagogical practices, as well as in the larger society as a whole.

At the same time, we need to acknowledge how inextricably language and culture (Chapter 3) are tied to one another if we hope to make meaningful use of our students' lived experiences in the course of working with them to fill their "quiver(s)" (Selfe, 2009, p. 645) with a provisional array of linguistic, cultural and semiotic resources that we as theorists, researchers and educators have identified. In tandem with their relationship to one another, language and culture in turn produce and are produced by the shifting identities (Chapter 4) that our students choose to appropriate and perform as they navigate and negotiate the varied social spaces they inhabit in the classroom, on campus and beyond. Finally, we need to think about how these three dimensions (language, culture and identity) can be utilized in our historically grounded efforts to cultivate citizenship (Chapter 5) among our students through the work we do together in the college classroom and in relationship to their other communities of belonging.

As we work collectively toward one of the most important outcomes of organized education—producing *citizens in the making* who are not only responsible in themselves and to others, but who are also committed to equity, inclusion and social justice—we must remain continuously aware of the key dimensions that inform this outcome. But because theoretical concepts have inherent constraints and limitations, we need to make sure we test our theories, if only in the most general sense. For that reason, the chapters in Part II demonstrate how the interactive elements I have just described manifest themselves in a single college writing classroom (Chapter 6) and in a first of its kind campus-wide Writing Across Communities initiative (Chapter 7) that attempts to integrate the individual college classroom, the campus and our students' other communities of belonging. There are few things more difficult to undertake through our scholarly work than lasting institutional change in the social spaces we occupy, but we will undoubtedly shortchange ourselves if we aim for anything less.

Language, Culture, Identity and Citizenship in College Classrooms and Communities should appeal to theorists, researchers, educators, graduate students and advanced undergraduate students in the fields of composition, literacy, rhetoric, multilingual, and education studies interested in exploring how to teach reading, writing and rhetoric in ways that acknowledge language difference, transcultural perspectives, identity formation and citizenship. Because the book reflects the growing alliance among scholars in first and second language studies, it should also appeal to anyone who is trying to find ways to address the needs of the growing number of migrant, immigrant and international students enrolling in postsecondary writing classes at an unprecedented clip. Theorists, researchers and educators on the international stage who are wrestling with many of these same issues will find that *Language, Culture, Identity and Citizenship in College Classrooms and Communities* provides them with conceptual ideas and examples of how we can best equip students with the repertoires of rhetorical and discursive practices they need to navigate and negotiate the complicated social and cultural circumstances they face in the late modern era.

One last thing: Except for the extended passage in Spanish and Spanish/ English that opens Chapter 2 and is translated in an endnote at the end of that chapter, the English translation of all Spanish words, phrases and sentences used in this book can be found listed in order of appearance in Spanish to English glossaries at the end of each chapter. In contrast to the typical practice in the field of inserting the English translation in brackets immediately after a passage in Spanish, I decided to include English translations in separate chapter glossaries to provide readers with the experience of encountering Spanish words, phrases and sentences in isolation. I am hoping this will allow readers with varied levels of competency in Spanish to take notice of the immediate tensions they experience as they struggle to translate and understand Spanish words, phrases and sentences at the very moment they encounter them in the book.

References

Guerra, J.C. (1997). The place of intercultural literacy in the writing classroom. In C. Severino, J.C. Guerra & J.E. Butler (Eds.), *Writing in multicultural settings* (pp. 248–260). New York, NY: MLA.

Guerra, J.C. (2000). The practice of transcultural repositioning: A possible alternative in education to assimilation and accommodation. Peabody College, Department of Teaching and Learning, Vanderbilt University.

Guerra, J.C. (2004). Putting literacy in its place: Nomadic consciousness and the practice of transcultural repositioning. In C. Gutiérrez-Jones (Ed.), *Rebellious readings: The dynamics of Chicana/o literacy* (pp. 19–37). Center for Chicana/o Studies: UC Santa Barbara.

Guerra, J.C. (2007). Out of the valley: Transcultural repositioning as a rhetorical practice in ethnographic research and other aspects of everyday life. In C. Lewis, P. Enciso & E.B. Moje (Eds.), *Reframing sociocultural research on literacy: Identity, agency, and power* (pp. 137–162). Mahwah, NJ: Erlbaum.

Kells, M.H. (2002). Linguistic contact zones in the college writing classroom: An examination of ethnolinguistic identity and language attitudes. *Written Communication*, 19(1), 5–43.

Kells, M.H. (2004). Understanding the rhetorical value of *Tejano* codeswitching. In M.H. Kells, V. Balester & V. Villanueva (Eds.), *Latino/a discourses: On language, identity and literacy education* (pp. 24–39). Portsmouth, NH: Boynton/Cook.

Kells, M.H. (2007). Writing across communities: Deliberation and the discursive possibilities of WAC. *Reflections*, 6(1), 87–108.

Kells, M.H. (forthcoming). *Vicente Ximenes and LBJ's Great Society: Twentieth-Century Mexican American Civil Rights Rhetoric*. Manuscript.

Kells, M.H., Balester, V. & Villanueva, V. (Eds.). (2004). *Latino/a discourses: On language, identity and literacy education* (pp. 24–39). Portsmouth, NH: Boynton/Cook.

Selfe, C.L. (2009). The movement of air, the breath of meaning: Aurality and multimodal composing. *College Composition and Communication*, 60(4), 616–663.

ACKNOWLEDGMENTS

My sincere thanks to the UW Office of Research for providing financial support through the Royalty Research Fund and the UW Office of the Dean of the College of Arts & Sciences for providing additional resources so that I could complete my work in a timely fashion. Without their generous backing, this project would never have come to fruition. For their part in approving the field research related to this project, I would also like to thank the UW Human Subjects Division for their patient and detailed responses to my queries and questions. The work many of us do at the UW would not be possible without their on-going help and support.

I am very grateful to have had the opportunity to work with my publishers (Naomi Silverman at Routledge and Kurt Austin at NCTE), my series editors (Valerie Kinloch and Susi Long), and their support staff (Merritt Duncan and Brianna Pennella) over the last three years. The work they did behind the scenes to make the publication of this book happen was spectacular. Special thanks, too, for the incredible feedback that outside reviewers provided after engaging an earlier draft of this book; their suggestions and ideas helped me think through a number of issues I was struggling with and reminded me to honor the work of scholars on whose shoulders I stand. I, of course, take full responsibility for any shortcomings this book may still have.

For their intellectual, emotional and spiritual support while I worked on this project, I would like to thank the following friends and colleagues: Anis Bawarshi, Nancy Bou Ayash, Limarys Caraballo, Sergio Casillas, Catherine Compton-Lilly, Patricia Enciso, María Fránquiz, Arline García, Allison Green, Carol Green, James Green, Gary Handwerk, Megan Faver Hartline, Bruce Horner, Michelle Hall Kells, Rebecca Lorimer Leonard, Min-Zhan Lu, Ann Shivers-McNair, Luz Murillo, Suhanthie Motha, Django Paris, Brian Reed, Angela Rounsaville,

Jacqueline Jones Royster, Mary Sheridan, Sandra Silberstein, Martha Townsend, Priscilla Wald and Christopher Wilkey.

My biggest thanks go to Michelle, who for the last 16 years has served as an intellectual partner whose scholarly work has enriched mine in inestimable ways. Michelle, your fingerprints are all over this book. Thanks for always being there. A very special thanks as well to Limarys for her invaluable contributions during our intense conversations when I was first conceptualizing the framework for this book, to Ann for taking over the transcription of the interviews when I found myself pressed for time, to Arline for help with the Spanish (and the English translations) I used throughout the book, and to Anis and Priscilla for generously reading earlier versions of the manuscript and providing tons of incredibly useful feedback.

Lest you think I have forgotten you, an enthusiastic shout out to the many Fellows and mentors in NCTE's Cultivating New Voices Among Scholars of Color program that I have been affiliated with for more than 12 years. You are without a doubt one of the best things that has ever happened in my professional life, and I will be forever grateful for your collegiality, your contributions to my personal and professional development and the painstaking work you do to contribute to our profession and to give back to our communities of belonging. Thank you all for being an integral part of my extended family.

Many thanks as well to my students in English 479 (Winter 2012) for sharing their writing and personal views, my colleagues in the Writing Across Communities program at the University of New Mexico for sharing their thoughts, documents and data, and my siblings in south Texas, Dallas, San Antonio and the Houston area for sharing their thoughts and their lives with me as well. Your willingness to take time out of your hectic schedules to sit with me while I pummeled you with interview questions is a measure of our mutual respect for all the differences we bring into the world. Each of you contributed more than just your oral and written words to this project; you gave it life and transformed it into something more than a theoretical treatise. A special thank you to the students who enrolled in my graduate course at the UW on Writing Across Difference in Spring 2013, Autumn 2013 and Spring 2015; our rich and engaging conversations in class provided me with the kind of feedback I needed to think through the ideas in this book.

As has been true during my more than 40 years as a theorist, researcher and educator in composition and literacy studies, everything I do professionally finds its greatest meaning in the support I have always received from my families in Seattle, Chicago and Texas. I want to thank you all for making the biggest difference. You have not only shared your lives with me in ways that provoked my continued interest in the roles that language, culture, identity and citizenship play in our lives, you have always demonstrated unwavering interest in and support for my professional work and my personal well-being. Your kindness, generosity and love have always sustained me, especially in trying moments when life became more than a notion. As always, a very special thanks to my wife, Diane, and my son, Sean, who have always been there for me. The two of you have always inspired me and have imbued everything I do with meaning, and always, your love has made me feel safe to take chances and to do everything I can to make our lives and the lives of others better than they would have been otherwise.

A version of Chapter 2 previously appeared as "From Code-Segregation to Code-Switching to Code-Meshing: Finding Deliverance from Deficit Thinking through Language Awareness and Performance" in the *61st Yearbook of the Literacy Research Association*. Copyright 2012 by the Literacy Research Association. Used with permission. A version of Chapter 3 appeared as "Invoking Modalities in the Writing Classroom" in *Time and Space in Literacy Research*. Copyright 2014 by Routledge. Used with permission. A version of Chapter 5 appeared as "Cultivating Transcultural Citizenship in a Discursive Democracy" in *Texts of Consequence: Composing Social Activism for the Classroom and Community*. Copyright 2013 by Hampton Press. Used with permission. A version of Chapter 7 appeared as "Enacting Institutional Change: The Work of Literacy Insurgents in the Academy and Beyond" in the *Journal of Advanced Composition*. Copyright 2014 by the *Journal of Advanced Composition*. Used with permission.

1

FIXITY AND FLUIDITY

The year is 1961. I am lying alone in a bed that I typically share with two younger siblings early on a Sunday morning reading a book I checked out from my elementary school library. I am engaged in the new—for me—social practice of reading, a habit I developed a couple of years earlier that compels me to immerse myself in fictional worlds created by various authors to escape the social, cultural and political constraints that conspire to keep me fixed, tied to a particular *chronotope* where "time, as it were, thickens, takes on flesh" and "space becomes charged and responsive to the movements of time, plot and history" (Bakhtin, 1981, p. 84). If, at that moment, we could have zoomed up into the sky from the bedroom and looked down as we are now able to do using the perspective Google Maps provides, we would have located that bedroom in one of 34 buildings laid out in a neat barracks-like matrix that together made (and still make) up *Los Vecinos*,[1] the housing project where my eight siblings and I grew up. Except for an Appalachian family that lived in the building immediately behind ours, every family living in the 29 four- and six-unit apartment buildings was Mexican or Mexican American. The families living in the 5 two-unit apartment buildings carefully segregated from our own were African American. We all knew our place so well at the time that in all my years living there I never once befriended an African American child, nor one of them me, even though I walked past their homes every day on my way to an overwhelmingly Mexican public elementary school that we did not share with them, located immediately south of the housing project.

If we were to zoom farther out, we would notice that *Los Vecinos* is located in Harlingen, a small rural town in the Lower Rio Grande Valley of South Texas methodically divided in half by railroad tracks that run through its middle. Like me, everyone (or so it seemed at the time) who lived west of those tracks in the

housing project or in one of the small, generally well-kept, but sometimes dilapi-
dated working-class homes on the west side of town was of Mexican origin. *Los
bolillos*—as housing project residents disparagingly referred to white people in
our town when they felt the need to put them in their place—lived east of the
railroad tracks in their comfortable middle-class homes with modestly mani-
cured lawns. I am certain—although I do not remember being aware of it at the
age of 11—that there must have been a few middle-class families of Mexican
origin living on the east side among the Anglos. West side residents referred to
them as *los vendidos*, a stinging rebuke used by adults in *el barrio* to describe those
they saw as having turned their backs on our shared language, culture and way
of life. Although I encountered both groups—*bolillos* and *vendidos*—on a regular
basis in the public junior high and high schools I attended later, like everyone
else in town, I pretty much hung out with my own kind. It was comfortable,
and it felt like home. But it was also the only thing we were permitted to do. We
had no other choice.

If we zoomed just a bit farther out, we would see precisely demarcated agri-
cultural plots of land spreading out in all directions from my hometown on
which an array of crops were and are still cultivated. Scattered among them you
would see the cotton and tomato fields where many of us in *Los Vecinos*—those
of us who did not head north late in the spring as part of the annual stream of
migrant farmworkers—labored to help our families make ends meet, earning 3
to 6 dollars (depending on how much we were able to pick) for a 12-to-14-hour
day of grueling work in the stifling heat and humidity of a south Texas summer.
In many cases, it was a life made even more difficult by a condition too many
of us had to deal with at home: alcoholism in the midst of poverty and all that
it entails.

Because of our current fascination in composition and literacy studies with
the role that fluidity plays in our day-to-day lives, we sometimes forget that the
rigid, stratified existence I just described is not a thing of the past, something
experienced only by those of us old enough to have lived in a pre-civil rights era
when every social, cultural, educational and political institution in this country
conspired to keep us segregated from one another on the basis of our language,
culture, identity and citizenship status. At the same time that it acknowledges
and provides a sense of the possibilities available to our students in a volatile
world where difference has replaced sameness and is now the new norm (Lu &
Horner, 2013), this book makes every effort to remind us that fixity continues
to be an inescapable element of our lives. But the book also fiercely argues that
we, as educators in composition and literacy studies, must delve into the intrica-
cies of what it means to live in social spaces[2] where nothing—not our languages,
cultures, identities, or citizenship status—ever stands still despite the best efforts
of institutional and ideological forces operating to hold us all—especially the
disenfranchised among us—in rigidly defined and stratified categories. In so
doing, I call on my own lived experience, first because the theoretical arguments

I plan to make will become too ethereal if they are not grounded in blood, flesh and bone, but also because anyone who is going to ask students to use their lived experience[3] to write themselves into being in college classrooms and other communities of belonging[4] must be willing to do the same.

A Deleuzian Dreamscape of Desire

Wherever we turn nowadays, we are practically overwhelmed by a Deleuzian dreamscape of desire informed by a rhizomatic interpretation of reality full of centers, but no beginnings or endings (Deleuze & Guattari, 1987). In ways that we may not have realized before, a Deleuzian orientation has infected our thinking in the field of composition and literacy studies and in an array of related disciplines. As a consequence, we are repeatedly reminded that everything around us in the physical, social, linguistic, cultural, political and virtual spaces we inhabit is in continuous motion despite the best efforts of conservative elements in our society to stop everything in its tracks, to contain the irreverent nature of life out of a deep-felt sense that centrifugal forces are tearing apart centripetal systems (Bakhtin, 1981) that have seemingly been in place forever. Motion and its cousin mobility (Urry, 2005, 2007) have always been terrifying, but in an era of unprecedented change reflected in transnational travel, multimedia overload and global marketplaces that influence our lifestyle choices and our work-related options, space and time seem to be picking up more speed with the announcement of each new technological innovation (Fairclough, 1999, p. 75). As a result, many among us often feel as if we are at the precipice, teetering on the edge of oblivion, lost in the muck of a new kind of space and time that more than ever refuses to stand still. In Deleuze and Guattari's words,

> We live today in an age of partial objects, bricks that have been shattered to bits, and leftovers. We no longer believe in the myth of the existence of fragments that, like pieces of an antique statue, are merely waiting for the last one to turn up so that they may all be glued back together to create a unity that is precisely the same as the original unity. We no longer believe in a primordial totality that once existed, or in a final totality that awaits us at some future date. We no longer believe in the dull grey outlines of a dreary, colorless dialectic of evolution aimed at forming a harmonious whole out of heterogeneous bits by rounding off the edges. We believe in totalities that are peripheral.
>
> *1983, p. 42*

As researchers, theorists and educators in composition and literacy studies, we are obligated to develop and provide our students with the strategic and tactical tools they need to navigate and negotiate the unprecedented levels of change they encounter in their lives as readers, writers and rhetoricians in college classrooms and other communities of belonging. It is also our responsibility to continuously remind them that they need to work on acquiring a "full quiver of semiotic modes," a rich repertoire of linguistic and cultural practices they can call on whenever they need to address the "wickedly complex communicative tasks" that we all face in an increasingly "challenging and difficult world" (Selfe, 2009, p. 645). In our collective effort to identify the various elements that inform the use of these modes and practices, we must work together with our students to help them develop the linguistic, cultural and semiotic tools they will need to employ to be more dexterous and agile, if only because every social space in which they will be putting these tools to use will be in a state of flux. It should come as no surprise that, through that lens, everything will seem as if it has become unhinged, and the center—the one thing everyone was counting on—has not held.

In more ways than ever, many of us are wildly romanticizing, even fetishizing, fluidity to counter the fixity that standardization has imposed on us (Lorimer Leonard, 2013) in much the same way that proponents of the New Literacy Studies fetishized the local over the global a few years back. At least until Brandt and Clinton (2002) pointed out that focusing exclusively on the local created methodological biases and conceptual impasses "by exaggerating the power of local contexts to define the meaning and forms that literacy takes and by under-theorizing the potentials of the technology of literacy" (p. 337). As was true back then, a question that immediately comes to mind is whether we have let the pendulum swing too far in a single direction and are finding ourselves unfairly criticizing valid representations of the challenging circumstances we all face instead of recognizing the degrees of difference that should inform any position we take. In working to become more precise in our description of what the world looks like now, we must be careful not to void historically important voices that have contributed to our understanding of the multiple forces that impinge on our curricular and pedagogical practices. The fact that they did not get everything right does not diminish the measure of their contributions to our understanding of how language and culture play themselves out in our lives as we perform our multiple *identities in practice* (Holland, Lachicotte, Skinner & Cain, 1998; Caraballo, 2011) in the process of becoming *citizens in the making.*

Take Leander and Boldt's critique of the New London Group's "A Pedagogy of Multiliteracies: Designing Social Futures" (1996), an essay they describe as a "disciplined rationalization of youth engagement in literacies" (2012, p. 22). They meticulously dismantle the basic arguments that the New London Group's groundbreaking essay introduced to the field of composition and literacy studies and whose effects continue to reverberate 20 years after its publication. In their analysis, they contend that the "vision of practice" promulgated by the essay involves "a domestication that subtracts movement, indeterminacy, and emergent potential" from the picture (p. 23). To the field's general detriment, they contend, the identities and futures that the New London Group (NLG) proposed "were understood as essentially the same as texts, all susceptible to being designed and redesigned as projects under the rational control of students and teachers" (p. 24). There is more than a hint of judgment here; there is also a purposeful reduction in the vitality that the NLG essay provided theorists, researchers and educators interested in understanding the role of reading, writing and rhetoric in the lives of students caught in the web of the social and cultural changes taking place at the time. Although there is certainly some truth in their critique—the NLG did indulge in the idea that text, reason and control would be our saving grace—I interpret Leander and Boldt's reading of the NLG's efforts to expand and smooth out grammars in the service of comprehending "the plurality of texts that circulate" in "increasingly globalized societies" (New London Group, 1996, p. 61; cited in Leander & Boldt, 2012, p. 24) as a purposefully designed effort to elevate the alternative model they offer above the NLG's.

In expanding and improving on the NLG's analytical frame of reference, Leander and Boldt (2012) call on the work of Massumi (2002), as well as Deleuze and Guattari (1987; see also Deleuze, 1994), to challenge what they see as the "overcoding structures" of "representationalism" (Deleuze & Guattari, 1987, p. 12; cited in Leander & Boldt, 2012, p. 25) inherent in the NLG project. To counter what they see as the NLG's relentless preoccupation with mechanical and static conceptions of text production, Leander and Bolt (2012) focus on the outside-the-classroom experiences of Lee, a 10-year-old boy who has been labeled a failing reader in school but has been described as an enthusiastic reader at home (p. 42). To test their alternative hypothesis, they follow Lee over the course of a day as he engages in reading and playing with text from *manga*, a Japanese comic book art form (p. 22). In the course of following him through his day, they focus their attention on Lee's profound immersion in a variety of social practices, including reading and writing, that are created and fed "by an ongoing series of affective intensities that are different from what the [NLG] describe[s] as the rational control of meanings and forms" (p. 26). In an effort to get away from what Lankshear and Knobel (2006) call "text-centricity" or "bookspace" (p. 52), Leander and Boldt (2012) conceive of Lee-as-body rather than Lee-as-text (p. 29), a critical strategy that in their minds produces more authentic data.

By locating Lee in an assemblage, a collection of things that are present in any given context and "have no necessary relation to one another" yet come together to produce "any number of possible effects" (p. 25), Leander and Boldt (2012) discover that what emerges is "the production of desire in which Lee does not aim to produce texts but to use them, to move with and through them, in the production of intensity" (p. 26). What they conclude from this "act of experimentation" (p. 25) is that the kind of activity Lee engages in "is saturated with affect and emotion; it creates and is fed by an ongoing series of affective intensities that are different from the [NLG's] rational control of meanings and forms" (p. 26). As difficult as it would be to transfer this kind of experience to the classroom, a challenge that Leander and Boldt (2012) acknowledge, they close with a couple of critical questions that we as scholars in composition and literacy studies must ask ourselves if there is any chance that what they propose will ever come to pass: "Can the teacher make space for fluidity and indeterminacy as the nature of things? Can he or she recognize difference, surprise, and unfolding that follow along paths that are not rational or linear or obviously critical or political?" (p. 44). The answer is yes, and no.

As much as I agree with Leander and Boldt's argument that the NLG's framework of analysis over-rationalizes literacy-as-text and in so doing misses an opportunity to imagine the emergent occasions that also inform any student's relationship to the work they do as readers, writers and rhetoricians, I am not persuaded that a complete shift away from the NLG's rational approach to the open-ended affective reading that Leander and Boldt (2012) propose is by itself adequate to address the challenges we all face as educators. I would argue that they commit the same error of omission they accuse the NLG of committing by privileging the affective over the cognitive. As attractive as the rhizomatic frame of reference Leander and Boldt (2012) propose is to many of us in composition and literacy studies, critics of the perspective that informs Leander and Boldt's position raise legitimate concerns about the either/or stance they take. In her critique of Massumi's *Parables for the Virtual: Movement, Affect, Sensation* (2002)—the bedrock text on which Leander and Boldt (2012) build their critique—Leys (2011) laments the fact that the process of producing the kind of nonrepresentational perspective they aim for creates

> a gap between the subject's affects and its cognition or appraisal of the affective situation or object, such that cognition or thinking comes "too late" for reasons, beliefs, intentions, and meanings to play the role in action and behavior usually accorded to them. The result is that action and behavior are held to be determined by affective dispositions that are independent of consciousness and the mind's control.
>
> *p. 443*

As I will demonstrate later in the next section of this chapter, if we hope to understand and make effective curricular and pedagogical use of the linguistic, cultural and political disruptions that recent developments in technology, modes of communication and globalization have had on the ideological approaches to language and cultural difference currently available to us in the classroom, we must be careful not to accent one element in any binary at the expense of the other. Instead, we need to find ways to focus on the dialectical tension their interplay produces. Before I do that, however, I think it would be useful to finish setting the stage by examining the work of another pair of theorists and researchers who seem to agree that Deleuzian desire must always inform the options available to all students, especially the disenfranchised, for shaping a fluid identity that responds critically to the inherent tendency in educational systems to assimilate them often through oppressive means.

In their review of the literature on the impact of linguistic and cultural ideologies on student identity formation, Lee and Anderson (2009) contend that
the "fluidity of both perceived and actual movements of persons and messages
makes it necessary to reconsider how identities are conceptualized and framed as
'mattering' in social interactions across different contexts" (p. 181). In their conceptual examination of why "identity is less about how and where you belong
and more about how transitions across contexts in the here and now render identities as boundary objects" (p. 185), Lee and Anderson (2009) analyze what they
refer to as two ontologically distinct heuristics that reflect contrasting theoretical
assumptions about the nature of mind and society: essentialist and social con-
structivist views of identity (p. 185). Against an essentialist view associated with
cognitivist and structuralist/mentalist constructions of a unified and coherent
self, of an individual who assumes a relatively stable identity that is "fixed, internal, and in direct correlation with measurable characteristics," Lee and Anderson
(2009) posit a fluid, social identity that is "variably related to contestable and
constructed categories and contexts" (p. 186).

In Lee and Anderson's (2009) view, linguistic and cultural minority students
in the various studies they reviewed selected one of three paths—assimilation,
opposition or straddling—in the course of negotiating the range of possible identities available to them in school settings. Not surprisingly, those who chose to
conform to the norms of the dominant group selected an assimilationist identity
and in so doing gained access to the social resources it is assumed all students
need to succeed academically. In the process, however, they often developed a
weak sense of ethnic identity and risked possible rejection by their co-ethnic
peers. Students who preferred to place more emphasis on their shared ethnic
history with their peers, on the other hand, chose an oppositional identity that
signaled their unwillingness to accept what they saw as the school's preconceived
assumptions about their abilities. In each case, students felt compelled to make an
either/or choice between the norms of the school and their ethnic or dominant
group. In that respect, both of these choices resulted in relatively stable identities
fixed by a particular set of values that limited the students' mobility.

According to Lee and Anderson (2009), members of the third group—Carter
(2005) refers to these students as *cultural straddlers*; Davidson (1996) calls them
transculturals—learned to utilize dominant frames of reference as needed but
managed to leverage the language use and cultural experience they brought
to the classroom from home to signal their affinity with peers who shared the
same ethnic history. These students, Lee and Anderson (2009) argue, "effectively utilized strategies that enabled them to cross racial, ethnic, class, gender, and linguistic boundaries" (p. 198).[5] Although the students who chose to
straddle linguistic and cultural differences were not described as possessing the
strong affective desires that Lee, the young boy in Leander and Boldt's (2012)
study experienced as a consequence of his active engagement in the world, Lee
and Anderson (2009) suggest that the cultural straddlers they identified in their

review of the literature demonstrated a penchant "for affirming their personal knowledge and skills as resources upon which to build" (p. 199) as they moved across a range of social spaces with the kind of dexterity we have all come to value as part of our effort to nurture linguistic and cultural practices among our students that respond to the fluidity of their lived experience.

While the seemingly irrevocable shift from fixity to fluidity that Leander and Boldt (2012) and Lee and Anderson (2009) advocate can help us imagine new ways to create conditions in any college writing classroom that are conducive to our students' ability to navigate and negotiate the challenges they encounter in the varied social spaces they inhabit in the course of their everyday lives, we need to acknowledge some of the unintended consequences this shift in curricular and pedagogical practices produces. The assumption, of course, is that students who are more linguistically and culturally dexterous and agile are in a better position to navigate the social spaces they inhabit and negotiate more productive relationships with the individuals they encounter there. Critics, however, have raised a number of concerns about how closely a progressive curriculum and pedagogy with these goals in mind aligns with the set of practices encouraged by proponents of what Gee, Hull and Lankshear (2000) refer to as new or fast capitalism. As Gee et al. (2000) point out in their effort to keep us from uncritically embracing difference, the fluid and flexible repertoire of skills we are increasingly cultivating in our students is being insidiously coopted and appropriated by what they call the "new work order."[6]

New capitalism, Gee et al. (2000) fervently argue, is hidebound to "create new social identities or new kinds of people: new leaders, new workers, new students, new teachers, new citizens, new communities, even new 'private' people who are supposed to dissolve the separation between their lives outside work and their lives inside" (p. xiii). In striking contrast to the "old school" capitalist paradigm, Gee et al. (2000) contend that this new capitalism

> is not about commodities or standardization, and very probably not about democracy. The new capitalism is, as we have seen, about *customization*: the design of products and services perfectly dovetailed to the needs, desires, and identities of individuals on the basis of their *differences*. . . . Thus, the new capitalism [as do many of the progressive curricular and pedagogical innovations that Deleuze-influenced scholars are proposing] celebrates diversity and abhors standardization.
>
> *p. 43, emphasis in original*

In the process, the new capitalism embraces—better yet, devours—the alternative habits and dispositions progressive educators seek to cultivate in their students in ways that severely contradict the values and beliefs progressive educators actually hold.

Faced with this conundrum, Gee et al. (2000) conclude that scholars in composition and literacy studies who share their perspective are left with the task of answering in a different way a basic question that has always preoccupied us: "What should we teach and learn, and why?" (p. 159). The question of goals in schools, they insist, can no longer be assessed on the basis of the traditional assumption that academic "disciplinary" knowledge is at the center of schooling. Instead, they argue, we need to understand how our educational goals are irrevocably transformed "when academic knowledge is pushed from the center of attention, as is happening today, in many respects, under the influence of the new work order" (p. 159). But it is also happening, as we will see in the next section, because—as a number of progressive scholars (Flower, 2008; Goldblatt, 2007; Guerra, 2008; Kells, 2007; Parks & Goldblatt, 2000; Weisser, 2002) have argued—the time has come for us to expand our interests in the teaching and learning of reading, writing and rhetoric beyond the academy and into the communities of belonging that feed it and from which it profits.

In response to these new circumstances, Gee et al. (2000) recommend that we implement four focus points that respond meaningfully to the question they pose. In conjunction with focus 1 (Thinking), Gee et al. (2000) declare that we want learners to develop the kinds of mental representations members of academic disciplines typically have in their heads; at the same time, we want to make use of whatever well-structured materials we may develop "to guide students through problems so that they can come to see and confront the difference between their everyday way of seeing things and the specialist way" (p. 160). Focus 2 (Tools), on the other hand, accents our need to provide groups of students working together, rather than as single individuals, with opportunities to discover and use the knowledge-handling tools associated with academic disciplines to do things, not in the way academics typically do, but in ways that respond to everyday circumstances beyond the academy (p. 160).

The goal of focus 3 (Culture) is to produce a community of practice "where students learn how to handle knowledge and language in ways that are like those in academic disciplines," but here yet again, the rhetorical and discursive approaches akin to disciplines must be "rendered relevant and suitable for particular communities of learners" (p. 161) inside and outside the academy. Finally, focus 4 (Critique) provides students with a critical awareness of how discourses have been constructed throughout history as a consequence of the particular ways of thinking, acting, interacting, talking and writing that occur in certain places and with certain tools. As is true of the other three, one of the key goals of focus 4 is "to understand how various specialist Discourses relate to and conflict with everyday Discourses, as well as various public sphere and global discourses connected to government, business, religion and the like" (p. 161).

Gee et al. (2000) are clearly suggesting that we need to use the kind of knowledge we and our students are exposed to in an academic setting to develop an oppositional, or better yet, an alternative Discourse that embodies resistance with the ultimate goal of social transformation (see Castells, 1997; Solórzano and Delgado Bernal, 2001) and is capable of challenging the inexorable force that fast capitalism and the new work order is imposing on our best efforts to prepare our students for what we hope will be unscripted futures neither constrained by the forces of standardization nor unfettered by false notions of difference. To initiate this critical process, Gee et al. (2000) propose that we juxtapose the new capitalism—which they describe as a new Discourse in the making—with other "competing, overlapping, mutually adjusting Discourses" similar to the ones they outline in their book and that I am laying out here. This new Discourse, Gee et al. (2000) insist, must "disavow the consumer determinism of the new capitalism" at the same time that it argues "for the reinvigoration of the local as against the 'faux' local of the new capitalism" (p. 166). The new Discourse also needs to "see critique as necessary to real learning and thus as part and parcel of critical thinking and the empowerment of workers" (p. 166). Above all, it must envision a new "global citizenship" that impresses on us all the need always to care about the poor in our local communities and elsewhere in the world. Here, Gee et al. (2000) echo Fairclough's argument that "as the shape of the new global social order becomes clearer," "so too does the need for a critical awareness of language as part of people's resources for living in new ways" (1999, p. 71). To accomplish this goal, Gee et al. (2000) propose that we place the Discourse of the new capitalism "within a 'Discourse map' of our societies and the world." This map can then be used to create a new "knowledge world" in which "learning and education become always and everywhere about being in, about comparing and contrasting, reflecting on and critiquing, Discourses—about the kind of people we are, are becoming, and want to be" (Gee et al., 2000, p. 166).

Se hace camino al andar[7]

In recent years, a wide array of scholars in composition and literacy studies (Flower, 2008; Genishi & Dyson, 2009; Gutiérrez, 2008; Gutiérrez, Bien, Selland & Pierce, 2011; Kells & Balester, 1999; Kells, Balester & Villanueva, 2004; Kerschbaum, 2014; Kinloch, 2010, 2011; LeCourt, 2004; Lee, 2007; Lewis, Enciso & Moje, 2007; Lu, 2004; Paris, 2011; and so many more) have knowingly and otherwise taken up Gee et al.'s (2000; see also Gee & Lankshear, 1995) call and introduced a rush of new ideas designed to address the multiplicity of challenges that all students—but especially those who have been disenfranchised because of race, class, gender, language, culture, ability, age, sexual orientation, lifestyle or citizenship status—face as they attempt to navigate and negotiate increasingly complex realities in local, regional, national and global communities that have been turned upside down and inside out by new capitalism. Their exploration of how students across grade levels can make more effective use of the repertoires of rhetorical and discursive practices they acquire in the course of their everyday interactions with others in the communities of belonging they inhabit signals a significant turn toward developing curricular and pedagogical practices for reading, writing and rhetoric classrooms that will equip students with the tactical and strategic tools they need to thrive in the fluid *and* fixed social spaces they inhabit over the course of their daily lives.

At the heart of much of this work, whether or not it is mentioned explicitly, is an emerging realization that what some call translanguaging (Canagarajah, 2011; García, 2009; García and Wei, 2014) and others call translingualism (Canagarajah, 2013; Horner, Lu, Royster & Trimbur, 2011a; Horner, NeCamp & Donahue, 2011b; Lu & Horner, 2013) must play an increasing role in our effort to understand the changes taking place as we shift from standardization to difference as the new norm. As most of this new work also demonstrates, a focus on language is necessary but insufficient to provide our students with the "capacity to aspire" (Appadurai, 2004) as they work to achieve recognition (Bourdieu & Wacquant, 1992; Honneth, 1995) and respect (Cintron, 1997) in their interactions with others. One of the signature goals of this book is to argue that we need to extend our interest beyond language to include culture, identity and citizenship as salient dimensions that also inform how we enact the curricular and pedagogical approaches various theorists, researchers and educators are proposing.

In the rest of this section, I want to describe four dimensions that to varying degrees all students, but especially those from disenfranchised communities, already have available to them to navigate and negotiate the varied college classrooms and other communities of belonging they are likely to inhabit over the course of their studies and beyond. I begin by laying out three well-defined ideological approaches to language and culture identified by several scholars in composition and literacy studies that together represent the choices available to us as we ponder how best to address the linguistic, cultural, identity and citizenship needs of our students. In the process, I argue that it is not language and culture writ large that informs our notions of identity, but the range of ideological perspectives reflected in each of these interrelated dimensions whenever we engage one another in the various fixed and fluid social spaces we inhabit at any given moment. To what end should we be interested in how language, culture and identity are conceptualized, much less how their intersection plays out in the world? I contend that various ideological formations of language, culture and identity eventually inform the kind of person we are or want to become, that is, the kinds of citizens in the making we imagine ourselves being as we gain and lose membership in the various local, regional, national and global communities with which we identify and to which we belong at different times and in different places.

In the course of conceptualizing approaches to language and cultural difference and pondering how best to organize a curriculum and develop a set of pedagogical strategies to enact it, a number of scholars in composition and literacy studies have identified a tripartite ideological structure that seeks to move beyond the binary formulations that have historically informed much of our thinking in the field. In their groundbreaking work, Horner et al. (2011b) make a distinction between what they refer to as *monolingual* and *traditional multilingual* models, two related but distinct approaches that conceptualize languages as fixed, discrete, binary and defined by specific forms. They then introduce what they call a *translingual* model, an alternative approach that conceives of languages and language boundaries as fluid and in constant revision. Where the monolingual model insists that fluency in other languages is deemed a threat to fluency in English, and the traditional multilingual model suggests that fluency in each discrete language is achieved by invoking what is appropriate at that distinct moment, the translingual model that Horner et al. (2011b) propose focuses on mutual intelligibility rather than fluency and reminds us that language use "has the potential to transform contexts and what is 'appropriate' to them" (p. 287). Finally, whereas fluency in multiple languages threatens intelligibility in the monolingual model and fluency in each discrete language determines membership in a language group in the traditional multilingual model, code-switching, code-meshing, borrowing, and the blending of languages represent the norm in the translingual model (p. 287).

Building on these ideas, Horner et al. (2011a) introduce a set of terms that adds some metaphorical nuance to our understanding of these concepts: the *monolingual* is described as traditional and eradicationist and the *multilingual* as tolerant and accommodationist. What they call the traditional approach takes as its norm "a linguistically homogeneous situation: one where writers, speakers, and readers are expected to use Standard English or Edited American English—imagined ideally as uniform—to the exclusion of other languages and language variations" (p. 303). The tolerant approach, on the other hand, seeks to distance itself from the traditional approach "by acknowledging differences in language use; codifying these; and granting individuals a right to them" (p. 306). In their view, however, the accommodationist approach proves just as constraining as the eradicationist because it assumes that "each codified set of language practices is appropriate only to a specific, discrete, assigned social sphere: 'home' language; 'street' language, 'academic' language . . . and so on" (p. 306). The translingual approach, which "sees difference in language not as a barrier to overcome or as a problem to manage, but as a resource" (p. 303), disrupts the dichotomizing relationship between the first two by acknowledging that "deviations from dominant expectations need not be errors; that conformity need not be automatically advisable; and that writers' purposes and readers' conventional expectations are neither fixed nor united" (p. 304).

While the role of culture is implied in discussions of translingualism, I believe that we need to examine its role more explicitly and apart from language because these two dimensions (language and culture) play equally significant roles in the kind of identity formation students, especially the disenfranchised among them, undergo as a consequence of their immersion in multiple languages and cultures. Fortunately, Kostogriz (2004) provides a description of the ideological forces impinging on culture that parallels the three approaches to language difference I just outlined. Using a conceptual framework similar to the ones used by Horner et al. (2011a) and Horner et al. (2011b), Kostogriz critiques the commonplace binary that literacy is *either* "centralized and decontextual-ized or decentered" *or* always situated. In his view, literacy neither "radiates out from an identifiable central place" nor is it "particular to bounded sociocultural places"; instead, as all proponents of a Deleuzian perspective argue, literacy is "fluid and relational" (p. 3). Because it is, Kostogriz (2004) challenges a conser-vative agenda grounded in a homogenizing ideology associated with universal-ism and national space, on the one hand, and a neoliberal conception of situated literacies associated with "particularism and local places" (p. 3), on the other. As an alternative, Kostogriz (2004) proposes a conception of literacy as *transcultural*, that is, as

> a cultural-semiotic practice happening in contact zones between "us" and "them", at different temporal scales, depending on cultural macro and micro politics, the degree of openness by ethnic communities to cultural changes, social mobility of their members and a variety of counter-strategies used by community leaders and media to resist these changes.
>
> *p. 8*

My conception of transcultural repositioning—which I defined in the preface as a rhetorical ability that many disenfranchised students have learned to enact as they move back and forth across "different languages and dialects, different social classes, different cultural and artistic forms, different ways of seeing and thinking about the increasingly fluid and hybridized world emerging all around us" (Guerra, 2007, p. 140)—parallels what Kostogriz describes here. It also has much in common with Anzaldúa's (1987) notion of *mestiza consciousness* and Braidotti's (1994) conception of *nomadic consciousness*.[8] As I have described it else-where (Guerra, 2004, 2007, 2013), this emerging habit of mind is effectively illustrated in Zamel's (1997) work on how second language writers enact what Ortiz (1947) first referred to as transculturation,[9] as well as in Lu's (1990) work on the important function of repositioning in the discursive lives of basic writers. In my view, the notion of transcultural repositioning provides a more effective way for educators to remind all students—but especially the disenfranchised among them—that they can and should make use of the prior knowledge and experi-ences they have accumulated and the rhetorical agility they have developed in the course of navigating and negotiating the various communities of practice to which they currently belong, have belonged in the past, and will belong in the future. For me, the term's explanatory power is reflected in the fact that the phrase simultaneously signals multiple places, literal and figurative, that individ-uals have to negotiate and continuously reorient themselves to in real space and time, especially if they come from marginalized communities and have always already had to figure out ways to reside intentionally and successfully in main-stream settings.

Based on my review of the three approaches to language *and* cultural difference I just described, I want to suggest that it is incumbent on us all to remind our students that they must deploy the rhetorical and discursive tools they have acquired through their lived experience and in congruence with one or more of the ideologies that I list in Table 1.1 below. The first six terms in each of the lists in Table 1.1 describe the different ways in which languages and cultures behave, the social and ideological forces that make them behave that way and our relationship to them. Each of these terms will be discussed in much greater detail in Chapters 2 and 3. The four terms included next in each list also focus on the different ways in which languages and cultures behave and our relationship to them, but because each of these is always already implicated in the ideologies that inform the approaches to language and cultural difference outlined here and in the broader social and political structures that inform them in turn, the rest of the book will be imbued by their influence, but that influence will be implied rather than explicitly noted.

In keeping with Gee et al.'s argument about the importance of placing the Discourse of new capitalism "within a 'Discourse map' of our societies and the world" (2000, p. 166), I would like to propose that we also need to offer our students an "ideological map" that makes visible the continuum of possible approaches to language and cultural difference available to them. These ideological forces do, after all, continuously impinge on and influence the choices students make, often without their being aware of it. The shift from a traditional binary to a tripartite structure begins with the original binary elements (Monolingual/Monocultural and Multilingual/Multicultural) in the first two vertical lists in Table 1.1, then adds a third (Translingual/Transcultural) that attempts to disrupt our tendency to bifurcate them. Where the first two lists represent a traditional binary relationship, the third reflects the liminal space between them. But instead of locating the alternative between the monolingual and multilingual as the inevitably preconceived product of a Hegelian dialectic, I

TABLE 1.1 Social and Ideological Approaches to Language and Cultural Difference

Monolingual/Monocultural	*Multilingual/Multicultural*	*Translingual/Transcultural*
Code-segregation	Code-switching	Code-meshing
Assimilation	Acculturation	Transculturation
Eradication	Accommodation	Hybridization
Language understanding	Language awareness	Critical language awareness
Cultural understanding	Cultural awareness	Critical cultural awareness
Life in the either/or	Life in the both/and	Life in the neither/nor
Conservative	Liberal	Progressive
Traditional	Modern	Postmodern
National	International	Transnational
Colonial	Neocolonial	Decolonial

set it at one end of the continuum to suggest its stronger location in a narrative of progress that often overrides our best efforts to remain ever vigilant and critical of not just one or two, but all three competing ideologies.

In the context of the four dimensions I am describing here—language, culture, identity and citizenship—that will provide a framework for imagining the ways in which students navigate and negotiate the varied rhetorical and discursive circumstances they encounter in college classrooms and other communities of belonging, I am locating identity as "the product rather than the source of linguistic and other semiotic practices and therefore [as] a social and cultural rather than primarily internal psychological phenomenon" (Bucholtz and Hall, 2005, p. 585). As I am describing it here, identity is part intentional, part habitual and less than fully conscious, but it is also, simultaneously, "an outcome of interactional negotiation, a construct of others' perceptions and representations, and an outcome of larger ideological processes and structures" (2005, p. 585). In the context of an identities in practice theory promulgated by Caraballo (2011; see also Holland et al., 1998), identity is above all else "multiple, intersectional, and contextual" (2011, p. 155), at the same time that it

> extends beyond a conception of the subject as totally discursively produced by ideologies and/or cultural and social norms, in which identity might be defined as the "meeting point," or "the point of suture" between discourses that call subjects into positions and the subjects' articulation or performance of these positions.
>
> *Caraballo, 2011, p. 165*

In other words, if students hope to learn how to "negotiate identities in their different social worlds," they will need to develop "linguistic and sociocultural competencies that afford them access to engaging in social opportunities for participation and to having that participation recognized by others" (Lee and Anderson, 2009, p. 183).

Finally, as Wan (2011) notes in an award-winning essay that highlighted the salience of citizenship in composition and literacy studies, "production of the citizen often remains at the center of recent discussions about higher education" (p. 28). What remains unarticulated, in her view, is the kind of citizen we hope to cultivate when we associate the notion of citizenship with our interest in literacy. Wan (2011) points out that scholars in our field typically allude to the importance of citizenship and democracy in such vague, ambiguous and generic terms—which she appropriately refers to as its "ambient nature"—that it renders the concept useless in our deliberations. In her critique of the limited ways in which we make use of the concept in our work, Wan highlights

> (1) the infinite flexibility that comes from shifting definitions of citizenship; (2) the pervasive belief that citizenship is an achievable status by

individuals who have the will for it; and (3) the implicit understanding that equality and social mobility are synonymous with and can be achieved through citizenship.

Wan, 2011, pp. 29–30

In summarizing her critique of these three issues, Wan invokes what she calls *habits of citizenship*. Although she does not present it as the answer to all our problems, she certainly acknowledges how much she appreciates the ways in which habits of citizenship

> take on more subtle meanings, not simply defined as explicit civic activity through participatory action, or as just legal boundaries. Rather, citizenship [gets] to be understood as also located in more everyday activities that may be mediated through habits and practices like the literate skills learned in classrooms and beyond. Perhaps one consequence of making this shift in thinking, for those teachers who hope to be more mindful of how to integrate citizenship into literacy instruction, is a shift in scale: rather than only try to amplify those citizenship habits that seem most obvious, we should also consider the other multiple ways that habits of citizenship are encouraged through literacy learning.
>
> *Wan, 2011, p. 45*

In their review of the literature on citizenship in educational studies, Fischman and Haas (2012) arrive at a similar conclusion:

> Citizenship education assumes that after a guided pedagogical process a new identity will emerge . . . however, the consolidation of any given identity . . . is always an "educationally" unfinished project, an unsolvable tension, that cannot be learned and understood through conscious rationality alone and thus not solved through the delivery of explicit instruction on what democracy is and how a good citizen should act.
>
> *p. 174*

As I will demonstrate in the next four chapters in Part I, the four dimensions I have just described—language, culture, identity and citizenship—are fluid, interactive and in the process of emerging at the same time as they are continuously constrained by competing ideologies that attempt to fix and hold them in place. Each in turn also plays a critical role in helping us understand how best to help our students develop the full repertoire of linguistic, cultural and semiotic resources they need to respond effectively to the reading, writing and rhetorical challenges they are likely to encounter in the academy and beyond. How this happens will be the focus of the final two chapters in Part II where I present and analyze data that I collected from case studies I conducted in a writing classroom

I taught at the University of Washington and in relation to a campus-wide writing initiative at the University of New Mexico. Together, the theoretical and applied work I present in the rest of this book unpacks a constellation of ideas that informs what I see as an emerging approach to the teaching and learning of reading, writing and rhetoric that values the interactive roles of language, culture, identity and citizenship.

Spanish to English Glossary

Los Vecinos [The Neighbors]
los bolillos [the white people]
los vendidos [the sell outs]
el barrio [the neighborhood]
Se hace camino al andar [The road unfolds as one walks]

Notes

1. As I noted in the Preface, except for the extended passage in Spanish and Spanish/ English that opens Chapter 2 and is translated in an endnote at the end of that chapter, the English translation of all Spanish words, phrases and sentences used in this book can be found listed in order of appearance in Spanish to English glossaries at the end of each chapter. In contrast to the typical practice in the field of inserting the English translation in brackets immediately after a passage in Spanish, I decided to include English translations separately to provide readers with the experience of encountering the Spanish words, phrases and sentences in isolation. I am hoping this will allow readers with varied levels of competency in Spanish to take notice of the immediate tensions they experience as they struggle to translate and understand Spanish words, phrases and sentences at the very moment they encounter them in the book.
2. According to Bourdieu (1989), a social space is a "system of relations." In his view, "we can compare social space to a geographic space within which regions are divided up. But this space is constructed in such a way that the closer the agents, groups or institutions which are situated within this space, the more common properties they have; and the more distant, the fewer. Spatial distances—on paper—coincide with social distances. Such is not the case in real space. It is true that one can observe almost everywhere a tendency toward spatial segregation, people who are close together in social space tending to find themselves, by choice or by necessity, close to one another in geographic space; nevertheless, people who are very distant from each other in social space can encounter one another and interact, if only briefly and intermittently, in physical space" (p. 16).
3. Throughout the book, I address the importance of affirming the lived experience that students bring to the classroom and of more effectively utilizing it in the course of their academic development. Depending on the particular circumstances, my discussion invokes such terms as "funds of knowledge" (Moll, Amanti, Neff & González, 1992; González, Moll & Amanti, 2005), "learning incomes" (Guerra, 2008) and "discursive resources" (Lu, 2004; Reiff & Bawarshi, 2011). Funds of knowledge refers to the "historically accumulated and culturally developed bodies of knowledge and skills essential for household or individual functioning and well-being" (Moll et al., 1992, p. 133) that students acquire in their local communities of belonging and that K-12 English Language Arts teachers utilize in their classrooms. The other two terms are more widely

used to identify the rhetorical and discursive practices that postsecondary students bring to the first-year writing classroom from their prior experience in school contexts and beyond. While the concept of learning incomes is used to remind writing teachers that the prior learning students bring to class is just as important as the learning outcomes the teacher has established as goals for a particular class, the concept of discursive resources acknowledges that students always and already possess and bring a rich cache of rhetorical and discursive skills to every formal learning opportunity as well.

4. I use the phrase "college classrooms and other communities of belonging" to highlight the fact that the college classroom is but one of many social spaces students inhabit in their everyday lives. In keeping with the ways in which the term is being increasingly used in the field of composition and literacy studies, I want to suggest that we think of *communities of belonging* as both real and virtual social spaces where individuals establish identities through their critical and collective engagement in the range of language, cultural and citizenship differences that inform their interactions. While the concept of communities of belonging has much in common with other terms that have been used in the field of composition and literacy studies, speech communities (Labov, 1972), discourse communities (Nystrand, 1982) and communities of practice (Wenger, 1998) among them, I use this term to invoke the sense of belonging one shares through self-reflective choice rather than through tradition or imposition. Belonging in this context, then, is not based on shared norms, values or assumptions only; it also reflects a willingness to engage one another despite, or because of, the differences each brings to the moment. As we must any time we use the term community in composition and literacy studies, we need to keep in mind Harris's caution that "since it has no 'positive opposing' term, *community* can soon become an empty and sentimental word" that "shifts [our view of the phenomenon at hand] subtly from the dynamic to the fixed—from something that a writer must continually reinvent to something that has already been invented" (1989, p. 13).

5. In their important work on student resistance, Solórzano and Delgado Bernal (2001) complicate Lee and Anderson's discussion of the ways in which *cultural straddlers* and *transculturals* are empowered to move across various boundaries of difference by shifting the focus instead to the values and beliefs that inform the ways in which students engage in resistance (rather than opposition) whenever they respond to constraining or oppressive conditions. Thus, instead of limiting their analysis to the process of social reproduction as Lee and Anderson (2009) do, Solórzano and Delgado Bernal take it a step further and unpack the role that *human agency*—the confidence and skills to act on one's behalf (p. 316)—plays when students engage in a form of resistance that they refer to as *social transformation*. In their view, student agency is not measured only by the degree to which students can effectively utilize strategies that enable them to cross racial, ethnic, class, gender, and linguistic boundaries (Lee and Anderson, 2009, p. 198), but also by the degree to which they are capable of critiquing oppressive conditions and structures of domination and committing themselves to social justice (Solórzano & Delgado Bernal, 2001, p. 319). As I will demonstrate later when I discuss the importance of critical language and cultural awareness, the distinction they make here reminds us to be careful not to fetishize fluidity and assume that it alone offers our students the kind of agency that will equip them to transform the oppressive conditions they may encounter in college classrooms and other communities of belonging.

6. In *Producing Good Citizens*, Wan (2014) alludes to this phenomenon when she describes what many administrators in higher education now see as the desired outcome of a college education: Students in college who learn "how to traverse languages, cultures, and nations toward a more cosmopolitan way of being" will learn how "to operate between and among nation-state boundaries and presumably to use highly literate skills in order to negotiate among these different spaces." In so doing, administrators in higher education argue, they will simultaneously demonstrate that they possess

the right qualifications for a future job and be more competitive in a global market (pp. 154–155).

7. This subtitle comes from a poem by Spanish poet, Antonio Machado, popularized in the late 1960s by Spanish singer, Joan Manuel Serrat. Although it translates literally as "the road unfolds as one walks," it figuratively suggests that one creates one's own destiny. Additional information on Machado and Serrat can be found on *Wikipedia*.

8. The concept of *transcultural repositioning* has much in common with Anzaldúa's (1987) *mestiza consciousness* and Braidotti's (1994) *nomadic consciousness*, but it more directly locates the phenomenon that all three terms describe in the context of current efforts to teach reading, writing and rhetoric. According to Anzaldúa (1987), "the work of *mestiza* consciousness is to break down the subject-object duality that keeps [the new *mestiza*] a prisoner and to show in the flesh and through the images in her work how duality is transcended" (p. 80). The consequences of this work, Anzaldúa makes clear, is not an "assembly . . . where severed or separated pieces merely come together. Nor is it a balancing of opposing powers." Instead, the self adds "a third element which is greater than the sum of its severed parts. The third element is a new consciousness—a *mestiza* consciousness—[whose] energy comes from continual creative motion that keeps breaking down the unitary aspect of each new paradigm" (pp. 79–80). Braidotti's (1994) nomadic consciousness, on the other hand, "combines features that are usually perceived as opposing, namely the possession of a sense of identity that rests not on fixity but on contingency. The nomadic consciousness combines coherence with mobility. It aims to rethink the unity of the subject, without reference to humanistic beliefs, without dualistic oppositions, linking instead body and mind in a new set of intensive and often intransitive transitions" (p. 32). Although transcultural repositioning describes a similar effort to overcome dualities, I argue that it shifts the focus to the ways an individual chooses to position or reposition him or herself within the evershifting matrix of transcultural landscapes, a process that requires one to make more than an either/or *or* a both/and choice.

9. According to Ortiz (1947), who originally coined the term, "the word *transculturation* better expresses the different phases of the process of transition from one culture to another because this does not consist merely in acquiring another culture, which is what the English word *acculturation* really implies, but the process also necessarily involves the loss or uprooting of a previous culture, which could be defined as a deculturation. In addition, it carries the idea of the consequent creation of new cultural phenomena, which could be called neoculturation. In the end, as the school of Malinowski's followers maintains, the result of every union of cultures is similar to that of the reproductive process between individuals: the offspring always has something of both parents but is always different from each of them" (p. 103).

References

Anzaldúa, G. (1987). *Borderlands/La frontera: The new mestiza*. San Francisco, CA: Aunt Lute Books.

Appadurai, A. (2004). The capacity to aspire: Culture and the terms of recognition. In V. Rao & M. Walton (Eds.), *Culture and public action* (pp. 59–84). Palo Alto, CA: Stanford University Press.

Bakhtin, M. (1981). *The dialogic imagination*. (C. Emerson & M. Holquist, Trans.). Austin, TX: University of Texas Press.

Bourdieu, P. (1989). Social space and symbolic power. *Sociological Theory, 7*(1), 14–25.

Bourdieu, P. & Wacquant, L. J. D. (1992). *An invitation to reflexive sociology*. Chicago, IL: University of Chicago Press.

Braidotti, R. (1994). *Nomadic subjects.* New York, NY: Cambridge University Press.

Brandt, D. & Clinton, K. (2002). Limits of the local: Expanding perspectives on literacy as a social practice. *Journal of Literacy Research,* 34, 337–356.

Bucholtz, M. & Hall, K. (2005). Identity and interaction: A sociocultural linguistic approach. *Discourse Studies,* 7(4–5), 585–614.

Canagarajah, S. (2011). Codemeshing in academic writing: Identifying teachable strategies of translanguaging. *Modern Language Journal,* 95(iii), 401–417.

Canagarajah, S. (2013). *Translingual practice: Global Englishes and cosmopolitan relations.* New York, NY: Routledge.

Caraballo, L. (2011). Theorizing identities in a "just(ly)" contested terrain: Practice theories of identity amid critical-poststructural debates on curriculum and achievement. *Journal of Curriculum and Pedagogy,* 8(2), 155–177.

Carter, P. (2005). *Keepin' it real.* London, UK: Oxford University Press.

Castells, M. (1997). *The power of identity.* Malden, MA: Blackwell.

Cintron, R. (1997). *Angels' town: Chero ways, gang life, and rhetorics of the everyday.* New York, NY: Beacon Press.

Davidson, A. (1996). *Making and molding identities in schools: Student narratives on race, gender, and academic engagement.* Albany, NY: State University of New York Press.

Deleuze, G. (1994). *Difference and repetition.* (P. Patton, Trans.). New York, NY: Columbia University Press.

Deleuze, G. & Guattari, F. (1983). *Anti-Oedipus: Capitalism and schizophrenia.* (R. Hurley, M. Seem & H. R. Lane, Trans.). Minneapolis, MN: University of Minnesota.

Deleuze, G. & Guattari, F. (1987). *A thousand plateaus.* (B. Massumi, Trans.). Minneapolis, MN: University of Minnesota Press.

Fairclough, N. (1999). Global capitalism and critical awareness of language. *Critical Awareness,* 8(2), 71–83.

Fischman, G. E. & Haas, E. (2012). Beyond idealized citizenship education: Embodied cognition, metaphors, and democracy. *Review of Research in Education,* 36, 169–196.

Flower, L. (2008). *Community literacy and the rhetoric of public engagement.* Carbondale, IL: Southern Illinois University Press.

García, O. (2009). Education, multilingualism and translanguaging in the 21st century. In T. Skutnabb-Kangas, R. Phillipson, A. K. Mohanty & M. Panda (Eds.), *Multilingual education for social justice: Globalising the local* (pp. 140–158). New York, NY: Multilingual Matters.

García, O. & Wei, L. (2014). *Translanguaging: Language, bilingualism and education.* New York, NY: Palgrave Macmillan.

Gee, J. P. & Lankshear, C. (1995). The new work order: Critical language awareness and 'fast capitalism' texts. *Discourse: Studies in the Cultural Politics of Education,* 16.1, 5–19.

Gee, J. P., Hull, G. & Lankshear, C. (2000). *The new work order: Behind the language of the new capitalism.* Boulder, CO: Westview Press.

Genishi, C. & Dyson, A. (2009). *Children, language, & literacy: Diverse learners in diverse times.* New York, NY: Teachers College Press.

Goldblatt, E. (2007). *Because we live here: Sponsoring literacy beyond the college curriculum.* Cresskill, NJ: Hampton Press.

González, N., Moll, L. & Amanti, C. (2005). Funds of knowledge: Theorizing practices in households, communities and classrooms. Mahwah, NJ: Erlbaum.

Guerra, J. C. (2004). Emerging representations, situated literacies, and the practice of transcultural repositioning. In M. Hall Kells, V. Balester & V. Villanueva (Eds.),

Latina/o discourses: On language, identity, and literacy education (pp. 7–23). Portsmouth, NH: Boynton/Cook.

Guerra, J.C. (2007). Out of the valley: Transcultural repositioning as a rhetorical practice in ethnographic research and other aspects of everyday life. In C. Lewis, P. Enciso & E. B. Moje (Eds.), *Reframing sociocultural research on literacy: Identity, agency, and power* (pp. 137–162). Mahwah, NJ: Erlbaum.

Guerra, J.C. (2008). Cultivating transcultural citizenship: A writing across communities model. *Language Arts*, 85(4), 296–304.

Guerra, J.C. (2013). Cultivating transcultural citizenship in a discursive democracy. In C. Wilkey & N. Mauriello (Eds.), *Texts of consequence: Composing social activism for the classroom and community* (pp. 83–115). Cresskill, NJ: Hampton Press.

Gutiérrez, K. (2008). Developing a sociocritical literacy in the third space. *Reading Research Quarterly*, 43(2), 148–164.

Gutiérrez, K., Bien, A., Selland, M. & Pierce, D.M. (2011). Polylingual and polycultural learning ecologies: Mediating emergent academic literacies for dual language learners. *Journal of Early Childhood Literacy*, 11(2), 232–261.

Harris, J. (1989). The idea of community in the study of writing. *College Composition and Communication*, 40(1), 11–22.

Holland, D., Lachicotte, W., Skinner, D. & Cain, C. (1998). *Identity and agency in cultural worlds*. Cambridge, MA: Harvard University Press.

Honneth, A. (1995). *The struggle for recognition: The grammar of social conflicts*. Cambridge, UK: Polity.

Horner, B., Lu, M.Z., Royster, J.J. & Trimbur J. (2011a). Language difference in writing: Toward a translingual approach. *College English*, 73(3), 303–321.

Horner, B., NeCamp, S. & Donahue, C. (2011b). Toward a multilingual composition scholarship: From English only to a translingual norm. *College Composition and Communication*, 63(2), 269–300.

Kells, M.H. (2007). Writing across communities: Deliberation and the discursive possibilities of WAC. *Reflections*, 6(1), 87–108.

Kells, M.H. & Balester, V.M. (Eds.). (1999). *Attending to the margins: Writing, researching, and teaching on the front lines*. Heinemann-Boynton/Cook.

Kells, M.H., Balester, V. & Villanueva, V. (Eds.). (2004). *Latino/a discourses: On language, identity and literacy education*. Portsmouth, NH: Heinemann/Boynton-Cook.

Kerschbaum, S. (2014). *Toward a new rhetoric of difference*. Urbana: NCTE.

Kinloch, V. (2010). *Harlem on our minds: Place, race, and the literacies of urban youth*. New York, NY: Teachers College Press.

Kinloch, V. (Ed.). (2011). *Urban literacies: Critical perspectives on language, learning, and community*. New York, NY: Teachers College Press.

Kostogriz, A. (2004). Rethinking the spatiality of literacy practices in multicultural conditions. Retrieved from www.aare.edu.au/04pap/kos04610.pdf

Labov, W. (1972). *Sociolinguistic patterns*. Philadelphia, PA: University of Pennsylvania Press.

Lankshear, C. & Knobel, M. (2006). *New literacies: Everyday practices and classroom learning, 2nd ed.* Berkshire, UK: Open University Press.

Leander, K. & Boldt, G. (2012). Rereading "a pedagogy of multiliteracies": Bodies, texts, and emergence. *Journal of Literacy Research*, 45(1), 22–46.

LeCourt, D. (2004). *Identity matters: Schooling the student body in academic discourse*. Albany, NY: SUNY Press.

Lee, C. D. (2007). *Culture, literacy and learning: Taking bloom in the midst of the whirlwind.* New York, NY: Teachers College Press.

Lee, J. S. & Anderson, K. T. (2009). Negotiating linguistic and cultural identities: Theorizing and constructing opportunities and risks in education. *Review of Research in Education,* 33, 181–211.

Lewis, C. J., Enciso, P. & Moje, E. B. (Eds.). (2007). *Reframing sociocultural research on literacy: Identity, agency, and power.* Mahwah, NJ: Lawrence Erlbaum Associates.

Leys, R. (2011). The turn to affect: A critique. *Critical Inquiry,* 37, 434–472.

Lorimer Leonard, R. (2013). Traveling literacies: Multilingual writing on the move. *Research in the Teaching of English,* 48(1), 13–39.

Lu, M.-Z. (1990). Writing as repositioning. *Journal of Education,* 172, 18–21.

Lu, M.-Z. (2004). An essay on the work of composition: Composing English against the order of fast capitalism. *College Composition and Communication,* 56(1), 16–50.

Lu, M.-Z. & Horner, B. (2013). Translingual literacy, language difference, and matters of agency. *College English,* 75(6), 582–607.

Massumi, B. (2002). *Parables for the virtual: Movement, affect, sensation.* Durham, NC: Duke University Press.

Moll, L., Amanti, L., Neff, D. & González, N. (1992). Funds of knowledge for teaching: Using a qualitative approach to connect homes and classrooms. *Theory into Practice,* 31(2), 132–141.

New London Group. (1996). A pedagogy of multiliteracies: Designing social futures. *Harvard Educational Review,* 66(1), 60–92.

Nystrand, M. (1982). *What writers know: The language, process, and structure of written discourse.* New York, NY: Academic.

Ortiz, F. (1947). *Cuban counterpoint: Tobacco and sugar.* (H. de Onis. Trans.). New York, NY: Alfred A. Knopf.

Paris, D. (2011). *Language across difference: Ethnicity, communication and youth identities in changing urban schools.* Cambridge, UK: Cambridge University Press.

Parks, S. & Goldblatt, E. (2000). Writing beyond the curriculum: Fostering new collaborations in literacy. *College English,* 62(5), 584–606.

Reiff, M. J. & Bawarshi, A. (2011). Tracing discursive resources: How students use prior genre knowledge to negotiate new writing contexts in first-year composition. *Written Communication,* 28(3), 312–337.

Selfe, C. L. (2009). The movement of air, the breath of meaning: Aurality and multimodal composing. *College Composition and Communication,* 60(4), 616–663.

Solórzano, D. G. & Delgado Bernal, D. (2001). Examining transformational resistance through a critical race and Latcrit theory framework: Chicana and Chicano students in an urban context. *Urban Education,* 36.3, 308–342.

Urry, J. (2005). The complexity term. *Theory, Culture & Society,* 22(5), 1–14.

Urry, J. (2007). *Mobilities.* Malden, MA: Polity Press.

Wan, A. (2011). In the name of citizenship: The writing classroom and the promise of citizenship. *College English,* 74(1), 28–49.

Wan, A. (2014). *Producing good citizens: Literacy training in anxious times.* Pittsburgh, PA: University of Pittsburgh Press.

Weisser, C. (2002). *Moving beyond academic discourse: Composition studies and the public sphere.* Carbondale, IL: Southern Illinois University Press.

Wenger, E. (1998). *Communities of practice: Learning, meaning, and identity.* New York, NY: Cambridge University Press.

Zamel, W. (1997). Toward a model of transculturation. *TESOL Quarterly,* 31(2), 341–352.

PART I

Building Theory through Lived Experience

2

LANGUAGE DIFFERENCE AND INEQUALITY

Cuando empecé mi primer año de escuela en el sur de Tejas en 1956, todos los niños en mi clase eran mexicanos o mexicanos americanos. Ninguno de nosotros hablábamos ni siquiera una sola palabra en inglés. En esa época, la televisión estaba en su infancia y era algo desconocido entre personas pobres que apenas tenían dinero para mantenerse. Había radios en nuestros hogares, pero como vivíamos por la frontera a menos de treinta millas de la boca del Río Grande, todas las estaciones que escuchábamos tocaban música norteña. En casa, en la comunidad, entre nosotros, el español era el idioma que usábamos para comunicarnos y para interpretar el mundo conocido. En la escuela pública ubicada en nuestra comunidad, todo estaba al revés: el uso del español era completamente prohibido.

Para cuando llegamos a la junior high school, *bien conocíamos la realidad en la cual existíamos. En casa hablábamos español* and at school we spoke English. *Los dos idiomas se mantenían segregados* just as we were kept segregated from *los gringos por una vía de ferro carril que dividía* the town in half. *Los gabachos* had their own communities and their own shopping establishments *en el* downtown *de la ciudad; nosotros vivíamos en nuestros barrios e íbamos de compras en nuestra placita.*

By the time we got to high school, *la division lingüística entre el español y el inglés* collapsed *completamente y* we began to blend the two languages *en una forma desconocida,* in a way that surprised our parents *y a nuestros maestros. Al mismo tiempo que nuestros padres aceptaron nuestra nueva forma de hablar,* albeit with some resistance, the public schools continued to prohibit *el uso del español y la combinación de los dos idiomas: el famoso espanglish. En casa y en la comunidad,* we artfully switched and meshed codes, borrowing from either language *lo que mejor nos servía para ser entendidos.*[1]

But the situation was very different in school. Because we segregated ourselves from Anglo students at the public junior high and high schools—or more to the point, were segregated from them by the racist system in place at the time—we thought we could speak our mother tongue among ourselves at school just as we did at home and in our community. But each time they caught us speaking Spanish in school, the teachers would take us to see the principal and he would either paddle us, put us in detention, or send us home with a note for our parents—which many of them could not read because it was written in English—telling them we were not allowed to speak Spanish in school. That is how they confused us, how they taught us that the clash between our languages and our cultures was going to create an identity problem that we would have to deal with for the rest of our lives.

I wish I could tell you that the autobiographical circumstances I just rendered bilingually are a relic of the past—a consequence of an unenlightened educational policy long ago overwritten by progressive forces that took hold and introduced an era of linguistic equity, inclusion and social justice in the United States. Unfortunately, disenfranchised children in this country today who speak a language other than English are still going through what I experienced more than 50 years ago as linguistic colonization. Matters are further complicated by the fact that children who speak or write a dialect other than Standard American English (SAE) face the same consequences. As hard as progressive theorists, researchers and educators have worked to improve conditions in the nation's public schools, we still find ourselves constrained by an anti-immigrant and anti-multilingual hysteria that has almost eliminated bilingual education programs in schools across the nation and has resulted in the successful passage of English Only legislation in 31 states. Despite our best efforts, the powers-that-be continue to fix and standardize the use of language in our English Only schools (Horner & Trimbur, 2002), further limiting the ability of students to develop and deploy a more complete and flexible repertoire of linguistic practices whenever they engage others deliberately and discursively in the various personal and public spheres they are likely to inhabit over the course of their everyday lives.

As scholars in composition and literacy studies caught in the web of a historical moment profoundly influenced by new capitalism (Fairclough, 1992, 1999; Gee & Lankshear, 1995), we find ourselves looking for ways to intervene in the lives of our students in a collective effort to provide them with the critical awareness of language they need to navigate and negotiate an increasingly complex and ever fluctuating set of circumstances. At the heart of our efforts is a desire to arm our students with an orientation—a new set of dispositions—toward language that will give them the ability to respond critically and self-reflectively to the competing ideologies that hail and interpellate them (Althusser, 2001, p. 115) as they make decisions about how to use the repertoire of languages and dialects at their disposal. While understanding what it means to instill a critical language awareness in our students is crucial to our endeavor, we cannot avoid wrestling with and taking a position on the various alternatives that have been posed in the current debate regarding the development of an approach to language difference that will equip our students with the rhetorical and discursive tools they need to navigate and negotiate the social spaces they routinely inhabit over the course of their everyday lives.

To accomplish these aims in the present chapter, I first review the development of critical language awareness by modern linguists as a strategy for equipping students (and their teachers as well) with a new set of self-reflective dispositions they can use to navigate and negotiate the various ideological approaches to language difference they are likely to encounter in classrooms, on campuses and in a range of other communities of belonging over the course of their studies and beyond. Along with Fairclough (1999), I argue that "as the shape of the new global social order becomes clearer, so too does the need for a critical awareness of language as part of people's resources for living in new ways" (p. 71). I then unpack what several theorists, researchers and educators have described as the three ideological approaches to the teaching of language difference—the *monolingual, multilingual* and *translingual*—with the specific goal of demonstrating how each of these addresses (or by itself fails to address) the educational needs of all, but especially disenfranchised, students. Because I consider the monolingual (code-segregation) approach generally debilitating and the translingual (code-meshing) approach necessary but insufficient, I conclude the chapter by explaining why I believe that our students must learn to deploy multilingual (code-switching) and translingual (code-meshing) tactics and strategies—at the same time that they learn how to respond proactively to the monolingual (code-segregation) constraints they inevitably face—in the varied rhetorical and discursive circumstances they are likely to encounter over the course of their personal, academic, civic and professional lives.

The Emergence of Critical Language Awareness

Critical Language Awareness (CLA)—a perspective originally postulated by Clark, Fairclough, Ivanič and Martin-Jones (1990, 1991; see also Clark & Ivanič, 1991, 1999; Fairclough, 1992, 1999; Gee & Lankshear, 1995) in the late 1980s as the best intervention for achieving the kind of critical consciousness (*conscientização*) Freire (1970) championed—grew out of the *Language Awareness* (LA) movement founded by Hawkins (1984, 1999) in the mid- to late-1970s. At around the same time that composition and literacy scholars in the US were calling for the establishment of a *Writing Across the Curriculum* approach to the teaching of writing, Hawkins and other likeminded scholars in the UK were calling for an even more ambitious *Language Across the Curriculum* approach that included foreign languages as well as the complete English Language Arts spectrum (speaking, listening, reading *and* writing). Hawkins (1984, 1999) reports that he and his colleagues were tremendously frustrated in their early efforts to institute a Language Awareness approach by the failure of the schools to encourage students and teachers to develop the self-reflective awareness they need to unravel the language differences they encounter in their academic and everyday lives. In a huff of exasperation, Hawkins describes how teachers of English at the 1978 National Congress on Languages in Education (NCLE) conference in the UK bitterly opposed a proposal that he and his colleagues put forth to improve the awareness of language use among students and teachers in the public schools (1999, p. 125).

In recounting its history, Hawkins (1999) points out that the concept of LA he and his colleagues proposed at NCLE had its roots in the work of a number of trailblazing scholars in the field of language studies. Shortly after the use of Latin experienced its growing demise in the 1950s as a university admission requirement in the UK, for example, it was modern linguists, such as Crowther and his colleagues, who raised the important question, "What should be put into the curriculum to 'do what Latin does'?" Their response, according to Hawkins, was to call for "rethinking the whole basis of the teaching of linguistics in the schools" (cited in Hawkins, 1999, p. 125) along the lines put forth by proponents of an emerging LA paradigm. As Halliday (1975), the first scholar in the UK to refer to the need for an "awareness of language," put it:

> [each one of us] has this ability (to use language) and lives by it; but we do not always become aware of it . . . [T]here should be some place for language in the working life of the secondary school pupil, and, it might be added, of the student in a College of Education.
>
> *cited in Hawkins, 1999, p. 125*

When the LA approach failed to take root as quickly as its proponents had hoped, they redoubled their efforts and forcefully accented the need for LA in schools, something that in time more theorists, researchers and educators started to take up in a collective effort to help students develop a fuller repertoire of language, cultural and semiotic resources.

Instead of having students focus their energies on the objective study of language, Hawkins and his followers called on teachers to get students to ask questions about language beyond the traditional focus on grammar and syntax. Moreover, instead of limiting their study to language's "pragmatic" function, which simply comments on what students already know about language, Hawkins (1999) encouraged educators to get students to focus on meaning making (pp. 135–136). Hawkins believed that educators could help students overcome "an uncertain attitude to language" that caused many of them to lose confidence "in using language for particular functions, especially for exploring new and strange, possibly challenging, realities" (p. 127). The ultimate goal in becoming aware of language, Hawkins and other modern linguists contended, was to get students to focus on what Halliday calls the mathetic function of language, that is, the metacognitive use of language "to learn about reality" (Halliday, 1975, p. 15). In Hawkins' view, the best way to measure how effectively students are learning a language is not by assessing their "mere ability to 'survive' in a series of situations," but by how well the experience of learning a language contributes "to *learning how to learn* through language" (p. 138, italics in original).

As powerful as an increased understanding of language can be in providing students and teachers with an orientation that encourages them to be more self-reflective about their language use and the language use of others, a number of scholars argued that LA as it was conceived by Hawkins and his colleagues remained too constraining because it failed to alert students to the role of power in language discrimination and standardization. To move the conversation forward, Fairclough (1992, 1999) and other scholars proposed instead that we cultivate in our students what they refer to as *Critical Language Awareness* (CLA). At the heart of CLA is a commitment to work together through the differences we face—especially when it comes to language—in every aspect of the lives we share with other human beings. The challenge, in Fairclough's view, is to remember that

> working across differences is a process in our individual lives, within the groups we belong to, as well as between groups. Working across differences entails semiotic hybridity—the emergence of new combinations of languages, social dialects, voices, genres and discourses. Hybridity, heterogeneity, intertextuality are salient features of contemporary discourse also because the boundaries between domains and practices are in many cases fluid and open in a context of rapid and intense social change.
>
> *(1999, p. 76)*

Fairclough's position here reflects an appreciation of the kind of Deleuzian desire I described in Chapter 1, but he also acknowledges the challenge of coping with what he calls a *technologisation of discourse* that "produces general formulas for change which tend to ignore differences of context, so that one effect of such cultural technologisation is normalisation, homogenisation and the reduction of difference" (1999, p. 77).

A number of scholars have extended our understanding of CLA by providing additional background information about its inception and its current value in helping all students navigate and negotiate the treacherous ideological waters they encounter in the college classroom and other communities of belonging. Clark and Ivanič (1999), who along with Fairclough and Martin-Jones originally coined the term in 1987 (see especially Clark et al., 1990, 1991), for instance, complain about how LA "ignores issues of ideology, subject-positioning and power" and becomes complicit in using language to maintain social inequities (p. 63). In their view, CLA—shaped by the same principles that inform the field of *Critical Discourse Analysis* (CDA)—trumps LA by professing that "language is shaped by and shapes values, beliefs and power relations in its sociocultural context." Language use, Clark and Ivanič (1999) add, can also contribute "to discoursal and social change" (p. 64).

Like other proponents interested in demonstrating how CLA can be integrated into classroom practices (see Janks, 1993, 1996), Clark & Ivanič developed a CLA approach to the teaching of academic writing that provides

> opportunities for students to examine and critique dominant academic discourse practices within linguistics and social science more generally. We aim to help students become more aware of the complex relationship between the institution, discourse, social power relations, identities and agency in shaping these practices. Raising critical awareness of these issues with our students allows us to focus on discourse choices and the way they position writers and readers.
>
> *1999, p. 66*

At the heart of the curriculum they propose are pedagogical principles that inform most progressive approaches: *socially situated learning, mainstreaming* (i.e., making something available to all students and not just the marginalized), and *a questioning approach* that is constantly asking the following kinds of questions: "Why are conventions/practices the way they are? In whose interests do they operate? What views of knowledge and representations of the world do they perpetuate? What are the possible alternatives?" (p. 66).

Few scholars in the field that I am aware of have made as valuable a contribution to our understanding of CLA as Males (2000) has in his pursuit of the question "What makes CLA critical?" Males (2000) initiates his inquiry by firmly supporting the pedagogical principles laid out by Clark and Ivanič (1999), arguing that "language education should have as a goal the achievement of a critical consciousness concerning the discourse practices found in the various communities to which students belong" (Males, 2000, p. 147). Males then uses three of Gadamer's (1993) conceptual notions (dialectic of experience, historically effected consciousness, and the dialectic of question and answer) as a frame of reference for describing how CLA can become a transformative tool when it is used effectively to cultivate a critical perspective on language. In any new experience, Males (2000) contends,

> consciousness recognizes what it knows through what is other or alien to its past experience [and this] consciousness of something as other than what experience anticipates leads to the reversal of consciousness itself in that what was other, what negates consciousness' anticipation, is experienced as a new unity through the reorganisation of past experience.
>
> *p. 149*

In contrast to earlier assumptions, the dialectic of experience "does not lead to a self-knowledge that culminates in Hegel's science or absolute knowledge but rather leads to a new orientation towards experiences" (p. 149). It produces a new understanding of why one must experience "a distance or separation of the self from the self in the process of integrating the alien, the new, the unexpected" (p. 153). It is, Males (2000) concludes, the space opened up by this distance or separation—this venturing into a liminal space between old and new experiences, if you will—that creates the critical instance (p. 153). In the next chapter, I will discuss a critical instance in greater detail when I look at the role that *Critical Cultural Awareness*, the flipside of *Critical Language Awareness*, plays in the process of locating one's self in the liminal space I have described here.

I would be remiss if I did not mention some of the criticism that scholars in the field have launched against CLA, especially since I agree with a number of them. In tying CLA to critical pedagogy, Wallace (1999) worries that if we see both only in terms of "resistance from the margins, the students may feel continuingly marginalized by the very pedagogies which are committed to their emancipation" (p. 101). For that reason, she argues, we need to make sure neither CLA nor critical pedagogy is "perceived as a marginalized activity—the particular concern of groups 'marked' by difference" (p. 101). If we hope to make CLA a meaningful, long-term educational project, Wallace insists that it needs to be seen as valuable by mainstream students as well (p. 102). It must also be guided, she insists, by an orientation that sees CLA as a form of resistance rather than opposition. In contrast to opposition, she points out, resistance "is a considered, reflected upon, rational stance, accompanied by justification and exemplification and open to the scrutiny of others." Such a stance, Wallace (1999) reminds us, "allows us a degree of detachment and distance from the kind of ideological prejudgments which some critics . . . have cautioned against" (p. 102). Based on what she learned from teaching a critical reading course founded on these principles, Wallace (1999) identifies several key aspects that reflect the kind of orientation she is proposing:

> a capacity to gain some distance from one's own identities, experiences and circumstances in light of greater understanding of those of others; an understanding of the nature of disadvantage and injustice beyond that personally experienced; being able to collaborate in discussion and debate to reach positions of consensus or agreement to disagree; and finally, having tools to articulate views rationally and coherently.
>
> *p. 104*

The rest of this chapter will use the key conceptual ideas I have outlined here to support my argument that all students, but especially the disenfranchised, must be made explicitly aware of the competing ideologies that inform their language use and the language use of others. Because I agree with Svalbert's (2007) observation that "uptake could be limited by [CLA's] confrontational nature" (p. 298), I must also temper my enthusiasm for CLA despite the fact that I consider it the most viable response to language difference currently available to us. Overall, I am quite impressed with the goals that proponents of an approach grounded in CLA have set for themselves and the way they are going about trying to achieve them. The one problem that remains for me is the insistence reflected in CLA that students should focus exclusively on understanding this approach as a single and isolated entity rather than examining it in the context of the tripartite network of ideological approaches that I outlined in Chapter 1. At the same time, I can understand this attitude because it is exactly what every competing ideology does: It typically presents itself as the only answer to whatever dilemma we are trying to solve.

As will become increasingly evident over the course of the rest of this chapter, I am also not completely persuaded by the number of arguments against appropriateness made by scholars who support CLA (Fairclough, 1999), code-meshing (Young, 2009; Young, Barrett, Young-Rivera & Lovejoy, 2014; Young & Martínez, 2011) and translingualism (Canagarajah, 2013; Horner, Lu, Royster & Trimbur, 2011; Lu & Horner, 2013b) because I continue to see appropriateness as one of the key elements that anyone engaging in language use must always acknowledge when confronted with the needs of a particular genre, audience or set of goals. Because appropriateness always informs the choices we make, I want to argue that it remains a consistent and inescapable force in our everyday lives. That, however, does not mean we should all behave appropriately all of the time. As Males (2000) and Wallace (1999) demonstrate in their work, resistance is often called for and should be acted on, but it needs to be balanced with a respect for the historically grounded and widely accepted values that continue to inform our language practices. Knowing when to do one thing (resist) or the other (accommodate) is what the approach to language difference that I am proposing here is all about.

Code-Segregation Revisited

What many of us living on the border between Texas and Mexico were put through as children in our public schools more than 50 years ago as I described it in the autobiographical passage that opens this chapter continues to be a problem. To this day, many of the children from my era and I carry the negative weight of our linguistic experiences in school with us; *una vergüenza tremenda* that continues to color our perspective on the world-at-large. Despite the fact that we have all become proficient in English—some of us to the point of becoming professors of the language of power in the U.S.—and have figured out why we were forbidden to speak our mother tongue in school in the first place, we still carry traces of the shame and self-doubt that our teachers—and especially the school system that trained them to behave as they did—planted in us. Today, because most children are no longer psychologically burdened by the pernicious ideology of code-segregation, that is, because they are no longer overtly told by their schools or their teachers that their first language or dialect is lacking in skill and grace, we consider ourselves enlightened. As a consequence, many of us think we are avoiding the damage and harm that a negative attitude among educators can visit on any child who speaks a language or dialect other than Standard American English. But are we really?

Code-segregation,[2] a term I coined because I was confused by the contradictory definitions of code-switching that have emerged in recent years, is a very familiar concept to any of us who grew up in pre-1960s America when racial segregation was the law of the land. As I noted in my autobiographical narrative at the beginning of this chapter, we were not only constrained to live in different communities based on linguistic, class and cultural differences; even when we all finally shared the same classrooms in middle school and high school, we were persuaded by the malevolent social, cultural, and political forces in play at the time to keep to ourselves and stay with our own kind. The personal narrative that began this chapter describes the attitudes of a school system supported by a state mandate that utterly refused to acknowledge any value in the linguistic practices children in the housing project I grew up in directly across the street from our public elementary school used at home and in the community. As the narrative makes clear, the ideology of code-segregation—founded on the basis of profound monolingual and monocultural values, beliefs and practices—encourages total assimilation by children who speak a language other than English, as well as varieties of English that have little status in the broader society. It demands that children strictly and without deviation completely adapt to a hierarchical world that has been carefully construed to avoid dealing with difference.

At least until the pre-civil rights battles of the 1960s, most educators in the United States were persuaded to enforce nativist assumptions inherent in the widely accepted practice of code-segregation. Because Standard American English was (and continues to be) firmly ensconced in our educational system as the code of power—a way with words expected of all our students—most educators and the institutions that managed and controlled their labor at the time had no qualms about eliding the alternative codes children brought with them to school from their varied communities of belonging. In Texas, where I was born and raised, for example, the use of Spanish was banned from public schools for many years after I graduated. In his award-winning essay, "*Spanglish* as Literacy Tool: Toward an Understanding of the Potential Role of Spanish-English Code-Switching in the Development of Academic Literacy," Martínez (2010) informs us that English-Spanish code-switching is now "common in schools throughout the Los Angeles Unified School District . . . and [is] also becoming increasingly common in school districts nationwide, as demographic shifts and changing immigration patterns continue to significantly reshape the nation's linguistic landscape" (p. 125). I hope this is true, but I suspect that because of the current anti-immigrant and anti-multilingual hysteria, as well as a deeply ingrained anti-Black racism in too many communities in this country, migrant and immigrant children who code-switch between their native language and English, and African American children who code-switch between Ebonics and

English, are still covertly and at times overtly discouraged from using both codes freely or simultaneously in the classroom.

The autobiographical narrative with which I began this chapter paints a bleak picture of what happens when schools keep students from using all the linguistic, cultural and semiotic resources available to them. It is code-segregation at its worst. It is also a manifestation of what I refer to as *language-in-stasis*, language as an entity that has become fossilized over time into a standardized variant that everyone is expected to emulate. Whether it is patterned after an ideology that grows out of a belief that sharing one language contributes to patriotism and love of country, or out of a suspicion of what others may be saying in a language someone else does not understand, the end result is the same: A negation of any other means of communication that challenges the standard by which everyone in a community is supposed to be assessed. Despite the fact that code-segregation has always been a problematic approach to teaching language and literacy to students of all ages, the disenfranchised in particular, it manages to persist in the insidious No-Child-Left-Behind tests and drills and continues to linger in the Common Core State Standards initiative currently being introduced in our public schools, both of which reinforce the depressing realization that code-segregation will never be completely excised from our educational practices. Fortunately, continuing dissatisfaction with this language-in-stasis model has given birth to code-switching and code-meshing, two alternative approaches to what language is and how it works. To better understand how we can effectively combat code-segregation in our efforts to develop meaningfully productive approaches to the teaching and learning of language and literacy, let us take a closer look at each of these alternatives in turn.

Code-Switching across Repertoires of Practice

In a thought-provoking essay titled "Nah, We Straight: An Argument Against Code Switching," Young (2009) criticizes what he sees as "the prevailing definition of code-switching that language educators promote as the best practice for teaching speaking and writing to African American and other 'accent- and dialect-speakers' of English." In his view, it represents an approach that "advocates language substitution, the linguistic translation of Spanglish or AAE into standard English," and "characterizes the teaching of language conversion" (p. 50). To support his critique, he examines the work of Wheeler and Swords (2006) who in a recent publication, *Code-Switching: Teaching Standard English in Urban Classrooms*, promote a pedagogy based on the argument that Black English and Standard American English are equal, that is, that each is considered prestigious in its respective community, then use the former only as transitional fodder for developing expertise in the latter. Young (2009) also criticizes prominent Black linguists Rickford and Rickford (2000) and Smitherman (1977), among others, for arguing that African American students must master Black English and

Standard American English, then learn to deploy them appropriately. Although his critique of Wheeler and Swords raises some valid concerns, I would argue that his critique of Rickford and Smitherman is misplaced because he conflates what I earlier described as code-segregation with code-switching based on appropriateness of language use, the latter of which, in contrast to his critique, can be construed as a powerful approach to addressing the weighty problems that we currently confront in our efforts to develop pedagogical support for the needs of all, but especially disenfranchised, students.

There is no question that anyone who advocates dismissing the linguistic, cultural and semiotic repertoires of practice that students use at home and in their communities of belonging as soon as they have served a transitional purpose in the classroom is engaging in a modern day form of code-segregation. To dismiss the role of race, class or gender as unimportant variables in the teaching and learning of language and literacy is to harken back to the day when Standard American English was assumed to be the only code worth learning. On the other hand, I must disagree with proponents of code-meshing who are unwilling to acknowledge the critical distinction that progressive scholars make when they argue that we must expand the repertoires of practice students bring with them to the classroom and encourage them to deploy their full arsenal tactically, strategically and appropriately as they navigate the multiplicity of linguistic and cultural contexts that they encounter in the course of their everyday lives. In so doing, these students are acknowledging a critical language awareness of the role that hierarchical power plays in the choices they are called on to make. Moreover, as I noted in my critique of Leander and Boldt's (2012) effort to dismiss the New London Group's contributions to the field in Chapter 1, I simply cannot ignore the critical contributions that some of the most highly acclaimed theorists, researchers and educators in the field have made to our understanding of how best to use the rhetorical and discursive resources disenfranchised students in particular bring with them from their homes and communities of belonging. This is why I believe that it is time for us to re-appropriate the term code-switching and rehabilitate it so that we can use it more productively in our work on language difference.

In K-12 settings, for example, a form of code-switching that advances the cause of social justice has manifested itself in the development of an array of carefully researched curricular and pedagogical approaches that value and use the languages and dialects students bring with them to the classroom from their communities of belonging. This particular form of code-switching—in contrast to what Young et al. (2014) describe as code-switching but I prefer to describe as code-segregation—acknowledges the important role that appropriateness plays in language use. Of the many researchers who have contributed to this work, I will focus on Lee (2007) and Gutiérrez (2008) because their strategies are assiduously crafted and have been widely adopted by progressive scholars in the field.

In her research, Lee has developed a *cultural modeling framework* that demonstrates how "powerful connections between African American students' everyday language practices and the skills required to interpret canonical literary texts . . . can be effectively leveraged in the service of academic learning" (Martínez, 2010, p. 127). Grounded in ethnographic research in an inner city high school setting, Lee (2007) uses her work on the African American rhetorical practice of signifying to develop an alternative to theories informed by what she describes as structural differences, cultural deficits, and cultural mismatches that ignore the value inherent in the funds of knowledge (González, Moll & Amanti, 2005; Moll, Amanti, Neff & González, 1992) students bring with them to school. Gutiérrez (2008), on the other hand, has studied the linguistic and cultural repertoires that Latino and Latina students bring with them as Spanish and English bilinguals in the context of what she calls the Third Space, "a transformative space where the potential for an expanded form of learning and the development of new knowledge are heightened" (p. 152). In her work, Gutiérrez (2008) provides a well-traveled and thought-out map for how we can help what she calls nondominant and I call disenfranchised students acquire repertoires of practice, that is, "both vertical and horizontal forms of expertise . . . [that include] not only what students learn in formal learning environments such as schools, but also what they learn by participating in a range of practices outside of school" (p. 149). In her carefully construed ecological approach, learning is organized in such a way that conversation, dialogue and examination of contradictions are privileged across learning activities with varied participation structures: tutorials, comprehension circles, writing conferences, *teatro*, minilectures and whole-class discussions (p. 154).

Unfortunately, what I refer to as code-segregation has manifested itself in more conservative terms that lie closer to Young et al.'s (2014) description of code-switching in first-year college writing programs and Writing Across the Curriculum settings, primarily because their proponents have generally assumed that students in higher education need to be initiated into more rigorous and demanding English Only academic contexts. While proponents of first-year writing approaches have noted the importance of valuing the linguistic and cultural repertoires that students bring to the classroom, until very recently, the inclination has been to focus on the demystification of academic language to make it easier for students to adapt to an array of academic discourses that grant little opportunity for the integration of the linguistic practices or the lived experiences students bring with them. This approach continues to be grounded in work that assumes disenfranchised students are being asked to learn a new dialect and new discourse conventions in the process of acquiring "a whole new world view" (Bizzell, 1986, p. 297). As Bartholomae (1986) put it when this perspective first emerged: Any student entering the academy "has to learn to speak our languages, to speak as we do, to try on the peculiar ways of knowing, selecting, evaluating, reporting, concluding, and arguing that define the discourse of our community" (p. 4). The almost exclusive devotion to academic discourse among proponents of Writing Across the Curriculum at the expense of the linguistic and cultural repertoires that students bring with them to the classroom has been no less stringent. In both instances, it is assumed that to be successful, students must learn how to code-switch (as Young et al. define the term) from their home languages and dialects to academic discourses and in the process leave the linguistic and cultural repertoires they bring with them at the door.

Along a continuum with code-segregation at one end and code-switching (as I define these terms) at the other, there is no question that the curricular and pedagogical practices used in college and university settings are much closer to the former than the practices invoked in K-12 settings. I would argue that this occurs because of the different institutional contexts and time constraints that inform each set of practices. It is also true that like code-segregation, code-switching (as I describe it) asks us to adapt to the world by behaving appropriately. There is no way around that. Educators who support a progressive form of code-switching certainly acknowledge the importance of having students develop a critical awareness of how language works in varied contexts. But where the ideology that informs code-segregation is based on a profound fear of change to the point of paralyzing language, that is, freezing it in place as some idealized standard language performance, code-switching (as I define it) acknowledges that change is inevitable and purports that the best option available to our students is for them to figure out how to use their "full quiver" of linguistic, cultural and semiotic resources to address what Selfe (2009) has described as the "wickedly complex communicative tasks" that we all face in an increasingly "challenging and difficult world" (p. 645). Unlike the form of code-switching promoted by such teachers and scholars as Wheeler and Swords, the brand of code-switching I advocate, which always goes hand in hand with code-meshing, is a manifestation of what I call *individuals-in-motion* because it is a tool our students can use nimbly, tactically, and self-reflectively rather than only intuitively to navigate and negotiate the curricular and pedagogical spaces they inhabit in our college classrooms, across our campuses and in an array of other communities of belonging as they move *from* one social space to another and *within* varied social spaces as well.

Code-Meshing as Pedagogical Alternative

In the back cover to their edited collection titled *Code-Meshing as World Englishes: Pedagogy, Policy and Performance*, Young and Martínez (2011) posit what they see as the most striking difference between their versions of code-switching and code-meshing:

> Although linguists have traditionally viewed code-switching as the simultaneous use of two language varieties in a single context, scholars and teachers of English have appropriated the term to argue for teaching

minority students to monitor their languages and dialects according to context. For advocates of code-switching, teaching students to distinguish between "home language" and "school language" offers a solution to the tug-of-war between standard and non-standard Englishes. . . . The original essays in this collection offer various perspectives on why code-meshing—blending minoritized dialects and world Englishes with Standard English—is a better pedagogical alternative than code-switching in the teaching of reading, writing, listening, speaking, and visually representing to diverse learners.

n.p.

According to Young (2004), who coined the term code-meshing as an alternative to code-switching and code-mixing (p. 713),[3] the ideology behind code-meshing "holds that people's so-called 'nonstandard' dialects are already fully compatible with standard English. [Thus,] code meshing secures their right to represent that meshing in all forms and venues where they communicate" (Young, 2009, p. 62). Although it acknowledges that standard principles for communication exist, a code-meshing approach "encourages speakers and writers to fuse the standard with native speech habits, to color their writing with what they bring from home" (pp. 64–65). Managed appropriately, Young contends, the implementation of a code-meshing approach "has the potential to enlarge our national vocabulary, multiply the range of rhetorical styles, expand our ability to understand linguistic difference and make us in the end multidialectical, as opposed to monodialectical" (p. 65).

Other proponents of code-meshing have reinforced and expanded Young's original conceptions of what is clearly a new and refreshing take on how educators can support the repertoire of linguistic, cultural and semiotic practices that students bring to the writing classroom. In keeping with Young's efforts to simultaneously acknowledge and destabilize the value of Standard American English by "extending the range of grammatical forms that students may use to express themselves," Barrett adds that "code-meshing recognizes the importance of *both* standard and undervalued varieties in contexts beyond the classroom (Young et al., 2014, p. 43, italics in original). But this can only happen, Barrett stresses, if educators in the field of composition and literacy studies are willing to acknowledge that

> *all* forms of language contain variation and that *all* forms of language are regular rule-based systems. Teaching Standard English in ways that exclude undervalued dialects from the formal aspects of school curricula and testing is destined to make children feel uncomfortable and unwelcome in academic environments. By fostering the use of multiple varieties of English, the code-meshing approach can be beneficial to students both

in teaching self-respect and in fostering the ability to communicate across a wider range of social contexts.

p. 51, italics in original

As Lippi-Green (2011)—another proponent of code-meshing—sees it, code-meshing is grounded in "the belief that it is possible for people to live their lives free of the compulsion to choose between language varieties" (p. xii). Code-meshing, then, is conceived of as a critical strategy that educators need to encourage students to consider in the writing classroom because it disrupts the range of constraints imposed by the forces of fixity and standardization at the same time that it provides them with opportunities to blend the repertoire of languages and dialects they bring from home with those they encounter in school.

In his contributions to the literature on code-meshing, Canagarajah locates Young's concept at the heart of current trends in composition and literacy studies—transcultural literacy, translingual writing, multiliteracies, translanguaging and plurilingualism, to name a few—that aim to disrupt forces of assimilation and standardization. According to Canagarajah (2011b), adherents of all these related approaches operate on the basis of several principles, among them the belief that

- Languages are always in contact and influence each other.
- All the codes in a multilingual user's repertoire are a continuum, not discrete elements.
- Multilinguals do not have separate competencies for separately labeled languages (as traditional linguistics assumes) but an integrated competence that is different in kind (not just degree) from monolingual competence.
- Although stable systems of language (in the form of registers, genres, and dialects) do evolve from local language practices, they are always open to renegotiation and reconstruction as multilinguals mesh other codes in their repertoire to achieve the voice they want.

pp. 273–274

At the same time that he reinforces many of the principles that inform a code-meshing approach, Canagarajah introduces a degree of caution that is often missing in the often overly optimistic renderings of the role that code-meshing can play in preparing students for the difficult rhetorical and discursive challenges they, like all of us, face in a world where the contestation of ideologies often produces more confusion than clarity, more diffidence than self-confidence. Scholars, he states bluntly, "must guard against romanticizing the concept" (2011b, p. 276). In my view, Canagarajah offers a more nuanced description of code-meshing that complements a number of the arguments I have made in this chapter. But in contrast to his claim that "codeswitching treats language alternation as involving bilingual competence and switches between two different systems" while "codemeshing treats the languages as part of a single integrated system" (2011a, p. 403), I contend that code-switching and code-meshing should be treated as complementary parts of a single integrated system rather than as dichotomous practices. Much of what he suggests in supporting his own contention, I would argue, parallels much of what proponents who embrace code-switching and code-meshing have claimed. For example, just as I do, Canagarajah contends that "students have to develop a critical awareness of the choices that are rhetorically more effective" (2011a, p. 402). After all, he reminds us, code-meshing is not "a mechanical activity independent of the specific communicative situation" in which it takes place. Moreover, he adds, "one has to carefully assess the extent to which one can codemesh in a given context" (p. 404). In other words, there will be times when students (as they do when they code-switch in the way I have been describing it) must downplay code-meshing entirely if the circumstances call for it.

Lu and Horner (2013a), who have clearly acknowledged the value of code-meshing in the past as well, recently commented on the on-going debate about the relationship between code-switching and code-meshing. Some writers, they note,

> appear to assume that taking a translingual approach to language would require that students engage in code-meshing, and that they avoid code-switching, in their writing, and that they avoid producing writing that appears to simply reproduce standardized conventions of syntax, notation, register, and organization. However, from our perspective, taking a trans-lingual approach does not prescribe the forms of writing that students are to produce. Instead, it calls on students (and their teachers) to develop specific dispositions toward languages, language users, contexts and consequences of language use, and the relations between all these, and to do so in all their engagements with reading and writing.
>
> *p. 29*

Although code-meshing is without a doubt a useful strategy that we need to teach all our students, its use must be tempered by the realization that rhetorical circumstances sometimes compel students to engage in code-switching, not because it is a compulsive response as Lippi-Green (2011) suggests, but because it happens to be the more appropriate response to a particular rhetorical situation.

Appropriateness and Appropriation

As I have demonstrated over the course of this chapter, some theorists, researchers and educators in the field of composition and literacy studies are convinced that code-switching (as code-meshing proponents have defined it) is anathema and code-meshing is our only viable alternative (Canagarajah, 2006, 2011b, 2013; Horner et al., 2011; Young, 2009; Young et al., 2014; Young & Martínez, 2011). Others (Guerra, 2012; Lu & Horner, 2013b), however, have begun to argue for accepting code-switching (as I have defined it in this chapter) and code-meshing as a legitimate tandem of approaches to language difference that together form a continuum rather than a binary. Lu and Horner (2013b) frame the argument in this way:

> [A]dopting the temporal-spatial framework of a translingual approach identifies agency in the production of what is recognized as code-switching and also what is recognized as code-meshing, as writers contribute in both these types of writing to the ongoing process of language sedimentation and the production of difference through recontextualization. To assign agency to only one of these kinds of practices results from a failure to locate the practices themselves temporally, as always emergent and necessarily subject to recontextualization with every utterance.
>
> *p. 600*

My 40 plus years as a writing teacher—many of them spent in college writing classrooms with some of the most underprepared students that Chicago's inner-city communities produced in the 1970s and 1980s—have persuaded me that code-switching *and* code-meshing, rather than code-meshing alone, unquestionably provide the best response at our disposal.

In the midst of the complex linguistic, cultural and semiotic challenges our students face in their everyday lives, the need to be rhetorically savvy trumps all other language practices. As much as many of us would like our students to engage in the lively practice of code-meshing on a continuous basis, we know from lived experience that context matters. We never speak or write the same way everywhere; we always adapt or adjust in appropriate ways that are always measured by degrees of difference. But whenever the moment calls for it, we do not hesitate to resist in ways that are measured by difference in kind. Let me illustrate what I am describing here by using the autobiographical narrative with which I began this chapter as a case study to explain what I see as the difference between adaptation and resistance. As you may recall, the first paragraph in this chapter is written entirely in monolingual Spanish and represents my first language, the one I spoke exclusively until I walked into my first grade classroom and our teacher Mrs. Rosales began to teach us English. In the context of the three ideological responses to language difference I outlined earlier in this chapter, the second and third paragraphs in the bilingual narrative illustrate code-meshing at its best. In both of these cases, I purposefully and dramatically resisted reader expectations. The fourth and final paragraph illustrates the act of code-switching that I am still engaged in as I write these words, at this very moment, right now, in real time. It is the response that I felt compelled to call on to make sure I would have a better chance of communicating my ideas with the largest number of anticipated readers: other scholars in my field of study.

Let us speculate for a second. What if I had decided to write in monolingual Spanish from the moment I began this chapter until its end? While a handful of readers may have praised me as the ultimate rebel for taking a definitive stance against the straight-jacketing constraints of the Standard American English and English Only academic discourses that U.S. scholars teach and traffic in, a larger number of readers would have been disappointed because I would not have met their expectations. On the other hand, if I had kept code-meshing throughout the chapter the way I did in the two middle paragraphs of the autobiographical narrative that I used to open this chapter, all non-Spanish or monolingual English readers would have managed to pick up at least half of what I wrote, but would have had difficulty following the logic of my inquiry because large chunks of information would have been inaccessible to readers with limited Spanish proficiency. As a consequence, we would have suffered a different kind of communication breakdown. In the end, I obviously decided to use what we recognize as academic English for the rest of this chapter because our ultimate goal as writers and rhetoricians enacting discourse is always to communicate as effectively as possible with whatever audience we have elected to address. That choice, to me, is what code-switching as I have defined it is all about. We read our audience, and we perform in a way that reflects the dynamic tension between a clueless conformity and a relentless rebellion. To put it another way, our decision as writers to engage in code-switching or code-meshing is guided by our continuous reading and re-reading of what is linguistically appropriate in any context and our willingness to appropriate language practices available to us and to use them in a particular rhetorical manner. The closer we choose to stick to convention in *any* setting, the more likely we are to engage in code-switching; the more we choose to be innovative in our language use, the more likely we are to engage in code-meshing.

If we are interested in creating conditions in classrooms under which students can acquire the tools they need to navigate and negotiate the troubled waters of their linguistic, cultural and semiotic existence, we must first encourage them to develop a critical awareness of how language works. While they should feel at home with their growing repertoire of rhetorical and discursive practices, they also need to be able to enact them with some degree of dexterity. In Bawarshi's (2003) words, we need "to teach our students how to become rhetorically astute and agile, how in other words, to . . . become more effective and critical 'readers' of the sites of action (i.e., rhetorical and social scenes)" (p. 165) within which—to borrow Young and Martínez's (2011) words—reading, writing, listening, speaking and visually representing take place. Our students must also learn how to adapt themselves to each rhetorical or discursive situation they encounter by calling on whatever languages, dialects or combinations thereof they deem most productive, knowing at the same time that it is their responsibility to resist the constraining limitations imposed by the rhetorical or discursive circumstances they find themselves in if they hope to make themselves fully heard. In short, it is not up to us as educators to tell our students how they should deploy their linguistic, cultural and semiotic resources; it is up to each of them to decide which of those resources they wish to invoke based on the rhetorical or discursive circumstances they happen to be facing. It is for this reason that I want to encourage us all to provide our students with the critical language awareness they need to make instantaneous decisions about how best to respond to any rhetorical or discursive situation they are likely to face. False dichotomies that cleave their options by framing them as either/or rather than both/and or neither/nor (more on this in the next chapter) are more likely to impede them and grant the decision-making power to us as their teachers rather than keeping it where it belongs: in our students' hands.

Spanish to English Glossary

una vergüenza tremenda [a tremendous shame]
teatro [theater]

Notes

1. Below is a translation of the passages in Spanish—in the context of the original English—that appear in the first three paragraphs of the autobiographical passage that opens this chapter. An English translation of all the other single Spanish words, phrases and sentences I use throughout the book appear in separate glossaries at the end of each chapter.

   When I started my first year of school in south Texas in 1956, all of the children in my classroom were Mexican or Mexican American. None of us spoke even a single word of English. Back then, television was in its infancy, and it was something relatively unfamiliar among poor people who were barely able to make ends meet. There were radios in our homes, but because we lived on the U.S.–Mexican border less than 30 miles from the mouth of the Rio Grande River, all the stations that our parents listened to played music from northern Mexico. At home, in the community, among ourselves, Spanish was the language we used to communicate with one another and to make sense of the known world. At the public school located in our community, everything was backwards. The use of Spanish was completely prohibited.

   By the time we got to junior high school, well we knew the reality of our situation. At home we spoke Spanish and at school we spoke English. The two languages were kept segregated from one another just as we were kept segregated from the Anglos by a railroad track that divided the town in half. White people had their own communities and their own shopping establishments in the downtown section of the city; we lived in our barrios and would go shopping in our little plaza.

   By the time we got to high school, the linguistic division between Spanish and English collapsed completely and we began to blend the two languages into an unrecognizable form, in a way that surprised our parents and our teachers. At the same time that our parents accepted our new way of speaking, albeit with some resistance, the public schools continued to prohibit the use of Spanish and the combination of the two languages: the famous Spanglish. At home and in the community, we artfully switched and meshed codes, borrowing from either language whatever best allowed us to make ourselves understood.

2. In the current debate about how we can best address matters of language difference in the writing classroom, the concept of code-switching has been defined in ways that have convoluted our understanding to the point where we often end up speaking at

cross purposes when we use the term. In an effort to provide some transparency, Barrett (Young et al., 2014) recommends that we make a distinction between *situational code-switching* and *metaphorical code-switching* to describe "the social aspects of alternating between languages" (p. 29). In her view, the first of these two describes "the use of one language variety in school and another language variety at home" (p. 30). This, she declares, is how we should use the term code-switching exclusively in our discussions. Barrett then contends that the term code-meshing has effectively replaced metaphorical code-switching to describe the blending of home and school identities through the process of "combining rather than switching between Englishes" (Young et al., 2014, p. 1). In this chapter, I will use the term code-segregation to describe what Barrett describes as situational code-switching and use the term code-switching to describe a very different set of circumstances. In my conception of code-switching, students do indeed shift from one language or dialect to another on the basis of their understanding of what is appropriate in a particular context. But in contrast to code-segregation, which devalues the home language or dialect and forces educators to get students to transition away from it and toward the exclusive use of Standard American English, my conception of code-switching acknowledges the fact that progressive educators value the home languages and dialects that students have already developed in other contexts and are devoted to expanding their existing repertoires of language and literacy practices in ways that will equip students to respond to the evershifting rhetorical situations they are likely to encounter in their everyday lives in a linguistic marketplace that values both difference *and* appropriateness.

3. Most of us in the field have no doubt assumed that Young coined the term code-meshing, but he humbly grants Gerald Graff credit for coining the term: "A little more than a decade ago, the term code-meshing came up in a conversation I had with literary critic and writing studies scholar Gerald Graff (aka Jerry). I was in his office discussing possible topics for my dissertation. As I wavered over a comparison of Native American and African American autobiographies, a rhetorical analysis of African American drama, or the failure of code-switching to provide African Americans equality, Jerry asked something like, 'What was that you were telling me about code-meshing and African American literacy?' 'Code-meshing?!' I thought. What a great term for what I had been describing to him for months as a blending of discourses, a diglossic, if not heteroglossic (multi-voiced) approach to speaking and writing. So the term code-meshing was really coined by Jerry Graff, and I acknowledge his generosity in allowing me to use it all these years" (Young et al., 2014, p. xiii).

References

Althusser, L. (2001). *Lenin and philosophy and other essays.* (B. Brewster, Trans.). New York, NY: Monthly Review Press.

Bartholomae, D. (1986). Inventing the university. *Journal of Basic Writing*, 5(1), 4–23.

Bawarshi, A. (2003). *Genre and the invention of the writer: Reconsidering the place of invention in composition.* Logan, UT: Utah State University Press.

Bizzell, P. (1986). What happens when basic writers come to college? *College Composition and Communication*, 37(3), 294–301.

Canagarajah, A.S. (2006). The place of world Englishes in composition: Pluralization continued. *College Composition and Communication*, 57(4), 586–619.

Canagarajah, A.S. (2011a). Codemeshing in academic writing: Identifying teachable strategies of translanguaging. *Modern Language Journal*, 95(iii), 401–417.

Canagarajah, A.S. (2011b). World-Englishes as code-meshing. In V.A. Young & A.Y. Martínez (Eds.), *Code-meshing as world English: Pedagogy, policy, performance* (pp. 273–279). Urbana, IL: NCTE.

Canagarajah, A.S. (2013). *Translingual practice: Global Englishes and cosmopolitan relations.* New York, NY: Routledge.

Clark, R. & Ivanič, R. (1991). Consciousness raising about the writing process. In P. Garret & C. James (Eds.), *Language awareness in the classroom* (pp. 168–185). London: Longman.

Clark, R. & Ivanič, R. (1999). Raising critical awareness of language: A curriculum aim for the new millennium. *Language Awareness,* 8(2), 63–70.

Clark, R., Fairclough, N., Ivanič, R. & Martin-Jones, M. (1990) Critical language awareness part I: A critical review of three current approaches to language awareness. *Language and Education,* 4(4), 249–260.

Clark, R., Fairclough, N., Ivanič, R. & Martin-Jones, M. (1991) Critical language awareness part II: Towards critical alternatives. *Language and Education,* 5(1), 41–54.

Fairclough, N. (Ed.). (1992). *Critical language awareness.* New York, NY: Longman.

Fairclough, N. (1999). Global capitalism and critical awareness of language. *Critical Awareness,* 8(2), 71–83.

Freire, P. (1970). *Pedagogy of the oppressed.* New York, NY: Continuum.

Gadamer, H.G. (1993) *Truth and method.* (J. Weinsheimer & D. Marshall, Trans.). New York, NY: Continuum Publishing.

Gee, J.P. & Lankshear, C. (1995). The new work order: Critical language awareness and 'fast capitalism' texts. *Discourse: Studies in the Cultural Politics of Education,* 16(1), 5–19.

González, N., Moll, L. & Amanti, C. (2005). *Funds of knowledge: Theorizing practices in households, communities and classrooms.* Mahwah, NJ: Erlbaum.

Guerra, J.C. (2012). From code-segregation to code-switching to code-meshing: Finding deliverance from deficit thinking through language awareness and performance. In P.J. Dunston & S.K. Fullerton (Eds.), *61st yearbook of the Literacy Research Association* (pp. 108–118). Oak Creek, WI: Literacy Research Association.

Gutiérrez, K. (2008). Developing a sociocritical literacy in the third space. *Reading Research Quarterly,* 43(2), 148–164.

Halliday, M.A.K. (1975). *Learning how to learn.* London: Edward Arnold.

Hawkins, E.W. (1984). *Awareness of language: An introduction.* New York, NY: Cambridge University Press.

Hawkins, E.W. (1999). Foreign language study and language awareness. *Language Awareness,* 8(3–4), 124–142.

Horner, B. & Trimbur, J. (2002). English only and U.S. college composition. *College Composition and Communication,* 53(4), 594–630.

Horner, B., Lu, M.Z., Royster, J.J. & Trimbur J. (2011). Language difference in writing: Toward a translingual approach. *College English,* 73(3), 303–321.

Janks, H. (1993). Developing critical language awareness materials for a post-apartheid South Africa. *English in Australia,* 106, 55–57.

Janks, H. (1996). *Why we still need critical language awareness in South Africa.* South Africa: SPiL Plus, University of Stellenbosch.

Leander, K. & Boldt, G. (2012). Rereading "a pedagogy of multiliteracies": Bodies, texts, and emergence. *Journal of Literacy Research,* 45(1), 22–46.

Lee, C.D. (2007). *Culture, literacy and learning: Taking bloom in the midst of the whirlwind.* New York, NY: Teachers College Press.

Lippi-Green, R. (2011). Foreword. In V.A. Young & A.Y. Martínez (Eds.), *Code-meshing as world English: Pedagogy, policy, performance* (pp. xi–xv). Urbana, IL: NCTE.

Lu, M.-Z. & Horner, B. (2013a). Translingual literacy and matters of agency. In A.S. Canagarajah (Ed.), *Literacy as translingual practice* (pp. 26–38). New York, NY: Routledge.

Lu, M.-Z. & Horner, B. (2013b). Translingual literacy, language difference, and matters of agency. *College English*, 75(6), 582–607.

Males, T. (2000). What is critical in critical language awareness? *Language Awareness*, 9(3), 147–159.

Martínez, R. A. (2010). *Spanglish* as literacy tool: Toward an understanding of the potential role of Spanish-English code-switching in the development of academic literacy. *Research in the Teaching of English*, 45(2), 124–149.

Moll, L., Amanti, L., Neff, D. & González, N. (1992). Funds of knowledge for teaching: Using a qualitative approach to connect homes and classrooms. *Theory into Practice*, 31(2), 132–141.

Rickford, J. R. & Rickford, R. J. (2000). *Spoken soul: The story of Black English*. New York, NY: Wiley.

Selfe, C. L. (2009). The movement of air, the breath of meaning: Aurality and multimodal composing. *College Composition and Communication*, 60(4), 616–663.

Smitherman, G. (1977). *Talkin' and testifyin': The language of Black America*. Detroit, MI: Wayne State University.

Svalbert, A.M.-L. (2007). Language awareness and language learning. *Language Teaching*, 40(4), 287–308.

Wallace, C. (1999). Critical language awareness: Key principles for a course in critical reading. *Language Awareness*, 8(2), 98–110.

Wheeler, R. S. & Swords, R. (2006). *Code-switching: Teaching Standard English in urban classrooms*. Urbana, IL: NCTE.

Young, V. A. (2004). Your average nigga. *College Composition and Communication*, 55(4), 693–715.

Young, V. A. (2009). Nah, we straight: An argument against code switching. *Journal of Advanced Composition*, 29(1–2), 49–76.

Young, V. A. & Martínez, A. Y. (2011). *Code-meshing as world Englishes: Pedagogy, policy and performance*. Urbana, IL: National Council of Teachers of English.

Young, V. A., Barrett, R., Young-Rivera, Y. & Lovejoy, K. B. (2014). *Other people's English: Code-meshing, code-switching, and African American literacy*. New York, NY: Teachers College Press.

3

NAVIGATING CULTURES IN FLUX

Although it is important for our students to develop a critical awareness of how language works, especially in the context of the various ideological approaches to language difference deployed in the college classroom and beyond, it is still not enough to guide the use of the rhetorical and discursive practices they have at their disposal. It is, therefore, incumbent upon us to encourage them also to consider the crucial role that *Critical Cultural Awareness* (Byram, 2012; Fenner, 2008; Agudelo, 2007) plays as they navigate and negotiate the various college classrooms and other communities of belonging they inhabit in the course of interacting with the world-at-large. This is how Dufva (1994) puts it:

> It has become increasingly evident that learning of languages is not a mat-
> ter of *language* only. Issues of *interaction* and *culture* are integral elements of
> language teaching. Therefore, it is not enough to make learners aware of
> language only. They must also be made interactively and culturally aware.
>
> *p. 19, emphasis in original*[1]

Equally important, in my view, is the role that memory plays in the formation of culture and awareness. The literature in the broader field of English Stud- ies offers no better way to examine this connection than through the concept of cultural memory,[2] which Bal (1999) tells us, "signifies that memory can be understood as a cultural phenomenon as well as an individual and a social one" (p. viii). It is also, she reminds us, "an activity occurring in the present, in which the past is continuously modified and redescribed even as it continues to shape the future" (p. vii). Like the figurations[3] (Braidotti, 1994) that I presented in the preceding two chapters and those I plan to present in future chapters, the ones I present in this one—*Critical Cultural Awareness* and *cultural modalities of memory*, among others—are part of the repertoire of rhetorical and discursive tools our students must have at their disposal each time they move *from* one social space to another and *within* social spaces as well (Bourdieu, 1989).

In explaining the integral role that culture plays in how we navigate and negotiate the real and imagined worlds we inhabit, and in response to Horner and Trimbur's (2002) recommendation that scholars in composition and literacy studies work across related disciplines in language education, this chapter begins by complementing the discussion of Critical Language Awareness in the previous chapter with a review of what scholars in foreign language education have come to call Critical Cultural Awareness (CCA). After unpacking the key elements that inform the construction and application of CCA, especially as it manifests itself through what Kramsch (2009, 2013) calls *Third Culture* and Gutiérrez (2008) and others call *Third Space*, I introduce *Life in the Either/Or*, *Life in the Both/And*, and *Life in the Neither/Nor*[4] as alternative metaphorical conceptions of the three approaches to cultural difference now commonplace in the field as theorists, researchers and educators work to overcome what Kostogriz (2004) describes as a space-place dichotomy and Lu and Horner (2013) describe as an absence of the temporal in our conceptions of literacy. My goal in doing so is to provide an alternative frame of reference for disrupting the binaries that typically constrain our ability to engage Otherness in unanticipated ways. I move next to Deleuze and Guattari's (1987) work on rhizomes to illustrate how space and time function in the new frame of reference that I am proposing.

Finally, after I review how cultural memory works and describe the cultural modalities of memory that our students have access to as they co-construct the *cultures in transition* (Caraballo, 2011) they inhabit in the company of others in their everyday lives, I analyze a series of brief autobiographical narratives from my own lived experience to illustrate how we work with the memories that inform who we are in the process of becoming. The narratives also demonstrate how we can train all students in our schools, but especially the disenfranchised among them, to reconfigure or reinterpret their own experiences in the social spaces they occupy during unsettled periods in their lives. In moments like these, I argue, CCA and cultural modalities of memory work especially well in helping students take on the challenges they encounter as they address the "wickedly complex communicative tasks" we all face in an increasingly "challenging and difficult world" (Selfe, 2009, p. 645). I conclude the chapter by intimating how language and culture contribute to identity formation, an active process each of us undertakes to claim recognition (Bourdieu & Wacquant, 1992; Honneth, 1995) and respect (Cintron, 1997) as we work to effect social change in the real and imagined worlds that we inhabit.

The Enactment of Critical Cultural Awareness

Although the concept has rarely if ever been used in the field of composition and literacy studies, CCA is widely discussed in foreign language studies as part of their long tradition of trying to understand how foreign language learners can make use of culture in the process of learning a new language. According to Fenner (2008), a paradigmatic change occurred in foreign language teaching in the 1970s as educators shifted from behaviorist, audio-lingual teaching to communicative language teaching as a consequence of the introduction of Chomsky's "theories of language and meaning" and the distinction he made "between linguistic competence and performance" (p. 275). As Fenner (2008) describes it, the introduction of sociocultural competence as an aspect of communicative ability persuaded scholars to regard culture, not only as "'information conveyed by the language' but 'as a feature of language itself'" (p. 276). In recent years, Byram (2012) contends, "a growing tradition of teaching to develop cultural awareness has been helped by definitions of intercultural competence, defined by Guilherme as 'the ability to interact effectively with people from cultures that we recognise as being different from our own'" (p. 6). In Byram's (2012) view, anyone can readily acquire "language competence and intercultural competence without the additional dimension of awareness," but it is only when they are able to analyze and reflect on the social and psychological dimensions of the language-culture nexus that they are then able to create a critical link between their linguistic and intercultural[5] competences (p. 7).

Just as Critical Language Awareness is deployed when we want to understand the characteristics that manifest themselves in one's language use at any given moment, as well as those that inform the language use of one's interlocutors, CCA is highly regarded by foreign language educators as a tool that students can enact "to understand other cultures without losing perspective of the local reality." In this scheme, the exploration of one's local culture becomes as valid and necessary as the exploration of a target culture (Agudelo, 2007, p. 187). According to Kramsch (2013), Byram and Zarate (1997) include CCA among "the five *savoirs* or capacities that constitute intercultural competence" to signal the important role that it plays in training students to understand local culture (p. 70). But while Byram and Zarate's (1997) discussion of the relationship between language and culture succeeds in framing its affordances in very helpful terms, Kramsch (2013) is nevertheless critical of their position because it inevitably ties culture to "the characteristics of native members of a national community who speak the national language and share in its national culture" (p. 70). Such a modern definition of culture, Kramsch contends, is readily challenged "by a lingua franca like English that knows no national boundaries and by global social actors who contest the supremacy of the native speaker as well as the notion of neatly bound speech communities" (p. 70). To offset Byram and Zarate's (1997) modernist tendencies, Kramsch (2013) offers an alternative, post-structuralist conception that she refers to as Third Culture.

In a fascinating essay titled "Third Culture and Language Education," Kramsch (2009) assiduously reviews theories of Thirdness in semiotics (Barthes, 1977; Peirce, 1898/1955), literary criticism (Bakhtin, 1981), cultural studies (Bhabha, 1994), foreign language education (Kramsch, 1993) and literacy pedagogy (Gutiérrez, Baquedano-López & Tejeda, 1999; Kostogriz, 2002). Along the way, Kramsch (2009) makes this important pronouncement:

> In language education there has always been a tension between the conventionally agreed upon and collectively shared ways of making meaning by members of a given culture, and the individual idiosyncratic uses of language by speakers and writers. In foreign language education, there is an additional tension within language learners who are by definition performers of a first language (L1) and a first culture (C1) and are becoming also performers of an L2 and C2. In both cases, there might be a conflict between the needs of the individual and the group, the demands of the self and the other. It is to break out of these dualities—individual-social, self-other, native-nonnative speaker, C1-C2—that the concept of "third culture" was conceived.
>
> *p. 233*

In light of the tremendous and on-going demographic changes taking place across the United States at all levels of schooling, I want to suggest that the additional tension Kramsch (2009) describes in foreign language education produced by C1 and C2 is no longer exclusively limited to her field of study. Because the tension between language and culture that foreign language scholars have identified is now present across the entire K-16 spectrum in the teaching and learning of English, it must also be considered a central concern in first-year college writing programs and Writing Across the Curriculum settings that more than ever are serving members of U.S. second language and international communities.

Kramsch's (2009) conception of Third Culture—which is not meant to eliminate dualities but instead to focus on the relationship between them (p. 238)—highlights the four major aspects that constitute what she refers to as "a 'third' perspective on the relation of self and other through language" (p. 246). The first, *subjectivity or subject positioning*, centers on how "[d]ifferent languages position their speakers in different symbolic spaces." According to Kramsch, "[s]ubject positioning has less to do with the calculations of rational actors than with a multilingual's heightened awareness of the embodied nature of language and the sedimented emotions associated with the use of this or that language, dialect or register" (p. 246). The second, *historicity or an understanding of the cultural memories evoked by symbolic systems*, reflects the ways in which cultures become what she calls "collective *lieux de mémoire* formed by the sedimented representations of a people" because they are actually remembered by individual members and serve as valid historical models in times of migrations and displacements. A third aspect that she refers to as *the capacity to perform and create alternative realities* reminds us that within an ecological perspective of human exchanges, "language is not merely the representation of thought but actually creates and performs thought in dialogue with others" (p. 245). This performative aspect of language, she notes, can be seen as having what Butler (1997) refers to as "political promise," that is, as potentially effectuating social change. *Stylistic variation*, the fourth aspect, signals current efforts in the field "to capture individual creativity in language use." Style in this context, Kramsch explains, must be understood as

> a general capacity of speakers to rework the utterances of others in their own personal style—a capacity that Coupland defines as "a subversive form of multi-voiced utterance, one that discredits hegemonic, monologic discourses by appropriating the voices of the powerful, and reworking them for new purposes."
>
> *Kramsch, 2009, p. 246*

Kramsch's (2009) post-structuralist alternative to the modernist position taken by Byram and Zarate (1997) reflects her understandable desire to accent fluidity over fixity in the context of my discussion of these two terms in the first chapter. It, therefore, comes as no surprise when she declares that culture under these circumstances must be seen "as heterogeneous, fluid, conflictual . . . a mode, not a place, of belonging; it is as imagined as it is real, a *lieu de mémoire* as much as a lived event" (pp. 247–248). To her credit, Kramsch (2009) reminds us that "because the metaphor of third culture is prone to romanticizing marginality and hybridity, it [continually] risks being easily re-appropriated by members of dominant first or second cultures as the exotic 'border-crossings' of polyglot cosmopolitan individuals." Moreover, it risks "becoming a static place between two dominant cultures . . ." (p. 248). Because the qualities Kramsch attributes to Third Culture are more familiar to scholars in composition and literacy studies through work that examines the concept of Third Space, let me now turn to a discussion of that concept.

From Third Space to Life in the Neither/Nor

As we continue to struggle with the untenable bifurcation of the oral and the literate, the specific and the universal, the local and the global, and the autonomous and the ideological, several scholars in our field (Gutiérrez, 2008; Licona, 2005; Moje et al., 2004; Kostogriz, 2004; Pahl, 2002) have posited new perspectives of a Third Space most widely popularized in the work of Bhabha (1994) and Soja (1996) that, as I noted a moment ago, parallel Kramsch's concept of a Third Culture. Although she was not aware of Bhabha's or Soja's work when she formulated her ideas, Gutiérrez's (2008) conception of a Third Space is very similar to their more theoretical, post-colonial iterations. Unlike Bhabha and Soja, however, Gutiérrez is interested in formulating a curricular and pedagogical tool kit that "nondominant" students can use to fashion a transformative sensibility in the English Language Arts classroom that will serve as the crucible for collectively nurturing the historical agency they need to nimbly, self-reflexively, and tactically navigate and negotiate the terrain of any given social space.

In earlier work (see Gutiérrez, 1995; Gutiérrez et al., 1999), Gutiérrez's "musings about the multiple social spaces of the classroom" helped her understand why it is important to account for "the interacting activity systems of people's everyday lives." This in turn led her to acknowledge the importance of attending to what she calls "the microgenetic processes of everyday learning across a range of contexts," especially those that involve the collective and individual sense-making activities taking place in the classroom (2008, p. 152). As she pondered the value in replacing traditional conceptions of academic literacy and instruction for students from nondominant communities with "forms of literacy that privilege and are contingent upon students' sociohistorical lives, both proximally and distally" (2008, p. 148), Gutiérrez became interested in designing a social environment—which she came to call a collective Third Space[6]—in which students could begin "to reconceive who they are and what they might be able to accomplish academically and beyond" (p. 148). From the outset, one of her key goals was to find ways to create curricular and pedagogical conditions in the classroom that would make it possible for students to use Gee's "social semiotic toolkit" (1996) to extend their repertoires of practice "in ways that [would] enable them to become designers of their own social futures" (Gutiérrez, 2008, p. 156).

In the course of describing what she learned from her empirical study of a program designed to prepare migrant students for college, Gutiérrez explores how Ave, a 16-year-old migrant student in the program, used the syncretic *testimonio* (a hybrid form of critical autobiography and *testimonio*) that she wrote while she was enrolled in the program to expand her repertoire of rhetorical and discursive practices and to situate her lived experience in the context of new historicized understandings (p. 153). Ave and her fellow students, Gutiérrez reports, used syncretic *testimonio* to tell "stories of movements across borders, across both new and familiar practices", which called "our attention to an important and unresolved dilemma in the learning sciences":

> How do we account for the learning and development embodied by and through movement, the border and boundary crossing of students who migrate to and throughout the U.S.? What new capacities and identities are developed in this movement? To what extent do these capacities and identities travel and shift across settings? And what new educational arrangements provoke and support new capacities that extend students' repertoires of practice?
>
> *p. 150*

I will return to Gutiérrez's work and the questions she asks here in my concluding remarks when I offer some of my own suggestions for how educators can use what we have learned from our conceptions of Third Culture, Third Space and Life in the Neither/Nor (a concept I will introduce in a moment) to develop navigational tools that all students, but especially the disenfranchised among them, can use to position and reposition themselves as the need arises.

While the concepts of Third Culture and Third Space that I just described provide us with lenses for understanding alternative contexts beyond the binary systems that inform how we typically construct the world around us, like any effort to understand complex processes, they have inherent limitations as theoretical tools because of the problematic ways in which some scholars use them. Williams (2003), for example, describes how an easy kind of "essentializing and naïve approach to the nature of hybridity and resistance has been embraced by multiculturalist thinking." In such instances, he argues, "the idea of a 'third space' has been employed to describe a benign and ultimately progressive and positivist multicultural synthesis that creates a new culture of pluralistic tolerance" (p. 600). Gutiérrez is certainly not guilty of misconstruing the concept in the ways that Williams describes because she employs Third Space to create opportunities for transformative experiences that result from the tension between two distinct forces or circumstances that produce it. In her conception, the Third Space is a place "where teacher and student scripts, the formal and informal, the official and unofficial spaces of the learning environment, intersect, creating the potential for authentic interaction and a shift in the social organization of learning and what counts as knowledge" (Gutiérrez, 2008, p. 152).

As useful as Kramsch's Third Culture and Gutiérrez's Third Space are in providing us with valuable insights into the nature of the liminal, the in-between or the hybrid, I want to offer a third lens to help us see the three approaches to cultural difference that I discussed in Chapter 1 in an alternative light. As you can see from Table 1.1 in the first chapter, the three figurations I want to introduce here—Life in the Either/Or, Life in the Both/And, and Life in the Neither/Nor—are ideologically aligned with particular approaches to cultural difference. Arguably the most salient characteristics of the first two—the binary either/or and the integrative both/and—is their unrelenting rigidity, on the one hand, and stability, on the other, especially in the context of recent efforts to disrupt the binary and dual frames of reference I discussed in Chapter 1. Whether we are locked in the midst of the black and white, the right and wrong of the former, or the synthetic/integrated quality of the latter, every one of us is able to navigate and negotiate these terrains with little trouble because they call on our agility with, and awareness and recollection of, highly prescribed cultural ways of being. In the conservative conception of Life in the Either/Or, we have little need to worry about the complexity of the social networks we traverse because everyone is assumed to know their place in the broader matrix that has been laid out for everyone to follow. In this context, we typically invoke what Bourdieu (1977) calls doxa, Giddens (1991) calls practical consciousness, and psychologists call working memory (Sulzen, 2001) as we follow the habitual patterns of our scripted lives. In their work, Deleuze and Guattari (1987) describe this "first type of book [as] the root book," which they contend is firmly grounded in the linear and hierarchical logic of what they call the root-tree (p. 5).

Navigation is slightly more challenging in Life in the Both/And, if only because we have a more varied array of different choices to make. Here, we are positioned by a liberal conception to combine contrastive patterns into new formulations, but in time, these new formulations also become rigid, stable and habitual. This reflects a different kind of essentialism-in-the-making. In the "radical-system, or fascicular root," Deleuze and Guattari (1987) note,

> the principal root has aborted, or its tip has been destroyed; an immediate, indefinite multiplicity of secondary roots grafts onto it and undergoes a flourishing development. . . . [But] whenever a multiplicity is taken up in a structure, its growth is offset by a reduction in its laws of combination.
>
> *pp. 5–6*

In other words, while a situated and multicultural frame of reference at first blush suggests that we have overcome the rigidity of a binary system, we soon discover that it is an illusion. The truth is we are still locked within a comparative frame of reference that is difficult to disrupt; we are still prisoners of a multiplicative process constrained by a totalizing unity.

Life in the Neither/Nor, on the other hand, is measured by its neverending fluidity, instability, and unpredictability. As such, it resembles a fragmented, discontinuous, and disorienting social space that the disenfranchised—post-colonial subjects in Bhabha's language—must learn to navigate and negotiate. To negotiate this location, "third-space subjects [must] put language into play by using disruptive discursive strategies that reflect our lived experiences as fragmented, partial, real, and imagined, and always in the process of becoming" (Licona, 2005, p. 106). Life in the Neither/Nor also mimics Deleuze and Guattari's notion of a rhizome, which, because it "has no beginning or end," becomes a particularly fascinating terrain. Deleuze and Guattari (1987) are not so much interested in the either/ors or the both/ands that mark the endpoints of a continuum. What really intrigues them are the degrees of difference in the middle, what they refer to as "between things, interbeing, *intermezzo*," the "coming and going rather than [the] starting and finishing." This middle, they contend,

> is where things pick up speed. Between things does not designate a localizable relation going from one thing to the other and back again, but a perpendicular direction, a transversal movement that sweeps one and the other away, a stream without beginning or end that undermines its banks and picks up speed in the middle.
>
> *p. 25*

What happens in this kind of middle, what they call a rhizome, others call Third Culture or Third Space, and I call Life in the Neither/Nor, awakens within each of us a *nomadic consciousness*[7] that requires a dynamic set of nimble, self-reflexive, and tactical capabilities (Braidotti, 1994, p. 23; Guerra, 2004, p. 24). How nomadic consciousness functions, as I explain in the next section, is best described by how we use cultural modalities of memory to navigate and negotiate disruptive or disorienting circumstances in the course of our everyday lives.

Cultural Memory as Lived Experience

One of the building blocks that makes a nomadic consciousness in Life in the Neither/Nor possible is what I referred to earlier as the cultural modalities of memory, that precious and as of yet generally unacknowledged navigational tool that we all possess but have not yet quite figured out how to use to transform ourselves. As most of us would agree, consciousness, like language and culture, is impossible without memory because, as Straub (2010) explains

> [m]emory and recollection are prominently involved in people's attempts to endow their experiences with sense and meaning that conforms to socio-cultural standards (values, rules in the form of norms or conventions, habits, goals, etc.). An important part of this process consists in a narrative arrangement and integration of events into generally intelligible stories. If it is required by one's own cultural, social, and psychological "logic," one leaves out one detail or another and adds something else here or there, changing things until they assume a more or less comprehensible guise.
>
> *p. 222*

Before I examine the cultural modalities of memory that contribute to the nomadic consciousness that disrupts the aforementioned tendency in memory to create a stable narrative and that we all invoke as we work to develop a critical awareness of language and culture, which together give birth to identity, I want to describe how cultural memory informs our ability to make sense of the real and imagined worlds that we inhabit.

In her discussion of memory, Bal (1999) makes a critical distinction between habitual, traumatic and narrative memories. Habitual memories rarely inform our self-conscious efforts to engage others because, as Bal argues, their "minimal protonarratives remain buried in routine; they contain no events that stand out. They arouse no suspense, and fail to flesh out a clear and distinctive vision" (p. viii) of who we are and our place in the world. Traumatic memories, on the other hand, "cannot become narratives, either because the traumatizing events are mechanically reenacted as drama rather than synthetically narrated by the memorizing agent who 'masters' them, or because they remain 'outside' the subject" (p. viii). Bal refers to traumatic reenactment as tragically solitary: "While the subject to whom the event happened lacks the narrative mastery over it that turns her or him into a proper subject, the other crucial presence in the process, the addressee, is also missing" (p. x). Only narrative memories, even of unimportant events, can be made memorable because they alone "are affectively colored" and "surrounded by an emotional aura." More often than not, "the string of events that composes a narrative (and narratable) memory offers high and low accents, foreground and background, preparatory and climactic events," as well as "some ordinary sense perception that evokes them" (p. viii).

Scholars invested in trying to understand the nature of cultural memory have focused, on the one hand, on how it operates as a biological or symbolic process, and on the other, on the complex relationship between language and memory. In reflecting on the former, Erll (2010) describes how at the first or biological level of operation, cultural memory is never purely individual. It is always inherently shaped by collective contexts: "From the people we live with and from the media we use, we acquire schemata which help us recall the past and encode new experience. . . . [Thus,] we remember in socio-cultural contexts" (p. 5). The second level of cultural memory is reflected in "the symbolic order, the media, institutions, and practices by which social groups construct a shared past." Metaphorically speaking, "identities have to be constructed and reconstructed by acts of memory, by remembering who one was and by setting this past Self in relation to the present Self" (p. 6). In a moment, when I describe what I have been referring to as cultural modalities of memory, we will see that cultural memory invariably "hinges on the notion of the medial, because it is only via medial externalization (from oral speech to writing, painting, or using the Internet) that individual memories, cultural knowledge, and versions of history can be shared" (Erll, 2010, pp. 12–13).

In his work, Echterhoff (2010) takes on the equally challenging question of whether language and culture are inherently conjoined or separate entities. On the one hand, he suggests, a number of theorists and researchers are convinced that "language provides the essence of human thinking and memory and the mental representations entertained in our minds are inextricably linguistic." This position is epitomized by the Sapir-Whorf hypothesis, which in its strong version suggests that "our experiences with the world are intrinsically linguistic and that cognition is inherently determined by the thinker's language" (p. 265). In other words, our interpretation and representation of the real and imagined worlds that we inhabit are always linguistically or discursively constructed. Scholars who hold the opposite view are convinced that "the contents and processes of the mind, including our knowledge and memory, are characteristically different and independent from the linguistic form that people use to communicate their thoughts and memories." They posit the existence of a universal and abstract "language of thought" that is different and separate from natural languages and is "used for internal rather than external communication" (p. 265). Echterhoff (2010) favors a middle ground supported by research in psychology that acknowledges the presence of "nonverbal modes of human cognition, such as representations based on visual, spatial, auditory, olfactory or motor information" that operate independent of language (p. 266). His conclusion, one that I share, is that this debate is both futile and fruitless. A more productive question worth asking, he tells us, is this one: How do nonlinguistic and linguistic representations interact or interfere with each other in the workings of the mind? (p. 267). While my forthcoming presentation and discussion will not answer this question fully, it will ponder the challenges the query suggests.

In the course of trying to figure out how best to conceptualize the notion of cultural memory in a way that would be more directly applicable to this project, I became intrigued by Erll's (2010) effort to distinguish between history and memory as two potentially different *modes of remembering* in culture. Troubled by what she saw as their useless opposition, Erll (2010) offers an alternative perspective that acknowledges the great degree of variation in our memories of past events, not only in terms of what is remembered (facts, data), but also for how it is remembered (p. 7). Because I am interested in trying to understand this critical relationship between sense and memory, I find Wallach and Averbach's (1955) contention that "there are memory modalities just as there are sense modalities" (p. 249) very compelling. Building on Wallach and Averbach's research, Sulzen (2001) has since developed a model of modality-organized cognition (see Figure 3.1) that describes a first level of modalities directly related to our senses (auditory, gustatory, haptic, kinesthetic, olfactory and visual) and a second level of non-sensory modalities (emotional/affective, linguistic and spatial) more directly related to our narratable memory. Although he is interested in understanding short-term rather than long-term memory (which is the focus of my own investigation), I believe that Sulzen's model can still be used as a heuristic for conceptualizing how cultural memory operates.

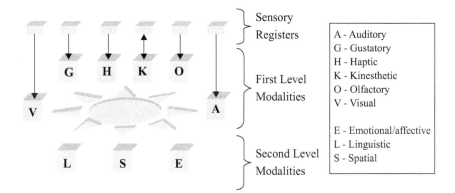

FIGURE 3.1 Modality-organized cognition
Source: Reprinted from Sulzen, 2001.

According to Sulzen (2001), each modality represents a complete cognitive processing system unto itself that includes its own working memory, long-term memory and processing capabilities. Each modality is also conceived as a "representational system" that represents processes, knowledge, perceptions and sensory experience in unique ways. For example, among the sensory-based modalities of memory, V represents knowledge in pictures and images, A in sounds, K in kinesthetic movement, and so on. Among the non-sensory modalities of memory, L is conceived of as "a pure linguistic system that represents knowledge and does its processing in terms of sequenced and syntactically ordered symbols," S as "a spatial system that represents spatial knowledge and performs spatial processing," and E as "our affective memories" (p. 5). Because every modality is connected to and capable of stimulating or receiving stimuli from every other modality, together, they "create the experience of cognition." Sulzen also suspects that there may well be a set of "tertiary" modalities that serves to organize social cognition or personality or other functions, but his model is not designed to extend the concept to that level (p. 4).

One of the things I find most intriguing about Sulzen's description of how modalities of memory function is the extent to which the processes he describes reflect elements of the multimodal conceptions that have been popularized in composition and literacy studies over the last 20 years as "the representation and communicational environment" that we all occupy has changed as a consequence of the relentless and on-going "shift from print as the primary medium of dissemination toward digital media" (Jewitt, 2014, p. 241). Not only have we come to realize that meanings are made, distributed, interpreted and remade "through many representational and communication resources, *of which language is but one*," (Jewitt, p. 246, emphasis added), we have also come to understand that while "all modes in a communicative event or text contribute to meaning, models of multimodality assert that all modes are partial" and "no one mode stands alone in the process of meaning making" (Jewitt, p. 246). As scholars in the field ponder how best to integrate the plethora of modes and media[8] available to us into the college writing classroom—among them "image, gesture, gaze, body posture, sound, writing, music, speech" (Jewitt, 2014, p. 246); "words, sounds, still and moving images, animation and color" (Lauer, 2009, p. 227); as well as the "digital, visual, spatial, [and] musical" (Sanders & Albers, 2010)—we must, as Alexander and Rhodes (2014) remind us, make sure that "the multiple rhetorical capabilities of the various media" and "the rich histories of those capabilities" are not elided (p. 3). A failure to historicize what we are doing could cause our celebratory embrace of modes and media to backfire on us.

As important as recent work on multimodalities and new media has been in reminding us of the plethora of tools we can make available to our students so that they can linguistically, culturally and semiotically represent their ideas in richly textured ways, I want to suggest that we need to remind ourselves that we also have an incredible array of opportunities at our disposal to help our students re-imagine the ideas embedded in the cultural memories they have access to if only they take the time to reflect on how the cultural modalities of memory I have just described can be used to integrate those cultural memories into the work they are doing in the college writing classroom and beyond. As Yancey reminded us in her chair's address at the 2004 Conference on College Composition and Communication, "we have separated delivery and memory from invention, arrangement, and style in ways that are counterproductive." The canons, she reminds us, are not discrete entities but instead are related to each other: "the canons interact, and through that interaction they contribute to new exigencies for invention, arrangement, representation, and identity. Or: they change what is possible" (pp. 316–317). As Romberger (2012) recently added, "The field of rhetoric and composition has for some time now been rethinking all of the canons for a multimodal pedagogy to open up the very type of composing modes that the New London Group has advocated" (p. 206). In what remains of this section, I would like to share a series of short autobiographical narratives to illustrate how I believe cultural modalities of memory make it possible for us to function in the social, discursive, material and imagined worlds that we occupy in Life in the Either/Or, Life in the Both/And and Life in the Neither/Nor, especially when it comes to our ability to navigate and negotiate these and other social spaces in a heightened state of consciousness.

No doubt each of us can remember moments in our lives when we felt very much like Sisyphus trudging up a mountain pushing a weighty stone, as well as those exquisite moments of nomadic consciousness when we discovered on the way down that same mountain, and later remembered many times over, the linguistic and cultural experiences that shaped our provisional identities in ways that we could have never imagined possible. In an effort to present some data that I can analyze and interpret using the tri-partite frame of reference I outlined earlier, I want to share publicly for the first time a series of short autobiographical passages that describe key moments in my life informed by a legal document that has haunted me for more than 50 years. My goal here is to illustrate how cultural modalities of memory can shape and reshape our identities as our memories themselves are shaped and reshaped, not by who we are but by who we are continuously becoming. Hall (1996) puts it this way:

> Though they seem to invoke an origin in a historical past with which they continue to correspond, actually identities are about questions of using the resources of history, language and culture in the process of becoming rather than being: not "who we are" or "where we came from," so much as what we might become, how we have been represented and how that bears on how we might represent ourselves.
>
> *p. 4*

In the pre-civil rights summer of 1959 when I was 9 years old, for the first time in my life, I rode my bike from the housing project in the Mexican part of my hometown of Harlingen, Texas across the railroad tracks to the white part of town to try out for little league baseball. A white coach who saw me trying out thought I had the skill to make it on his team, so he came over and asked if I could bring him my birth certificate to prove I was old enough to play. I went home and excitedly told my mother that I needed something called a birth certificate to prove my age if I wanted to play baseball. My mother hesitated for a moment, suspicious about why anyone would need to see what she obviously considered one of the most important documents in her possession, then, told me she would give it to me the following day.

The next day after I reminded her that I needed my birth certificate, my mother left the room for a few minutes, came back with a white envelope, and told me not to share it with anyone but the coach. I said okay, got on my bike, and took it to the baseball park where the coach removed my birth certificate from the white envelope, glanced at it, then, gave it right back to me. "Okay," he said, "I'll see you here at our first practice on Monday after school." After I took the envelope and thanked him, I got on my bike and started home. Probably more out of curiosity than anything else, I stopped on my way home, leaned the bike against a tree, sat on the ground and took the birth certificate out of the envelope.

The birth certificate was an ordinary piece of blue paper, folded several times over, with information printed and typed on it. As I felt the piece of paper between my fingers, I noticed it had a raised seal on the left-hand edge with a signature over it. I also noticed and became curious about the information typed in the first series of boxes listed next to CHILD. First name: Juan. Middle Name: Cruz. Last Name: Guerra. The middle name caught me by surprise because I had never heard that word uttered in my life. The next set of boxes listed next to FATHER had question marks in them. My mother's name was typed into its respective boxes. First name: Teresa. Last name: Guerra. I had known for some time that the individual who lived with my mother, my two older Mexican-born sisters, my three younger siblings and me, was not my father—he had told me that himself—but I had never been told and had never asked who my biological father was or what had happened to him.

At the bottom left-hand corner in a box numbered 21, I came to a final section that had a strange sounding word with a question mark after it: Legitimate? Typed in the box that this strange word occupied, I found another word in capital letters: NO. Not knowing what to make of it, I folded the document, put it in the envelope and headed back home on my bike. Along the way, I pondered the blank space where my biological father's name should have been and the word NO in the box numbered 21. When I got home, my mother immediately took the white envelope from me and asked if anyone else but the coach had looked at it. "*No, mami,*" I lied. I then went to my bedroom, took out a dictionary and looked up that strange word. Legitimate: "Being in compliance with the law. Genuine. Authentic. Born of legally married parents."

Because I was a monolingual Spanish speaker who had never read, written or heard a single word of English until the first grade, almost three years before the birth certificate incident, I'm not sure how much I can trust my recollection that I took out a dictionary and looked up that ominous word. After all, as Vivian (2010) notes, our memories "subsist in a state of dispersion [rather than] in the form of a unified or stable presence" (p. 126). On the other hand, I vividly remember consulting a dictionary after my last confession in the Catholic Church a few years later at the age of 13 when the priest asked me in English if I had offended God, and I didn't know how to respond because I could not figure out what the word meant in that context. Peeved at my ignorance, the priest told me to go home and not return to church until I had an answer.

In a moment I still recall vividly and viscerally, I ran home and after lying on my bed in tears and saying "*pendejo, pendejo, pendejo*" to myself under my breath, I got a dictionary and looked up the word. Offend: "To arouse anger, resentment, or indignation in." Now whether I did or did not consult a dictionary at age 9 is in many ways secondary; the fact that I remember having done so suggests the extent to which our memories are not foundational but continuously revised on the basis of our later experiences. While the cultural modalities of memory influence the ways in which we narrate our past experiences, they are in turn shaped by the current circumstances of our lives as we work to develop a cohesive sense of the world.

Eight years later in 1966 when Bertha, one of my older sisters, invited me to spend the summer with her in Chicago, my godfather drove my mother and me to the bus station for the beginning of my 48-hour, fifteen-hundred-mile journey. After my bag was stored in the bus's lower compartment, I stood in the early evening drizzle and said goodbye to my godfather and mother. When my godfather stepped away to give us a moment of privacy, my mother took out a white envelope from her purse and said to me, "*Lleva esto contigo, mi'jo. Es tu certificado de nacimiento. Por si acaso alguien te pregunta si naciste en este país.*" "*Gracias, mami,*" I said. Before I had a chance to take a step to board the bus, my mother asked me if I had a pencil. "*Si, aquí,*" I said as I pulled one out of my pocket. "*Escribe esto, mi'jito. Mayúscula S-a-l-o-m-é. Mayúscula C-r-u-z. Ese es el nombre de tu apá.*" I nodded my head, gave her a final hug and boarded the bus.

Once I took my seat on the bus, I glanced out the window and saw my mother and godfather waving goodbye to me through the rain-stained window, and I waved back as the bus pulled out of the station. Within minutes of getting on the road, I pulled out the envelope with my biological father's name written on it, took out my pencil and, with salty tears stinging my eyes and blurring my vision, erased it in a futile effort to regain a past that had provided the parameters of the life I had come to know. What I realized some time later, of course, is that once something is written down, once something is produced by the cultural modalities of memory, it can no longer be erased, can no longer be extinguished. From the moment it is brought to consciousness, it becomes an integral element of our navigational equipment and informs our emerging identities.

Over the next 48 hours, I sat on that bus as it traveled from my hometown in rural south Texas to Chicago, at the time the second largest city in the United States. During my journey, I also became part of a larger phenomenon: the diaspora of black and brown people migrating from the south to the north, a migration that had begun in earnest for Latinos and Latinas the year before with the passage of the Immigration and Nationality Act of 1965.[9] At each stop, I found myself—as I had in that moment when I had opened the envelope on my way home from the baseball park eight years earlier—caught in an ephemeral moment between my past and my future, increasingly conscious of my place in the world. In both instances, I momentarily found myself inhabiting Life in the Neither/Nor, caught in a liminal space and time where I was continually coming and going and not yet arrived. Like one of Licona's (2005) third-space subjects, I was slipping and sliding "across both sides of a border to a third space between the authentic and the inauthentic, the legitimate and the illegitimate, the pure and the impure, the proper and the improper," trying "to uncover Other ways of being, and of knowing, in order to make meaning of the everyday" (p. 106).

So what lessons do these autobiographical memories bring to mind for me about the different ways that we navigate and negotiate the challenges of Life in the Either/Or, Life in the Both/And and Life in the Neither/Nor? On the one hand, I see myself at the beginning of that first narrative caught in the certitude of Life in the Either/Or, living a life pre-ordained by the social, cultural and political forces that constrained who I was and could be at the time. As I traveled on my bike from the housing project where so many of us lived seemingly futile lives and crossed the railroad tracks to the white part of town where children were being prepared for very different lives, I caught a momentary glimpse of Life in the Both/And. Because that transitional instance was too brief, I had no reason to question my place in the carefully laid out racist matrix or to imagine my life would ever be any different than it was at that very moment. On the other hand, when I opened that envelope and saw, for the first time, my life documented so boldly by the very state that governs our every move, I momentarily experienced Life in the Neither/Nor and was no longer able to locate myself either in the life I had always known in the housing project or the new and very different life that I was about to come to know in that baseball park on the white side of town. For the first time in my remembered life, cracks began to form in the cage that contained me—if only because I finally knew that I was recognized as illegitimate, illegal, momentarily beyond the reach of the two worlds I had traversed. As I traveled on that bus to Chicago eight years later, carrying the birth certificate with me, I again found myself in Life in the Neither/Nor, witnessing a world in transition as a wide spectrum of poor and working-class people from Texas, Louisiana, Mississippi, Tennessee, Missouri and Illinois crossed paths with me on the bus. Because both of these experiences were unexpected and unprecedented, they created opportunities for me to know what life could be like when we momentarily escape the habitual practices of our daily rituals.

These memories continue to shape and reshape the historical moments surrounding them in ways that have contributed to the constitution and reconstitution of the provisional identities I have embraced ever since, especially when it comes to my relationship with literacy. Sitting here near the end of a career as a scholar and educator that has spanned more than 40 years, I am left to ponder what made it possible for the little boy in the stories I just told to morph into the man I have become. No doubt the many other moments I have experienced along the way that have momentarily heightened my consciousness and allowed me to break out of the confines of Life in the Either/Or and Life in the Both/And have contributed their own aspirational insights to the process. It is, I suspect, not much different for the increasing number of disenfranchised students currently enrolling in our colleges and universities. How we can use what we know about the cultural modalities of memory to help students navigate and negotiate their way through their educational experiences is something I will turn to in a moment, but first, it may be worthwhile for me to ponder how the autobiographical narratives that I just shared made effective use of cultural modalities of memory to elicit in me a set of feelings connected to those moments and a connection with readers through their inherent use of sensory and non-sensory means.

Unlike traditional academic discourses that tend toward the abstract and rarely invoke sensory or affective responses in readers because of their profound commitment to reason, the autobiographical narratives that I just shared invoke what we can refer to as cultural modalities of memory to produce responses in readers (including myself) on several levels. In so doing, they remind us that while written language represents a single medium, it makes use of as wide a range of modalities as the new media our students are learning to use in many college writing classrooms. Cultural modalities of memory are not monomodal; they elicit a range of sensory and affective responses that remind us of the many ways that we interact with the world. My autobiographical narratives, for example, demonstrate kinesthetic movement as I venture on a bike and a bus; touch when I describe the raised imprint on the birth certificate; the taste and sting of salty tears; the sound produced by voices engaged in dialogue; spatial and temporal configurations as I move from my neighborhood to a white neighborhood and later travel across the country by bus. Above all, the autobiographical narratives produce an affective response because readers who can relate to the stories I am telling feel, or at least empathize with, the range of emotions that I experienced at different points in the telling and in the actual experience. In a way that we often forget when we diminish the power of written language by juxtaposing it to the rich and varied new media now at our disposal as a consequence of technological advances, we are reminded that multimodalities have always been present; they are not new, as Alexander and Rhodes (2014, p. 3) remind us. Equally important, they can be used to bridge our students' lived experience with the array of modalities and media now available to them in many of our college writing classrooms.

Pedagogical Memories

In "Pedagogical Memory: Writing, Mapping, Translating," Jarratt, Mack, Sartor and Watson (2009) invoke the work by Bal (1999) on cultural memory that I reviewed earlier in this chapter and use it to describe what they call *pedagogical memory*, a concept that in many ways parallels the concept of cultural modalities of memory that I just presented. According to Jarratt et al., pedagogical memory consists of the information that "students [remember] of their early college writing instruction," which students could potentially use "to chart their own paths from first-year to discipline-based writing and beyond" (p. 48). Unlike students in their study who declined to narrate and tended "to remember learning to write as fixed in an indefinite past" (p. 53), successful students demonstrated "a stronger ability to narrate their writing experiences, to see themselves in relationship to writing teachers and other audiences, and to confront the emotional challenges writing poses" (p. 66). Like the perspective I have been presenting in this chapter, the approach to writing instruction that Jarratt et al. (2009) describe underscores "the inclination toward reflective writing already well accepted in the field" and constructs "such opportunities not as validation of already determined institutional goals but as tools for use by individual students to map their own idiosyncratic pasts and to imagine future writing lives" (pp. 66–67). If there is a major difference between what they describe as pedagogical memory and what I describe as cultural modalities of memory, it is one of scope or scale. While pedagogical memory focuses specifically on what students remember about learning to write in school, cultural modalities of memory aims for memories of a broader range of lived experiences that extend beyond the college writing classroom and out into the wider social spaces that inform their everyday lives.

In that respect, the autobiographical narratives that I just shared are meant to remind us and our students that, when it comes to pedagogical spaces, the trees that we sit under and the buses that we ride are as important and critical to our lives as the classrooms that we share. At the same time, it is not enough for any student to come to terms with their historical past, especially those deeply hidden and shameful moments that raise the pain threshold in ways that, if we are lucky, heighten our consciousness. What I want to suggest instead is that students need to call on their cultural modalities of memory and imagine connections between them and the multimodalities available to them through the range of new media now at their disposal in the college writing classroom.

While we want to encourage our students to invoke their personal histories, to bring their lived experience into the classroom and to use it as a tool to navigate and negotiate the terrain of their unfolding lives, we also want them to think of these autobiographical moments, not as opportunities for confession in the Foucauldian sense, but as opportunities to constitute and reconstitute themselves in the process of becoming (Hogan, 2005, p. 151). When we represent aspects of our lived experience in the context of confession as a genre, we are constrained by the need to frame them as familiar narratives that display an internal coherence designed to strip them of their multiple contradictions. Students need to learn to use cultural modalities of memory to highlight the rhizomatic nature of their lived experience, to wrestle with the multiple contradictions that Life in the Neither/Nor in particular brings to light. When we constitute or reconstitute ourselves, we purposefully disrupt the need that we feel to make sense of the world in coherent and highly prescribed terms.

In her pedagogical work, Gutiérrez (2008) provides a well-traveled and thought-out map for how we can help disenfranchised or nondominant students acquire these repertoires of practice, that is, "both vertical and horizontal forms of expertise . . . [that include] not only what students learn in formal learning environments such as schools, but also what they learn by participating in a range of practices outside of school" (p. 149). At the same time that it focuses on the sociohistorical influences on its students' language, literacy, and learning practices, the UCLA Migrant Student Leadership Institute (MSLI)—the subject of Gutiérrez's research—addresses their social, economic, and educational realities. As she notes, the curriculum and its pedagogy "are grounded in the historical and current particulars of students' everyday lives, while at the same time oriented toward an imagined but possible future" (p. 154). In Gutiérrez's carefully construed ecological approach, learning is organized in such ways that conversation, dialogue, and contradiction are privileged across learning activities with varied participation structures: tutorials, comprehension circles, writing conferences, *teatro*, minilectures and whole-class discussions (p. 154). In describing this terrain, Gutiérrez (2008) reminds us not to think of the collective Third Space as a utopian narrative because "work in these spaces is difficult and filled with contradictions, setbacks, and struggle" (p. 160). Instead, she wants us to think of it as "an example of what is possible when educators and educational researchers arrange educational environments in ways that incite, support, and extend students' repertoires of practice by organizing the frequency, co-occurrence, and difficulty of cultural practices and forms of mediation" (p. 160).

What I want to respectfully add to Gutiérrez's highly nuanced description of the tools that disenfranchised students need to navigate and negotiate the provisional pedagogical spaces they inhabit in our schools, colleges and universities, and communities of belonging is another set of tools that students must also acquire and use nimbly, tactically and self-reflexively rather than only intuitively, to move *from* one physical space to another and *within* varied social spaces as well. What I hope my discussion adds is a different frame of reference, a different figural representation of the contexts that all students inhabit as they move from one social, cultural, discursive, material and imagined space to another in their everyday lives. I want us to remind students that the spaces they occupy have been framed in different ways by the different ideological forces that shape and influence the institutions responsible for their education. I want to argue that it is important for them to know that the tools they learn to use in Third Culture, Third Space or Life in the Neither/Nor can also be used to navigate life in a range of other social spaces, most of which tend to sedate them into automatically enacting the habitual patterns of our pre-formulated lives.

Finally, as educators, we need to think of our students, and we need to encourage them to think of themselves, as *nomadic subjects* who are continuously in the process of becoming (Braidotti, 1994, p. 25). They need to know that while they will spend a good part of their lives in Life in the Either/Or and Life in the Both/And, they will also—particularly if they are disenfranchised—continue to live critical portions of their lives in Life in the Neither/Nor as well. Ave, the 16-year-old migrant student whose syncretic *testimonio* Gutiérrez (2008) shares with us in her essay, writes:

> I grew up believing I was invisible and I learned that my vocation was that of an outside observer. . . . I learned to simply observe everything and everyone, but even that bothered people. I was never taught to fight, so instead I did what I was best at, stay quiet and take it all in. The silence somehow sent them the message that I was dumb and stupid.
>
> *p. 151*

In our autobiographical narratives, Ave and I both call on our cultural modalities of memory to draw forth experiences that I suspect neither one of us had ever shared publicly with anyone before. We engage in what Hogan (2005) has described as "a kind of identity formation that is not coerced, but is a freely chosen subjective exploration of experience" (p. 121). We also learn to successfully navigate Life in the Neither/Nor by becoming assemblers of our own lived experience, which in turn alerts us to the new possibilities available to us in Life in the Either/Or and Life in the Both/And as well.

It took me more than 50 years to take command of and share painful moments of heightened consciousness with you in this chapter. Fortunately for all of us who support the kind of work that the Migrant Institute staff and students in their program have done, Ave shared similar moments in the context of a collective Third Space at the age of 15. My hope is that Ave is well on her way to learning how to use the tools that she acquired at the Migrant Institute to navigate and negotiate the multiplicity of pedagogical spaces she will inhabit in the course of her life. Our task as educators is to make sure we continue to create conditions in our classrooms that provide students like Ave with endless opportunities to share and shape their lives as they come and go.

Spanish to English Glossary

No, mami [No, mom]
pendejo, pendejo, pendejo [idiot, idiot, idiot]

Lleva esto contigo, mi'jo. Es tu certificado de nacimiento. Por si acaso alguien te pregunta si naciste en este país. [Take this with you, my son. It's your birth certificate. Just in case someone asks you if you were born in this country.]

Gracias, mami [Thanks, mom]

Sí, aquí [Yes, here]

Escribe esto, mi'jito. Mayúscula S-a-l-o-m-é. Mayúscula C-r-u-z. Ese es el nombre de tu apá. [Write this, my young son. Capital S-a-l-o-m-é. Capital C-r-u-z. That's the name of your father.]

teatro [theater]

testimonio [testimonial]

Notes

1. As I argued in the preceding chapter, we have to be careful not to limit our scholarly conversation to language; we also need to speak of culture in the same breath. Dufva's position, which is widely supported by scholars in the field of foreign language education, is one that we in composition and literacy studies also need to adopt.

2. I chose to use the concept of cultural memory instead of the concept of autobiographical memory (for a description of the latter, see Klein, German, Cosmides & Gabriel, 2004) in framing my argument in this chapter because by definition the former includes the latter.

3. Braidotti (1994) defines a figuration as a politically informed account of an alternative subjectivity designed to help us "learn to think differently about the subject, invent new frameworks, new images, new modes of thought" (p. 1). Because this figurative mode functions according to what she calls "the philosophy of 'as if'"—"as if some experiences were reminiscent or evocative of others" (p. 5)—a figuration has the potential to open up, "through successive repetitions and mimetic strategies, spaces where alternative forms of agency can be engendered" (p. 7). I consider a number of the concepts that I present over the course of this book—transcultural repositioning, code-segregation, critical language awareness, critical cultural awareness, cultural modalities of memory, Life in the Neither/Nor, etc.—figurations because they provide us with opportunities to reimagine the conceptual notions that we typically invoke in relation to the subject matter I discuss along the way.

4. I want to thank Angela Rounsaville (2011) for introducing me to Third Culture Kid discourse (Pollock & Van Reken, 2009), which makes use of the term "neither/nor" to describe a disposition related to the metaphor of interstitial space. I adopted the term, framed it as "Life in the Neither/Nor," then expanded it to include "Life in the Either/Or" and "Life in the Both/And" because of the parallels that I saw between these three conceptual notions and the tripartite framework used to describe the different approaches to language and cultural difference that I discussed in Chapter 1.

5. According to Fenner (2008), the term *intercultural* has gradually replaced the term *cultural* in foreign language studies because "learners encounter the foreign culture as members of their own cultural community, and the encounter thus implies two cultures" (p. 277). While the term intercultural is widely used in second language studies, it is rarely used in composition and literacy studies (see Guerra, 1997), where we seem to prefer to use transcultural as its equivalent.

6. The concept of third space has also been effectively deployed in research related to first-year college writing classrooms in ways that parallel Gutiérrez's conceptualization to imagine its utility for understanding how students can develop what Sandoval (2000) calls a differential consciousness as they navigate and negotiate the competing ideologies related to language difference that they inevitably confront in the academy

and beyond. Building on Anzaldúa's (1987) work on *mestiza consciousness*, which Anzaldúa defines as "a consciousness of duality" that embraces "ambiguity and contradiction" and permits one to reconcile different, sometimes conflicting identities (p. 59), Licona (2005) posits a third space that can be understood as both a practice and a location. As a practice, she contends, "it reveals a differential consciousness capable of engaging creative and coalitional forms of opposition to the limits of dichotomous [mis]representations. As a location, third space has the potential to be a space of shared understanding and meaning-making" (p. 105).

7. In Braidotti's view, nomadic consciousness is akin to what Foucault called countermemory. It "combines features that are usually perceived as opposing, namely the possession of a sense of identity that rests not on fixity but on contingency. The nomadic consciousness combines coherence with mobility. It aims to rethink the unity of the subject, without reference to humanistic beliefs, without dualistic oppositions, linking instead body and mind in a new set of intensive and often intransitive transitions" (1994, p. 31). For a slightly different take on nomadic consciousness, see Guerra, 2004.

8. According to Lauer (2009), the difference between multimodal and multimedia is largely a difference between *modes* (design/process) and *media* (production/distribution). Modes can be understood as ways of representing information, or the semiotic channels we use to compose a text. Examples of modes include words, sounds, still and moving images, animation and color. Media, on the other hand, are the "tools and material resources" (see Kress & Van Leeuwen, 2001, p. 22) used to produce and disseminate texts. Examples of media include books, radio, television, computers, paint brush and canvas, and human voices (Lauer, 2009, p. 227).

9. According to the *Center for Immigration Studies*, the Immigration and Nationality Act of 1965 "phased out the national origins quota system first instituted in 1921" and replaced it "with a system based primarily on family reunification and needed skills." The legislation unexpectedly led to "one of the greatest waves of immigration in the nation's history—more than 18 million legal immigrants since the law's passage," most of whom came from Asia and Latin America (2013, n.p.).

References

Agudelo, J. J. (2007). An intercultural approach for language teaching: Developing critical cultural awareness. *Íkala: revista de lenguaje y cultura*, 12(18), 185–217.

Alexander, J. & Rhodes, J. (2014). *On multimodality: New media in composition studies*. Urbana, IL: NCTE.

Anzaldúa, G. (1987). *Borderlands/La frontera: The new mestiza*. San Francisco, CA: Aunt Lute Books.

Bakhtin, M. (1981). *The dialogic imagination*. (C. Emerson & M. Holquist, Trans.). Austin, TX: University of Texas Press.

Bal, M. (1999). Introduction. In M. Bal, J. Crewe & L. Spitzer (Eds.), *Acts of memory: Cultural recall in the present* (pp. vi–xvii). Hanover, NH: University Press of New England.

Barthes, R. (1977). *The third meaning: Image-music-text*. (S. Heath, Trans.). New York, NY: The Noonday Press.

Bhabha, H. K. (1994). *The location of culture*. New York, NY: Routledge.

Bourdieu, P. (1977). *Outline of a theory of practice*. Cambridge, UK: Cambridge University Press.

Bourdieu, P. (1989). Social space and symbolic power. *Sociological Theory*, 7(1), 14–25.

Bourdieu, P. & Wacquant, L. J. D. (1992). *An invitation to reflexive sociology*. Chicago, IL: University of Chicago Press.

Braidotti, R. (1994). *Nomadic subjects.* New York, NY: Cambridge University Press.

Butler, J. (1997). Queer transexions of race, nation, and gender. *Social Text,* 52/53, 265–277.

Byram, M. (2012). Language awareness and (critical) cultural awareness – Relationships, comparisons and contrasts. *Language Awareness,* 21(1–2), 5–13.

Byram, M. & Zarate, G. (1997). Defining and assessing cultural competence: Some principles and proposals for the European context. *Language Teaching,* 29, 14–18.

Caraballo, L. (2011). Theorizing identities in a "just(ly)" contested terrain: Practice theories of identity amid critical-poststructural debates on curriculum and achievement. *Journal of Curriculum and Pedagogy,* 8(2), 155–177.

Center for Immigration Studies. (2013). Three decades of mass immigration: The legacy of the 1965 Immigration Act. Retrieved from www.cis.org/1965Immigration Act-MassImmigration

Cintron, R. (1997). *Angels' town: Chero ways, gang life, and rhetorics of the everyday.* New York, NY: Beacon Press.

Deleuze, G. & Guattari, F. (1987). *A thousand plateaus.* (B. Massumi, Trans.). Minneapolis, MN: University of Minnesota Press.

Dufva, H. (1994). Language awareness and cultural awareness for language learners. *Jyvaskyla,* 19–32.

Echterhoff, G. (2010). Language and memory: Social and cognitive processes. In A. Nünning & A. Erll (Eds.), *A companion to cultural memory studies* (pp. 263–274). Berlin: De Gruyter.

Erll, A. (2010). Cultural memory studies: An introduction. In A. Nünning & A. Erll (Eds.), *A companion to cultural memory studies* (pp. 1–15). Berlin: De Gruyter.

Fenner, A.-B. (2008). Cultural awareness in the foreign language classroom. In J. Cenoz & N. H. Hornberger (Eds.), *Encyclopedia of language and education, 2nd ed., vol. 6: Knowledge about language* (pp. 273–285). Springer Science + Business Media LLC.

Gee, J. P. (1996). *Social linguistics and literacies: Ideology in discourses, 2nd ed.* London, UK: Taylor & Francis.

Giddens, A. (1991). *Modernity and self-identity: Self and society in the late modern age.* Stanford, CA: Stanford UP.

Guerra, J. C. (1997). The place of intercultural literacy in the writing classroom. In C. Severino, J. C. Guerra & J. E. Butler (Eds.), *Writing in multicultural settings* (pp. 248–260). New York, NY: MLA.

Guerra, J. C. (2004). Putting literacy in its place: Nomadic consciousness and the practice of transcultural repositioning. In C. Gutiérrez-Jones (Ed.), *Rebellious readings: The dynamics of Chicana/o literacy* (pp. 19–37). Center for Chicana/o Studies: UC Santa Barbara.

Gutiérrez, K. (1995). Script, counterscript, and underlife in the urban classroom: Constructing a Third Space. Paper presented at the Fourth International Literacy and Education Research Network Conference on Learning, Townsville, QLD, Australia.

Gutiérrez, K. (2008). Developing a sociocritical literacy in the third space. *Reading Research Quarterly,* 43(2), 148–164.

Gutiérrez, K., Baquedano-López, P. & Tejeda, C. (1999). Rethinking diversity: Hybridity and hybrid language practices in the third space. *Mind, Culture, and Activity,* 6(4), 286–303.

Hall, S. (1996). Introduction: Who needs "identity"? In S. Hall & P. du Gay (Eds.), *Questions of cultural identity* (pp. 1–16). Thousand Oaks, CA: Sage.

Hogan, K. J. (2005). Student subjectivity and the teaching of literature: The possibility of free space. Unpublished doctoral dissertation, University of Washington, Seattle.

Honneth, A. (1995). *The struggle for recognition: The grammar of social conflicts.* Cambridge, UK: Polity.

Horner, B. & Trimbur, J. (2002). English only and U.S. college composition. *College Composition and Communication,* 53(4), 594–630.

Jarratt, S. C., Mack, K., Sartor, A. & Watson, S. E. (2009). Pedagogical memory: Writing, mapping, translating. *WPA: Writing Program Administration,* 33(1–2), 46–73.

Jewitt, C. (2014). Multimodality and literacy in school classrooms. *Review of Research in Education,* 32, 241–267.

Klein, S. B., German, T. P., Cosmides, L. & Gabriel, R. (2004). A theory of autobiographical memory: Necessary components and disorders resulting from their loss. *Social Cognition,* 22(5), 460–490.

Kostogriz, A. (2002). Teaching literacy in multicultural classrooms: Towards a pedagogy of "Thirdspace." Annual Conference of the Australian Association for Research in Education, Brisbane, Australia. Retrieved from www.aare.edu.au/02pap/kos02346.htm

Kostogriz, A. (2004). Rethinking the spatiality of literacy practices in multicultural conditions. Retrieved from www.aare.edu.au/04pap/kos04610.pdf

Kramsch, C. (1993). *Context and culture in language teaching.* Oxford, UK: Oxford University Press.

Kramsch, C. (2009). Third culture and language education. In V. Cook & L. Wei (Eds.), *Contemporary applied linguistics* (pp. 233–254). London, UK: Continuum.

Kramsch, C. (2013). Culture in foreign language teaching. *Iranian Journal of Language Teaching Research,* 1(1), 57–78.

Kress, G. & van Leeuwen, T. (2001). *Multimodal discourse: The modes and media of contemporary communication.* Oxford, UK: Oxford University Press.

Lauer, C. (2009). Contending with terms: "Multimodal" and "multimedia" in the academic and public spheres. *Computers and Composition,* 26, 225–239.

Licona, A. C. (2005). (B)orderlands' rhetorics and representations: The transformative potential of feminist third-space scholarship and zines author(s). *NWSA Journal,* 17(2), 104–129.

Lu, M.-Z. & Horner, B. (2013). Translingual literacy, language difference, and matters of agency. *College English,* 75(6), 582–607.

Moje, E. B., Ciechanowski, K., Kramer, K., Ellis, L., Carrillo, R. & Callazo, T. (2004). Working toward a third space in content areas literacy. *Reading Research Quarterly,* 39(1), 38–70.

Pahl, K. (2002). Habitus and the home: Texts and practices in families. *Ways of Knowing Journal,* 2(1), 45–53.

Peirce, C. S. (1898/1955). *Philosophical writings of Peirce.* (J. Buchler, Ed.). New York, NY: Dover Publications.

Pollock, D. C. & Van Reken, R. E. (2009). *Third culture kids: Growing up among worlds.* Boston, MA: Nicholas Brealey Publishing.

Romberger, J. (2012). Multimodality, memory and evidence: How the treasure house of rhetoric is being digitally renovated. In C. Whithaus (Ed.), *Multimodal literacies and emerging genres* (pp. 204–222). Pittsburgh, PA: University of Pittsburgh Press.

Rounsaville, A. (2011). Figuring transnational literacies: Rhetorical negotiations in a global paradigm. Unpublished doctoral dissertation, University of Washington, Seattle.

Sanders, J. & Albers, P. (2010). Multimodal literacies: An introduction. In P. Albers & J. Sanders (Eds.), *Literacies, the arts, and multimodality* (pp. 1–25). Urbana, IL: National Council of Teachers of English.

Sandoval, C. (2000). *Methodology of the oppressed.* Minneapolis, MN: University of Minnesota.

Selfe, C. L. (2009). The movement of air, the breath of meaning: Aurality and multimodal composing. *College Composition and Communication, 60*(4), 616–663.

Soja, E. (1996). *Thirdspace: Journeys to Los Angeles and other real-and-imagined spaces.* Malden, MA: Blackwell Publishers.

Straub, J. (2010). Psychology, narrative, and cultural memory: Past and present. In A. Nünning & A. Erll (Eds.), *A companion to cultural memory studies* (pp. 215–228). Berlin: De Gruyter.

Sulzen, J. (2001). Modality based working memory. School of Education, Stanford University. Retrieved from http://ldt.stanford.edu/~jsulzen/james-sulzen-portfolio/classes/PSY205/modality-project/paper/modality-expt-paper.PDF

Vivian, S. (2010). *Public forgetting: The rhetoric and politics of beginning again.* University Park: Pennsylvania State University Press.

Wallach, H. & Averbach, E. (1955). On memory modalities. *American Journal of Psychology, 68*(2), 249–257.

Williams, B. (2003). "Speak for yourself? Power and hybridity in the cross-cultural classroom. *College Composition and Communication, 54*(4), 586–609.

Yancey, K. B. (2004). Made not only in words: Composition in a new key. *College Composition and Communication, 56*(2), 297–328.

4

THE RHETORIC AND IDEOLOGY
OF SELF-REPRESENTATION

As I noted in the opening chapter, my siblings and I grew up in a housing project that physically isolated us from other linguistic and cultural groups in our home-town of Harlingen, Texas. Except for a group of African American families that lived on the periphery of the housing project in a half block area between us and the public elementary school that we attended, almost everyone else in the housing project was Mexican or Mexican American. Because of the social and political forces that worked to contain us all, we rarely interacted with anyone else in the larger community outside of school (and in my case, little league baseball) who did not share our language, cultural practices or lifestyle. One afternoon when I was about 16 years old and lying in bed in an upstairs bedroom reading a book, I heard a voice call out from our front yard, "*¡Oye, Chico, ven pa' fuera, hombre!*" When my younger brother, Chico, failed to respond immediately, the voice called out again: "*¡Andale, Chico, apúrate!*" After another moment went by, I heard a second voice—my mother's—respond: "*¿Y quién habla?*" The first voice responded, "*¡Habla* Horace*!*" Surprised by the person's non-Spanish first name, I bolted up from the bed and looked out the window to see an 11-year-old African American boy standing outside our apartment. A few seconds later, Chico came out the front door, greeted Horace—"*¿Qué pasó,* Horace*?*"—then walked off with him to join a group of friends. That moment marks the first time I recall wit-nessing anyone of my siblings, including myself, interacting with a non-Mexican or non-Mexican American outside of a church, school setting or baseball field.

Since then, as several of my siblings and I have left our hometown and moved to other communities in Texas and beyond as part of the Latino/Latina diaspora that began in this country after the Immigration Act of 1965, the exceptional moment of linguistic and cultural contact that I just described has been repeated by each of us to varying degrees, depending on where we settled and how our individual identities evolved after we left home. For example, when she moved to Chicago in the mid-1960s, my older sister Bertha found herself in a diverse metropolitan area where for the first time in her life she met and befriended Anglos, Puerto Ricans and African Americans as social and cultural equals. When I followed Bertha to Chicago a couple of years later and got a manual labor job in a factory where she did office work, I, too, found myself in the midst of an array of individuals very different from any I had ever interacted with back home. Some years after I left, my brother Chico moved to San Antonio and my two youngest siblings—Esmeralda and Joe—moved to Dallas where they integrated themselves into broader social and cultural networks through work, leisure and neighborhood connections. Meanwhile, several of my sisters—Gracie, Peggy, Isabel and Irene[1] stayed in our hometown where they remained connected to family and friends through networks that more generally reflected the social, cultural and linguistic affiliations we had all shared before some of us had moved away. As a consequence of the varied changes each of us experienced, our language practices, class status, lifestyles and how we identified ethnically shifted as we each adapted to different geographical settings and more varied social, cultural and linguistic relationships.

In this chapter, I want to explore some of the layers that make the concept of identity as difficult to ascertain as the other dimensions—language, culture and citizenship—that inform this project. I want to do this, not by taking a look at how students in our college classrooms engage in identity construction or performance as many scholars in the field have done (Kells, 2002; Kerschbaum, 2014; LeCourt, 2004; Norton, 2013), but by looking at something closer to the kind of lived experience I have been weaving into the story that I have been telling in this book: the varied identities my siblings report having performed or deployed "in practice" (Caraballo, 2011) in the course of their everyday lives. In the process, I want to examine the identity categories and markers of difference (Kerschbaum, 2014) they have performed, have had imposed on them or that have unexpectedly emerged of their own accord to understand the complex choices we make each time we position or reposition ourselves in the social spaces that we inhabit. In addition to several key conceptual notions that Kerschbaum (2014) describes in her award-winning book, *Toward a New Rhetoric of Difference*, and the synthesis that Bucholtz and Hall (2004, 2005) provide of the various ways sociocultural theorists have conceptualized the notion of identity, I use van Dijk's (1995) discussion of the role discourse plays when we deploy our always ideologically-grounded identities to frame my analysis and discussion of a series of interviews that I conducted with my siblings[2] to examine the different ways they engage in the rhetorical and ideological practice of self-representation.

In the context of my discussion of language difference in Chapter 2, I first examine the array of linguistic practices—Spanish, English and code-switching[3]—my siblings used during our interviews to situate themselves rhetorically and discursively in relation to the position I occupied as the interviewer. In so doing,

I demonstrate how *identities-in-practice*,[4] even when they emerge from similar bilingual and multidialectal contexts, are subject to myriad relational and intersecting ideological, contextual, rhetorical, affective, embodied, material, and historical experiences and affiliations, all of which challenge easy assumptions about how, when, or if individuals are going to code-switch or, to use the term Young (2004) coined, code-mesh. In the context of my discussion of culture in Chapter 3, I take the singular concept of "Mexicanness" to demonstrate how many degrees of difference are always present in the ways individuals within a single community—or in this case, a single family—choose to represent themselves. I later connect this to the parallel phenomenon educators are experiencing more and more as a consequence of the increasing number of multilingual and multicultural students in our classrooms. Finally, I describe several interactions my siblings and I had with linguistic and cultural others who asked us the bold questions—usually one or the other—that anyone who does not fit a mold inevitably gets asked in the U.S.: What are you? Where are you from? I conclude each subsection with some remarks about how my discussion of identity can help educators figure out ways to learn about and integrate the plethora of lived experiences students bring with them into classroom activities. My overall goal in this chapter is to identify the range of identity markers individuals may use in any community of belonging to represent themselves and to grant value to the kinds of rhetorical and discursive features (reflected in my siblings' language differences) students would likely display in our college writing classrooms, if these were not continually displaced by our institutional commitment to academic discourses and the English Only language practices that create and sustain them.

Finding Difference beyond the Politics of Identity

In *Toward a New Rhetoric of Difference*, Kerschbaum (2014) presents an approach to understanding difference that uses "a flexible means of examining and reexamining the interplay between identity categories and the communicative performances and contexts in which those categories become meaningful" (p. 4). In so doing, she identifies two strategies used in writing research that "take identity categories as a central unit of analysis and interpretation" (p. 6). The first approach, which involves *taxonomizing difference*, accentuates "intersections among various identity categories" that effectively recognize and acknowledge "the variety of ways that people can be identified and named" (p. 8). This strategy, which broadens the range of interpretive possibilities I described in the introduction to this chapter, encourages educators to think of their students "not in terms of single identifiers but as the embodiment of a complex set of identifications that must be considered together, rather than independently from one another." The second approach—*categorical redefinition*—deemphasizes multiple categories and their intersections and instead "focuses on producing more refined and careful interpretations of a specific category" (p. 10). As productive as these methodological strategies have been in complicating our understanding of the range of identity categories or axes of differentiation (Braidotti, 1994) our students embody and that we must always take into consideration when we interact with them, Kerschbaum contends that they inadvertently contribute to the problem of "fixing difference in order to study it" by treating difference "as a stable thing or property that can be identified and fixed in place" and by attempting "to fix—that is, improve—the way difference is understood" (p. 6).

To remedy these shortcomings, Kerschbaum (2014) proposes *markers of difference* as an alternative conceptual orientation that "make[s] visible the dynamism, the relationality, and the emergence of difference" because they help us "mediate between broad conceptual tools for talking about difference and the unique qualities of individual moments of interaction" (p. 7). Marking difference, Kerschbaum explains,

> is a rhetorical lens—rhetorical because it emphasizes the relationship between speaker/writer and audience as well as the situated nature of all communication activity—that acknowledges the important role identity categories play in interactions at the same time that it attends to difference as it is performed during the moment-to-moment vicissitudes of communication.
>
> *p. 67*

Building on Bakhtin's work on "noncoincidence in being," Kerschbaum shifts the focus on difference from "something to be named or described" to "a relation between two individuals that is predicated upon their separateness from one another. . . . Difference-as-relation," she surmises, "drives communicative efforts because it is part of the interplay between identification and differentiation" (p. 66). In Kerschbaum's view, this move is a critical one for educators to make because it shifts the emphasis away from *learning about others* (which we do when we think of a student as a simple constellation of identity categories) to *learning with others* (which we do when we personally interact with them in shifting contexts and pay attention to as many of the identity categories, categorical redefinitions and markers of difference that emerge in the process) (p. 74). Because their ephemerality balances the preconceived nature of the identity categories and categorical redefinitions we depend on to understand our students (p. 70), markers of difference help "bridge the conceptual gap between *knowledge about difference* and interactional *involvement with difference*" (p. 67, emphasis added) that can help us generate a fuller understanding of our students' identities-in-practice (Caraballo, 2011, 2012).

Like Kerschbaum (2014), Bucholtz and Hall (2004, 2005) frame identity "as a relational and sociocultural phenomenon that emerges and circulates in local discourse contexts of interaction rather than as a stable structure located primarily in the individual psyche or in fixed social categories" (2005, pp. 585–586). In deliberately broad and open-ended terms, Bucholtz and Hall define identity as "the social positioning of self and other" (p. 586). Reflected in this definition is the widely shared view that identity is a sociocultural, multi-faceted, situated, contingent and ideological practice. In their synthesis of research in several related disciplinary areas in language study, Bucholtz and Hall develop five principles that in their view "represent the varied ways in which different kinds of scholars currently approach the question of identity" (p. 607):

1. Identity is best viewed as the emergent product rather than the pre-existing source of linguistic and other semiotic practices and therefore as fundamentally a social and cultural phenomenon (p. 588).
2. Identities encompass (a) macro-level demographic categories; (b) local, ethnographically specific cultural positions; and (c) temporary and interactionally specific stances and participant roles (p. 592).
3. Identity relations emerge in interaction through several related indexical processes, including: (a) overt mention of identity categories and labels; (b) implicatures and presuppositions regarding one's own or others' identity position; (c) displayed evaluative and epistemic orientations to ongoing talk, as well as interactional footings and participant roles; and (d) the use of linguistic structures and systems that are ideologically associated with specific personas and groups (p. 594).
4. Identities are intersubjectively constructed through several, often overlapping, complementary relations, including similarity/difference, genuineness/artifice, and authority/delegitimacy (p. 598).
5. Any given construction of identity may be in part deliberate and intentional, in part habitual and hence often less than fully conscious, in part an outcome of interactional negotiation and contestation, in part an outcome of others' perceptions and representations, and in part an effect of larger ideological processes and material structures that may become relevant to interaction. It is therefore constantly shifting both as interaction unfolds and across discourse contexts (p. 606).

In addition to describing what happens when the identity categories that Kerschbaum examines are disrupted and the dynamic characteristics of what in another context Caraballo (2011, 2012) calls identities-in-practice come into play, Bucholtz and Hall remind us that our identities are always partial, emergent and negotiated.

Although Bucholtz and Hall's discussion adds texture to Kerschbaum's conceptual framing, it does not provide an adequate frame of reference for understanding the critical role that ideology plays in identity formation. For that reason, I find van Dijk's (1995) work on how discourse and ideology influence one another in a multiplicity of contexts better correlated with my own interests in that respect. Unlike everyone else I have cited thus far, van Dijk uses the group rather than the individual as the unit of analysis. In his sociocognitive and discursive perspective, van Dijk (1995) defines ideologies as "basic systems of fundamental social cognitions and organizing attitudes and other social representations shared by members of groups" that "indirectly control the mental representations (models) that form the interpretation basis and contextual embeddedness of discourse and its structures" (p. 243). More specifically, van Dijk (1995) conceives of ideologies "as some kind of group self-schema that consists of a number of basic categories organizing the evaluative propositions" that define a particular group. For our purposes, the one category worth mentioning here is what he refers to as identity or membership in a group because it responds directly to a critical question we always ask to differentiate insiders from outsiders: "Who belongs to the group and who does not?" Whether this question is asked by someone who embraces racist, ethnocentric, xenophobic or nationalist ideologies, on the one hand, or ideologies of resistance, for instance, of ethnic minority groups or feminists, on the other, van Dijk (1995) contends that this category "typically features the self-defined fundamental (e.g., inherent or more or less permanent) properties of the group," among them "Origin, Appearance, Ethnicity, Gender, Language, Religion, and so on" (p. 249).

In a first sketch of a more explicit and theoretical framework, van Dijk (1995) proposes that all ideologies share a number of characteristics. All ideologies, for example, are "socially shared 'interpretive frameworks' that allow group members to understand and make sense of social reality, everyday practices and relations to other groups" (p. 245). In contrast to perspectives that purport to identify one ideology as superior to all others, van Dijk (1995) argues that ideologies are neither true nor false because every ideology represents "the possibly partisan, self-serving 'truth' of a social group" (p. 246). Because ideologies "involve mental objects such as ideas, thoughts, beliefs, judgments and values" that reflect "the abstract, 'axiomatic' oasis of the socially shared belief systems of groups" (p. 244), van Dijk (1995) also believes that there is no such thing as a personal ideology. By its nature, every ideology is social, cultural and interactive. Finally, in addition to simultaneously exhibiting "contextually variable manifestations" (p. 246) as well as a degree of "relative stability and continuity" (p. 247), ideologies are the basic axioms "of a naïve, implicit social theory of a group about itself and its position in society" that group members use to monitor "social interpretation and interaction" (p. 246).

Recognition, Misrecognition and Other Acts of Identity

¿Pues, quién y qué soy yo? From the moment I was conscious enough to be aware of my social and physical surroundings, I have asked myself this question because every time I looked in the mirror as a child, I saw myself as something and someone very different from those around me in my immediate family and in the highly segregated housing project in which my siblings and I grew up. Long

before my mother intimated that I had been born out of wedlock, I knew that I was different from everyone in my household, a household made up of a veritable rainbow coalition of bodies as a consequence of two older sisters born in Mexico before me and six younger siblings[5] born in the United States after me, all of us to the same woman but to three different fathers. Because I was one of the more light-skinned children in the family, my mother and her blood relatives in Texas and Mexico often referred to me as *"puro* Guerra" to reflect the admiration that light skin carries among many families of color and to cast me as a reflection of my tall and light-skinned grandfather. Regrettably, I met him but once in my life at the age of seven when my family traveled to his home in *La Villa de Allende,* a small village outside of *Monterrey, Nuevo León* in northern Mexico some 90 miles from our home in Harlingen, Texas. Because my grandmother died before I met my grandfather that one time and I never once met my biological father or his parents, my mother's father was all I had connecting me to the furthest reaches of my past.[6]

So, who and what am I? It is, if the literature on identity I reviewed in the preceding section is any indication, a difficult question for any one of us to answer; yet, we are all prone to ask it at some point in our lives to explain and understand our place in the world. It is, of course, also a question students, no matter what language, culture, race, ethnicity, class, gender, age, ability, sexual orientation or lifestyle they choose to embrace or we happen to impose on them, also ask themselves in an effort to locate and explain the presence of the varied linguistic and cultural voices that emerge in the course of their reading, writing and rhetorical engagement with others in the academy and beyond. In the preceding two chapters, I implicated myself through several autobiographical passages in the tangled conversations about the role of language and culture in the lives of the students we meet in our writing classrooms. In this chapter, I want to use the interviews that I conducted with my siblings to explore more fully how rhetoric and ideology, and the identities-in-practice they inform, play themselves out in the context of our everyday lives. My hope is that an understanding of how various identity markers or axes of differentiation inform our rhetorically and ideologically imbued efforts at self-representation will shed light on the challenges that we all face as educators interested in understanding the multiplicity of identities our students deploy in the college writing classroom.

In the analyses and discussions that I present in the three ensuing subsections, the range of competing and complementary conceptions of identity I outlined above serve as multiple lenses for understanding how my siblings and I have deployed varied axes of differentiation to position or reposition ourselves in our interactions with others. They also provide me with an opportunity to examine the kinds of assumptions educators often make about the backgrounds and lived experiences students bring to the college classroom, especially as these are reflected in their language, culture, race, ethnicity, gender, class, age, ability, sexual orientation, lifestyle and citizenship status. An examination of my siblings as members of the same family who can be assumed to share a history and a multitude of lived experiences that have influenced their identity formation, I argue, can provide critical insights not available in a comparable study of a group of students in a classroom setting. I begin my analysis by considering the kinds of assumptions interlocutors often make about someone's language use on the basis of the various axes of differentiation they are able to identify. I then caution against the kinds of easy assumptions educators often make about someone else's cultural practices in light of what they take to be that individual's generic racial or ethnic background. Finally, I consider one of the most problematic acts of misrecognition that interlocutors engage in when they prejudge someone's identity on the basis of their physical appearance. Taken together, the forthcoming analyses and discussions remind us of the challenges we face when we attempt to know who someone is on the basis of always limited information about their identity.

Language Use and the Intersection of Identity Categories

Every time I go back home to visit my family in the Lower Rio Grande Valley of South Texas, I find myself having to self-consciously adjust linguistically to a way of life I recognize as dramatically different from the one I lived in Chicago for 22 years and the one I have lived in Seattle for the past 25. Like most transitions from one sociocultural and sociolinguistic context to another, the rhetorical and discursive adjustments I have to make are often stark, but sometimes relatively subtle. My cadence and intonation change ever so slightly in some cases, and more dramatically in others, as I engage in the give and take of our conversations, no longer dominated by English or by the ethos surrounding it. These changes, of course, vary depending on my conversational partner. With my 95-year-old mother, I speak Spanish almost exclusively. She has learned some English over the years and will sometimes sprinkle her speech with it, especially if she knows that her interlocutor does not speak much Spanish, but she generally prefers the comfort of her first language. On the other hand, I tend to code-switch in conversations with my oldest sister, Gracie, and my middle siblings, Peggy, Isabel and Chico, all of whom dropped out of school at one point or another and are Spanish dominant bilinguals.[7] Conversations with my other older sister Bertha, who also dropped out in the ninth grade, but later received a GED, are very different. No doubt part of it has to do with the fact that she went back to college later in life and earned a bachelor's degree in English. Like Gracie, she was born in Mexico; unlike Gracie, who has never lived anywhere else but Harlingen, Bertha has lived in Chicago and the Houston area for many years. My conversations with my three youngest siblings—Irene, Esmer, and Joe—are yet again different, more English dominant, and like my conversations with Bertha, typically more academic in orientation. Because they grew up speaking a lot of Spanish with my mother, Irene and Esmer are also very comfortable code-switching between English and Spanish when the occasion calls for it.

Interestingly, during our interviews, Bertha, Esmer and Joe did not use any Spanish whatsoever; Irene and Gracie uttered a total of 9 Spanish words between them (Irene, 4 and Gracie, 5).[8] Although Bertha is probably the most bilingual member in the family (in my opinion, she speaks both standardized forms of English and Spanish better than anyone else), she tends to code-switch less than the rest of us because she typically prefers to speak continuously in English or Spanish. Probably because she perceived the interview as a formal encounter, despite my instructions to the contrary, she decided that it called for an English Only response. Even though she is among the youngest children in the family and one could easily expect her to have limited Spanish-speaking proficiency, Esmer is as bilingual as the rest of us because she grew up in my mother's presence at a time when my mother spoke very little English. It probably helps that Esmer still has the habit of speaking with my mother on the phone several times a day; this has no doubt reinforced her use of Spanish. As a consequence, like Bertha, she tends to speak in one language or the other, although code-switching comes easily to her when the occasion calls for it. As the youngest sibling in the family, Joe learned to speak the least Spanish at home and speaks it less today than anyone else. No doubt the fact that he criticized our mother for not speaking English when she went to school to meet with his teachers or when his friends came over to visit colored his attitude toward learning the language in the first place. On the other hand, it is because of Joe that our mother learned to speak English as well as she does.

A review of their language use in our interviews also readily demonstrates the different degrees to which my three middle siblings, who as a group are the most working class among us, code-switch effortlessly and continuously in a variety of situations. As they do regularly in the context of their everyday lives, Peggy, Isabel and Chico displayed a fluid mix of English and Spanish in our interviews that will likely seem dramatic and challenging to monolingual English readers. Readers who are bilingual Spanish/English speakers and are familiar with what is euphemistically called "Spanglish" will no doubt also notice the Spanish register they use; it reflects a grammar and vocabulary described as Chicano Spanish by linguists (see Peñalosa, 1980; Sánchez, 1983) and a set of rhetorical and discursive practices profoundly informed by their working-class histories as life-long residents of south Texas. When I asked Peggy (a clerk at a convenience store in Harlingen at the time of our interview) how she would identify herself when people asked her about her race or ethnicity, she said:

> I just say I'm *mexicana*. Mexican *nomás*. I don't know. I've always liked the way they talk, the people from over there. *Hablan bien bonito.* And their language is different from ours. *Y son bien* close *ellos. Digo yo.* They're very united and they talk different. *Y dicen, "Ay corazoncito, ay papacito,"* con *mucho amor,* and I like that.

In this passage, Peggy's word choice is two-thirds English and one-third Spanish. Despite the assumption that many readers are likely to make, as Peñalosa (1980) and Sánchez (1983) have demonstrated, her mixing of the two languages is strategically managed and displays her command of the syntax and vocabulary that informs each. In other words, her language use is not haphazard; Peggy switches effortlessly depending on the degree of her rhetorical and discursive identification with her interlocutor.

Like Peggy, Chico and Isabel also demonstrate an affinity for code-switching. To my surprise, however, Isabel spoke at length in Spanish even when she was describing concepts like *Chicanismo*, which I had anticipated at the time would have triggered her tendency to code-switch. In describing his own involvement with Chicanismo, a social movement that emerged in the late 1960s and became a battle cry for individuals who had decided they no longer wanted to be called Mexican American, Chico (a heating and air conditioning installer in San Antonio when I interviewed him) had the following to say:

> We wanted equal rights for us Mexicans. . . . The *bolillos* got this, we don't. And you know *que* we would go out and rally, so I guess that's where it came from when I was growing up. . . . I used to go to rallies. A guy would go out there and talk, and I would be there supporting the guys. *Ahí en la placita*. Different places. There was, *¿cómo se llamaba?* *La Raza Unida* from Pharr. . . . I was in the 8th or 9th grade.

In this passage, only about 15% of Chico's vocabulary is in Spanish, but again even a sprinkling of words in Spanish gives the passage a different flavor and represents a very different sensibility than if every word had been in English. Again, as Peñalosa (1980) and Sánchez (1983) have demonstrated in their work, this kind of meshing is unpredictable in that it is impossible to anticipate what words will be expressed in one language or the other. Code-switching, or what some scholars nowadays call code-meshing (Young, 2004), is a creative and unpredictable process because it only comes into being at the very moment of its inception. There is no standard formula to follow; in a manner of speaking, the two languages take on a life of their own as they mingle with one another in unpredictable yet very systematic ways.

In her conversation with me, Isabel exhibited the exact opposite response in terms of her language use. In describing her own understanding and lack of involvement with the Chicano movement, Isabel (a telemarketer for Direct TV in Harlingen when I interviewed her) shared her sense of what it meant for someone to consider themselves Chicano or Chicana:

> *Mira, estabas hablando de los Chicanos. ¿Sabes quiénes son los Chicanos? Los Chicanos y las Chicanas son los que se iban para el norte. Esas son las Chicanas porque en ese tiempo tenían huelgas y todo.* Chicano power! Chicano power!

> *¿Te acuerdas? Las Chicanas y los Chicanos eran los que se iban para el norte.*
> *Porque hablé con una* girlfriend *que ella también se iba para el norte, y dijo "Ay,*
> *yo soy Chicana, porque toda la gente que se va para el norte semos Chicanos."*

Out of 85 words in this passage, only three are in English, and two of those words were part of a phrase (Chicano power) that she was quoting. Except for her working-class dialect use of the word *"semos"* (*"somos"* in Standard Spanish), Isabel's Spanish is fairly standardized and exhibits a degree of familiarity with Standard Spanish that many of us in the family do not typically demonstrate. Again, in reviewing all of the transcripts, I was surprised that Isabel spoke in Spanish at greater length than I had anticipated. This is the kind of response I would have expected from Bertha or Esmer, both of whom are more prone to speak in one language or the other.

In the context of my discussion of the various approaches to language difference in Chapter 2, my description of how varied my siblings' language use is in English and Spanish illustrates the challenges that writing teachers face when they make assumptions about the language use of any of their migrant, immigrant or international students. Even when a group of individuals is raised in the same household and exposed to very similar multilingual and multidialectal practices, it is impossible to predict how or if they are going to code-switch (i.e., code-mesh). For this reason, it behooves those of us responsible for teaching and training writing teachers to remind ourselves and them that the most important thing we can do is to alert our students to the competing ideological approaches to language—i.e., help them develop critical language and cultural awareness—so that they can decide for themselves whether or not, and if so, to what extent they wish to engage in either code-switching or code-meshing in the sense that I described them in Chapter 2. Pedagogical approaches designed specifically to encourage code-meshing on the assumption that it is good for our students may well backfire among some students who will feel put upon instead of being allowed to make their own decisions about how to use their language practices in the college writing classroom.

Deconstructing "Mexicanness"

A few years ago, I became curious about how the language and cultural practices my siblings and I shared had influenced our tendencies to use various ethnic markers to label ourselves and to perform different identities depending on the circumstances in which we found ourselves. I knew from personal experience that I tended to shift my use of ethnic markers to describe myself depending on the individuals with whom I was interacting. As I noted in "Emerging Representations, Situated Literacies, and the Practice of Transcultural Repositioning,"

> There was a time, in the days of my youth, when I thought of myself as *puro chicano*. Having served proudly in affiliation with Rodolfo "Corky"

Gonzáles and the Crusade for Justice in Denver, Colorado, no other label of self-identification made sense to me. But times have changed, and so have the ways I describe myself. In Chicago, most of the time but not always, *soy hispano o latino*. In Texas, *soy tejano*. In Mexico, *soy mexicano Americano*. In Washington state, *soy chicano*. When I am out of my element, I refer to myself as Mexican or *mexicano*. And when I am around Anglos who are not quite sure what all of these words ending in "o" mean, I tell them—and yes, I admit that I still grit my teeth and bite my tongue before I speak this phrase—that I am Hispanic. At this point in my life, I want to believe that whatever singular label I may prefer to use to define myself in theory is no longer as important as the multiple labels I must choose to identify myself in practice.

Guerra, 2004, p. 7

As Kerschbaum (2014) points out, emphasizing multiple categories and their intersections in the process of taxonomizing difference, as I did in the previous subsection, can provide us with a more complicated sense of the ways in which identity categories intersect and influence the varied linguistic and cultural identities individuals adopt. Equally useful is what Kerschbaum (2014) refers to as the process of redefining a particular category to produce more refined and careful interpretations of how a generic category functions in identity construction. In this subsection, I review the various axes of differentiation that incline my siblings and me to think of ourselves as having a shared linguistic and cultural past at the same time that we demonstrate through our use of localized ethnic identifiers how different we have become from one another beyond what is stereotypically thought of as our shared "Mexicanness."

In contrast to that overriding stereotype, individuals of Mexican origin in Texas have an incredible array of ethnic and regional labels at their disposal to demonstrate different degrees of affiliation with their Mexicanness: Mexican, *mexicano/ mexicana*, Mexican American, *mexicano americano/mexicana americana*, Chicano/ Chicana, *tejano/tejana*, Hispanic and Latino/Latina. The decision among most of my siblings to identify themselves as Mexican or *mexicano/mexicana* makes sense; although only my two oldest siblings were born in Mexico, all of us feel an affinity for Mexicanness to varying degrees because we all grew up 10 miles from the U.S.–Mexico border in a highly segregated community that embraced that identity as a counter to the "Americanness" label embraced by Anglos in our hometown. More recently, however, Mexican American and Chicano/Chicana, on the one hand, and Hispanic and Latino/Latina, on the other, have been introduced as terms to describe diametrically opposed ideological identities in the broader Mexican-origin community. While the terms Mexican American and Hispanic are considered ideological labels that reflect conservative values and are therefore typically adopted by individuals in the community who tend to lean to the right, Chicano/Chicana and Latino/Latina are thought to reflect progressive values and are adopted by individuals who tend to lean to the left. The extent to which each of my siblings and I have embraced either or both of the terms available in each pair to demonstrate ideological identification or differentiation among one another will become apparent in the course of my discussion and analysis.

Not surprisingly, the five oldest siblings among us typically use Mexican or *mexicano* to describe ourselves to others; at the same time, none of the youngest four siblings reported using these terms at all. It makes sense that my two older sisters—Gracie and Bertha—would feel a close affinity to these terms because they were both born in Mexico. Gracie (a clerk at Target in Harlingen at the time of our interview), for example, firmly and unambiguously identifies herself as Mexican because she was born there and reports that "[I use that label because] it's a *costumbre*." While Gracie reports occasionally identifying herself as Mexican American, Bertha strictly identifies herself as Mexican. When I asked her if she ever used a term like Hispanic or Latina to self-identify, Bertha (an investigator for the U.S. Department of Labor in McAllen, Texas when I interviewed her) said:

> No, I don't use the word Hispanic. I feel that I do not fall under that category. I'm Mexican and I want to be identified with Mexico. If I say I'm Hispanic, then, that means anything else. It could mean Puerto Rican, it could mean Honduran, it could mean Guatemalan. And not that I have anything against any of those countries; it just means that I want to be identified as Mexican because that's what I am.

As the third in line in the birth order and the first born in the U.S., I probably use Mexican or *mexicano* to describe myself as often as any other descriptor, mainly because it is what I grew up thinking of myself and it is a term that almost anyone I interact with is likely to find familiar. Although they both mentioned it in passing (Peggy: "I just say I'm *mexicana*. Mexican, *nomás*." Isabel: "*No, nomás, este, digo yo* Mexican."), I am surprised that Peggy and Isabel use the term because they came of age during the Chicano movement's heyday. On the other hand, gender clearly plays a major role in their case because in its original incarnation the Chicano movement reflected the gendered masculine values inherent in a Mexican-origin identity.

The term Mexican American also suggests an interesting ideological pedigree among us as everyone but Peggy claims to use it. In Peggy's case, however, the absence of the term in her vocabulary seems to reflect a degree of confusion on her part. "When I'm filling out a form," she notes, "I put down American instead of Mexican American because I'm from the United States. I thought Mexican American was, like, *no sabía que era*." When I asked her what she thought a Mexican American was, she responded, "*Que era de México y se hizo* American, *¿qué no?*" As I noted earlier, Gracie firmly and unambiguously identifies herself as Mexican because she was born there, but she (surprisingly) generally prefers the label Mexican American because, as she put it: "I'm from

Mexico, but I've been here since I was 40 days old,[9] so I consider myself, not an American, but almost." The only time Isabel is likely to use Mexican American, on the other hand, is when she is filling out an application form: "Yes. *Cuando estoy en una* office filling out *una* application, *pongo* Mexican American." My brother, Chico, on the other hand, always refers to himself as Chicano (more on that in a moment) whenever he is in conversation with Latinos/Latinas or other individuals of Mexican origin. When I asked him if he ever referred to himself as Mexican American, this is what he had to say: "Like with white people, I say I'm Mexican American." Finally, Esmer uses Mexican American because it "reflects mom's and dad's heritage. So in my mind when I say Mexican American, I'm honoring, you know, my heritage."

Chicano and Chicana, on the other hand, are highly contested terms in my family, as they are in many families of Mexican origin in the U.S. Not surprisingly, in light of the term's historical development, the word Chicano is as I noted a moment ago highly gendered in my family, which is probably why my brother Chico and I are the only ones who feel comfortable using the term to describe ourselves. Joe, on the other hand, does not use it at all probably because the term had lost its popularity by the time he came of age. In an effort to highlight his use of the term, Chico described his response to inquiries about his ethnic identity from strangers in this way: "*Me preguntan, '¿Pos, eres mexicano?' Les digo que soy* Chicano. Chicano is what I say. 'Are you from Mexico?' *No, hombre,* I'm from Texas. I'm Chicano." In explaining why he primarily uses Chicano as an identity marker, Chico reflected on his growing up in south Texas at a time when the term was emerging in a political atmosphere thick with protest and demonstration. When I asked my sisters whether they identified with the terms Chicano or Chicana, they explained at length that they had not earned the right to use it. This is how Bertha put it: "Chicana, to me, is a political identification. Because I've not been active in any politics, I've not had an opportunity to use that label. I'd hate to take that term loosely because I haven't done anything. I think I would use it if I were involved in politics." As I noted a moment ago, like Bertha, Isabel sees the term as something that only people who migrate north and participate in labor issues have a right to use.

More recently, the competing terms Hispanic and Latino/Latina also entered our shared vocabulary as ethnic descriptors. As I noted at the outset of this subsection, I prefer the term Latino over Hispanic but on occasion—especially when I decide that my interlocutor might not be as familiar with the array of terms ending in an "o"—I grudgingly use the latter. Of all the terms available to us, Hispanic is least correlated with age, gender or place of residence among my siblings: Gracie, Isabel and I, as well as my three youngest siblings have used it. On the basis of what they report, its use reflects the term's introduction through government forms that require one to self-identify racially or ethnically. As Isabel put it, she often uses it because "in reality, we're supposed to be, what, Hispanic, no? Well, I call myself Hispanic." Irene (an elementary special education teacher in Harlingen at the time of the interview), on the other hand, notes that where she almost always used the term Mexican American in the past, she now almost exclusively uses the term Hispanic to describe herself ethnically: "I think in the past it used to be Mexican American. Now, it's more Hispanic. It's becoming more popular." In her view, the term Hispanic became popular in the Rio Grande Valley about 15 years ago: "The term Hispanic has become more popular for forms that you have to fill out and stuff. What race are you? That's one of the choices. So, now, I just tend to say Hispanic [no matter who I'm talking with]." Joe (a software engineer at Texas Instruments in Dallas at the time I interviewed him) concurred: "I think from most of the applications that I have filled out, it's from that, it's from what I've been exposed to in the past that's been the majority of the things that ask what are you and most of them have picked out Mexican American. The newer ones are starting to switch over to Hispanic." While Esmer (a purchaser at Texas Instruments in Dallas when I interviewed her) also feels compelled to use Hispanic, she reports (the only sibling besides me) that she occasionally uses Latina as well: "When I say Hispanic, it's like the politically correct thing to say here in Texas. You're Hispanic, you know. When I'm with my Latina friends, who can be from Colombia, Brazil, El Salvador, from other Latin American countries, I say we're Latinas. So, yeah, when we're altogether, it's cool to be a Latina."

As is clear, ethnic identity labels are complex and riddled with contradictions. In the context of the shifting nature of one's cultural modalities of memory that I described in Chapter 3 and the shared assumption among many educators that racial and ethnic labels typically represent one's cultural identification in a nutshell as well, my discussion of how, when and why my siblings and I use the varied ethnic labels I just described should give us pause. I suspect that I am not much different from most of my colleagues in that I readily make certain judgment calls on the basis of the constellation of identity categories I accumulate about my students. As self-aware as I like to think I am, it really is difficult for me to ignore what I learn about my students through information I get from them or the university about how they identify themselves. My discussion in this subsection is meant to remind us that as helpful as this information is in getting to know our students, it is—as Kerschbaum (2014) points out—necessary but insufficient. It is only by getting to know our students through as well as beyond the identity markers we pick up that we can avoid making the mistake of assuming that we know our students when in truth we just happen to know something about them. It also reminds us, I think, that the racial and ethnic identity terms they use to position or reposition themselves are always in flux depending on local circumstances or variables they encounter when they are asked to self-identify. It is incumbent upon us all, then, to tread lightly early on when we are still in the process of getting to know our students so that we do not inadvertently misread them by misinterpreting whatever we happen to learn about them in isolation from the more complex network of identity markers that may become apparent over time.

Countering Presuppositions about Ethnic Appearance

As revealing as the process of locating ourselves in the range of varied languages and cultural categories available to us can be in the process of constructing our identities, one of the more interesting issues that emerged during my interviews with my siblings was the extent to which individuals who we interacted with at work, school and other public settings made assumptions about who and what we were, racially and ethnically speaking, on the basis of our physical appearance. As a light-skinned member of the family—a *güerito*—I have always been put off by the surprise that some people I meet express when they first encounter me and are curious to know why someone who looks like me is named Juan. As anyone who has experienced this particular response knows, there is always an initial dancing around the question as interlocutors try to read different bodily aspects and continue to gather information about us. Eventually, those who get stumped ask me who or what I am. Because I want to keep it simple, I almost always refer to myself as Mexican in those cases because I consider it the most widely recognized identity category among the options at my disposal. "But you don't look Mexican" is their typical response. I usually suggest as casually as I can that they must not know many Mexicans because we as a people display a broad range of skin colors and other physical attributes that range from strikingly Iberian to strikingly indigenous in appearance. When that is not enough, I tell them about the carnival I attended in my early 20s near my grandparents' village in Mexico where everyone I saw was blond-haired and blue-eyed. That usually does it. Because my siblings cover the full spectrum of color (dark to light skinned) and appearance (indigenous to Iberian), several of them told me during the interviews how incredulous others often were when interlocutors learned that a particular sibling was of Mexican-origin.

Bertha, who is as fair-skinned and Iberian looking as I am, described a conversation she had with a co-worker in Fort Worth, Texas who asked her the inevitable question: Who or what are you? This is Bertha's take on their exchange:

> I'm Mexican American. "No, you can't be." Yes, I am. "No, you can't be. Well, you must not be full Mexican American." I was born in Mexico and I'm full Mexican. I became a U.S. citizen later on. She called a supervisor and said, "Come over here. Bertha says she's Mexican. Right, she doesn't look like she's Mexican? She must not be all Mexican."

Here we have a clear example of what Bucholtz and Hall (2005) refer to as "presuppositions regarding one's own or other's identity position" (p. 594). As Kerschbaum (2014) is careful to remind us, "category identifications are always a part of interactional processes, so much so that for some categories people may explicitly solicit category identifications if group affiliation is not immediately perceivable" (p. 73). The obvious problem with the kind of exchange that Bertha had with her coworker is that it reflects a tendency in many of us to use identity markers as static and predetermined categories. Because these kinds of perspectives are ideologically grounded, they are difficult to change even in the face of someone adamantly defending who or what they see themselves as in racial or ethnic terms. Despite her best efforts, Bertha never succeeded in persuading the woman that she was indeed Mexican because in the woman's eyes she did not look like one and therefore did not fit the profile.

One would think that my siblings who are marked by others as physically more ethnic looking in appearance than Bertha and I would not have to address these kinds of questions; one would be wrong. In Harlingen and the Rio Grande Valley in general, Peggy has never been asked about her race or ethnicity as residents are generally able to read her features because of their broad experience with individuals who look like her. Outside of south Texas, however, Peggy's physical appearance is read very differently and in the context of the experiences her interlocutors bring to their interactions with her. More than once in Chicago where she lived for several years, for example, Peggy was assumed to be a member of an entirely different racial or ethnic group:

> They ask me if I'm from another land, if I'm like, from, *¿cómo se dicen esas?*, I have a friend, those nurses *que*—[Filipina?]—Yes. "I think you're a Filipina, you're a nurse, and you don't belong here," *me dicen. Cuando estaba en* Chicago*, también todo el tiempo me dicían,* "I think you're Filipina. . . . Yeah, because of your eyes."

Irene, on the other hand, is often assumed to be Chinese, again, because of her eyes: "I think a lot of times, they think I'm Chinese. They think I'm Oriental because of my eyes." She does, however, immediately correct them: "I tell them that I'm Hispanic." In both cases, interlocutors take a single feature (the eyes) and ignore all others to arrive at their stereotypical assumption.

Esmer and Joe are not immune either. In both their cases, individuals have approached them and asked them if they are originally from India or the Middle East. Here is how Joe describes it: "I was in one situation [where] this lady asked me if I was from India cause I have, because Hispanics, some Hispanics have very similar features [to them]. There's been one other situation when a lady from Egypt asked me if I was from there." Joe routinely smiled and said, "No, I'm Hispanic. Mexican American." Because of her almond shaped eyes and olive skin, Esmer is often assumed to be from India:

> I had a lady who was doing a spot treatment on my face one time. . . . And she was from India. And she asked me, "Are you from India? Are you Indian?" And I said, "No, I'm not," I said, "I'm Hispanic. I'm, you know, Mexican American." And then she said, "Oh, but you look so much like you're from our culture!" I said, "Oh, well, I did not know that." I said, "We

have the same skin tone, you know, so I can understand why some Latinas are maybe familiar to your culture because of our skin tone."

In a race conscious society like ours where it is important for both White and non-White individuals to locate someone they are interacting with in terms of their race or ethnicity, these kinds of responses are of course not unexpected. When one is the recipient of these kinds of inquiries, it is impossible not to feel slightly discombobulated, especially when your interlocutor denies you the opportunity to assert your racial or ethnic identity.

One of the elements that all of the situations I just described have in common is that they all occurred outside of south Texas. Because I was considered light skinned but not Anglo when I was growing up in Harlingen, no one ever asked me those questions. Everyone pretty much knew I was Mexican American by the way I dressed, the way I behaved and the way I spoke. Since then, strangers have on occasion asked my wife or a friend if I was Anglo because I did not fit their stereotype of what a Mexican should look like. In each case, the person who asked was not local. They either came from Mexico or some other region of the country. When I asked her if she had ever been asked about her ethnic background, Gracie speculated that no one ever had because she has not traveled widely and has lived in Harlingen all her life. Gracie did, however, relate a story about an experience her daughter had in Dallas very similar to those I have described. During our interview, Gracie told me about an experience that her oldest daughter, who moved to Dallas to live with my sister Esmer when she was in her early 20s, shared with her: "After she moved to Dallas, she said she was in a restaurant and a lady said, 'So what nationality are you?' Because her eyes are like, look a little bit Asian. 'What nationality are you, Asian or something like that?' 'Oh, no,' she said, 'Oh, no, I'm Mexican.'" Gracie then went on to explain where her daughter might have picked up that particular physical feature: "My grandmother and my father have those kinds of eyes. Well, nobody else has them."

The stories I just shared readily suggest that, before anything else, we need to figure out how to ask the right questions in the college writing classroom if we hope to successfully shift our orientation from what Kerschbaum (2014) calls learning *about* others to learning *with* others. Kerschbaum provides several questions that illustrate each of these approaches. The *learning about* questions, for example, generate the kinds of stereotypical identity markers Kerschbaum identified in her study:

- What differences are present in the classroom?
- What groups do individuals belong to?
- What names or labels can describe particular individuals or associate them with others?
- What can we learn about the individuals in the classroom?
- What information about the self is being communicated in talk? (p. 74)

The answers to these questions will no doubt be relatively static and one-dimensional, but if those answering them provide lots of detail, a better composite picture will emerge. But that, Kerschbaum suggests, is not enough. It is for this reason that Kerschbaum (2014) urges us to consider a different set of questions, one that looks at process rather than state of being and elicits more complex and dynamic responses. These questions also do a better job of getting at the truth without repeatedly prejudging others:

- How do individuals position themselves alongside others?
- How are individuals positioned by others?
- How do individuals acknowledge similarities and differences between themselves and others?
- What differences are made salient through classroom interactions?
- How are students and teachers learning with others in the classroom?

As Kerschbaum notes about the students in her study, while "their interactions with one another were not silent regarding how they positioned themselves and others," students were "verbally silent on many issues of race and other contested identities" (p. 18). As rich and insightful as the data from her micro-level study are, I can only imagine how much more complex the data would have been if students had engaged the hard issues in the classroom. Just as my siblings and I did during my series of interviews, we need to find ways to create conditions in our classrooms that will give students and us an opportunity to talk about our most salient differences in as respectful a manner as we are able to manage. Just as we need to give students the opportunity to decide how they wish to invoke their language and cultural differences in the course of representing themselves rhetorically and discursively, we need to provide them with opportunities to perform as limited or broad a range of identities as they so choose.

Spanish to English Glossary

¡Oye, Chico, ven pa' fuera, hombre! [Hey, Chico, come outside, man!]
¡Andale, Chico, apúrate! [Come on, Chico, hurry up!]
¿Y quién habla? [And who's calling?]
¡Habla Horace*!* [It's Horace calling!]
¿Qué pasó, Horace*?* [What's up, Horace?]
¿Pues, quién y qué soy yo? [So, who and what am I?]
puro Guerra [pure Guerra]
La Villa de Allende [The Village of Allende]
Monterrey, Nuevo León [city of *Monterrey* in the state of *Nuevo León*]
mexicana [Mexican]
Mexican *nomás.* [Mexican and nothing else.]
Hablan bien bonito. [They talk real pretty.]

Y son bien close *ellos. Digo yo.* [And they're very close. That's what I say.]

Y dicen, "Ay corazoncito, ay papacito," con mucho amor [And they say, "Oh, my little love, oh, my little daddy," with so much affection]

bolillos [White people]

que [that]

Ahí en la placita. [Over there in the little plaza.]

¿cómo se llamaba? La Raza Unida [what was it called? The United Race]

Mira, estabas hablando de los Chicanos. ¿Sabes quiénes son los Chicanos? Los Chicanos y las Chicanas son los que se iban para el norte. Esas son las Chicanas porque en ese tiempo tenían huelgas y todo. Chicano power! Chicano power! *¿Te acuerdas? Las Chicanas y los Chicanos eran los que se iban para el norte. Porque hablé con una* girlfriend *que ella también se iba para el norte, y dijo "Ay, yo soy Chicana, porque toda la gente que se iba para el norte semos Chicanos."* [Listen, you were talking about the Chicanos. Do you know who the Chicanos are? The Chicanos and the Chicanas are the ones who went north. Those are the Chicanos because in that time they had strikes and everything. Chicano power! Chicano power! Do you remember? The Chicanas and the Chicanos were the ones who went north. Because I talked with a girlfriend who also went north, and she said "Ah, I'm Chicana because all of the people who went north are Chicanos."]

semos/somos [we are]

puro chicano [pure Chicano]

soy hispano o latino [I am Hispanic or Latin]

soy tejano [I am Texan]

soy mexicano americano [I am Mexican American]

soy chicano [I am Chicano]

mexicano [Mexican]

mexicano/mexicana [Mexican]

mexicano americano/mexicana americana [Mexican American]

tejano/tejana [Texan]

costumbre [custom]

nomás [only]

No, nomás, este, digo yo Mexican. [No, I just, uh, say Mexican.]

no sabía que era [I didn't know what it was]

Que era de México y se hizo American, *¿qué no?* [Someone who was from Mexico and she became an American, isn't that right?]

Cuando estoy en una office [when I'm in an office]

una application, *pongo* [an application, I put]

Me preguntan, "¿Pos eres mexicano?" Les digo que soy Chicano. [They ask me, "So, are you Mexican?" I tell them that I'm Chicano.]

No, hombre [No, man]

güerito [light skinned]

¿cómo se dicen esas? [what do you call those?]

que [that]
me dicen. Cuando estaba en Chicago, *también todo el tiempo me dicían* . . . [they tell me. When I was in Chicago, they would always tell me . . .]

Notes

1. The names I am using are not pseudonyms; they are my siblings' actual names and nicknames. As will become clear over the course of this chapter, many of our names were anglicized, or in the case of Facundo, Jr. (Chico) and Esmeralda (Esmer), occasionally simplified. Over the years, some of us have exhibited a greater preference for the English version of our names (Gracie/Graciela; Peggy/Pilar; Irene/E-ré-ne; and Joe/José Luis), while some of us have demonstrated a preference for the Spanish version (Bertha, with a silent "h" in Spanish; Juan; Isabel).
2. I interviewed my siblings in 2004 as part of a project on the rhetoric of self-representation that emerged out of my plans at the time to undertake an ethnographic study to unpack "the explanatory power of the concept of transcultural repositioning by moving beyond an analysis of my siblings' literacy practices to a more complicated analysis of how they have used their rhetorical skills to navigate the range of trans-cultural circumstances they have faced" (Guerra, 2007, pp. 159–160). The interview questions were designed to elicit stories and information about the terminology my siblings used to describe themselves ethnically, as well as examples of the languages and/or dialects they used in telling their stories or reporting that information to me. Three of the interviews (Chico, Esmer and Joe) were conducted over the phone; the rest were conducted face-to-face during several visits back home. All of the interviews lasted from 30 minutes to an hour.
3. In this chapter, I use code-switching in the more traditional linguistic sense (instead of the more modern term code-meshing) to indicate intra- and inter-sentential shifts between Spanish and English.
4. Much of the theoretical work on identity understandably focuses on the role that ideology plays in its formation. Because I agree with Caraballo (2011) that discussions of identity are problematic when they construct the subject as "totally discursively produced by ideologies and/or cultural and social norms, in which identity might be defined as the 'meeting point,' or 'the point of *suture*' between discourses that call subjects into positions and the subjects' articulation or performance of these positions (Hall, 1996, p. 5)," I invoke the concept of *identities-in-practice* to acknowledge that the subject "also acts upon these discursive positions in generative ways" (Caraballo, 2011, p. 165) informed by their embodied interaction with material reality in what Caraballo and others describe as figured worlds. Holland, Lachicotte, Skinner and Cain (1998) define a figured world as a "realm of interpretation" in which particular identities or positions "are recognized, significance is assigned to certain acts, and particular outcomes are valued over others" (p. 52).
5. Because my mother raised her grandson—José Luis (Joe)—from birth, I have included him in this number even though he is not one of my mother's biological children. I do so because most of my siblings and I have always thought of Joe as more of a brother than a nephew.
6. Curious to learn more about my ancestry, I decided to submit a DNA sample to Ancestry.com three years ago to see what I would learn. According to their analysis, I am 41% Iberian, 28% Native American and 6% Italian/Greek. The rest is a mixture of Middle Eastern, African, West Asian and Western European in declining order. Because some of my siblings and I were curious to know our parents' heritage, we decided to submit a DNA sample for my mother and my stepfather as well. In percentages very similar to mine, my mother is 49% Iberian, 23% Native American and

10% Italian and Greek with a smattering of Middle Eastern and African. My stepfather, whose bloodline runs through the six youngest siblings in our family, is 98% Native American with a very slight but equal smattering of Polynesian and East Asian. Although these DNA results are problematic and questionable, at the very least, they provide some insight into the *mestizaje* or miscegenation reflected in the broad range of physical differences among members of my family that I describe and discuss in this chapter.

7. Of the six oldest children in the family, I was the only one who graduated from high school. Gracie dropped out in the eleventh grade and got married; the other four (Bertha, Peggy, Isabel and Chico) all dropped out in the ninth grade. (Gracie, Bertha and Chico later earned their General Equivalency Diploma, and Bertha also eventually earned a bachelor's degree in English.) This is probably also one of the reasons why most, if not all, of them are Spanish dominant bilinguals.

8. Although it was not as apparent in the interviews, both Gracie and Irene also code-switch extensively in their everyday lives because they are profoundly immersed in the linguistic and cultural rhythms of life in south Texas where code-switching is an ever-present border phenomenon (see Anzaldúa, 1987). No doubt, my mother—who as I noted speaks some English and code-switches on occasion—is a critical influence in this respect because all my siblings still living in Harlingen (Gracie, Peggy, Isabel and Irene) interact with her on a regular basis.

9. Right before Gracie—the oldest child in the family—was born, my mother left Mercedes, Texas where she was living with her sister and returned to her family's village in Mexico to give birth and spend the first 40 days of Gracie's life with her parents as was customary at the time.

References

Anzaldúa, G. (1987). *Borderlands/La frontera: The new mestiza.* San Francisco, CA: Aunt Lute Books.

Braidotti, R. (1994). *Nomadic subjects.* New York, NY: Cambridge University Press.

Bucholtz, M. & Hall, K. (2004). Theorizing identity in language and sexuality research. *Language in Society,* 33(4), 469–515.

Bucholtz, M. & Hall, K. (2005). Identity and interaction: A sociocultural linguistic approach. *Discourse Studies,* 7(4–5), 585–614.

Caraballo, L. (2011). Theorizing identities in a "just(ly)" contested terrain: Practice theories of identity amid critical-poststructural debates on curriculum and achievement. *Journal of Curriculum and Pedagogy,* 8(2), 155–177.

Caraballo, L. (2012). Identities-in-practice in a figured world of achievement: Toward curriculum and pedagogies of hope. *Journal of Curriculum Theorizing,* 28(2), 43–59.

Guerra, J.C. (2004). Emerging representations, situated literacies, and the practice of transcultural repositioning. In M. Hall Kells, V. Balester & V. Villanueva (Eds.), *Latina/o discourses: On language, identity, and literacy education* (pp. 7–23). Portsmouth, NH: Boynton/Cook.

Guerra, J.C. (2007). Out of the valley: Transcultural repositioning as a rhetorical practice in ethnographic research and other aspects of everyday life. In C. Lewis, P. Enciso & E.B. Moje (Eds.), *Reframing sociocultural research on literacy: Identity, agency, and power* (pp. 137–162). Mahwah, NJ: Erlbaum.

Hall, S. (1996). Introduction: Who needs "identity"? In S. Hall & P. du Gay (Eds.), *Questions of cultural identity* (pp. 1–16). Thousand Oaks, CA: Sage.

Holland, D., Lachicotte, W., Skinner, D. & Cain, C. (1998). *Identity and agency in cultural worlds.* Cambridge, MA: Harvard University Press.

Kells, M. H. (2002). Linguistic contact zones in the college writing classroom: An examination of ethnolinguistic identity and language attitudes. *Written Communication*, 19(1), 5–43.

Kerschbaum, S. (2014). *Toward a new rhetoric of difference.* Urbana, IL: NCTE.

LeCourt, D. (2004). *Identity matters: Schooling the student body in academic discourse.* Albany, NY: State University of New York Press.

Norton, B. (2013). *Identity and language learning: Extending the conversation, 2nd ed.* New York, NY: Multilingual Matters.

Peñalosa, F. (1980). *Chicano sociolinguistics, a brief introduction.* Rowley, MA: Newbury House.

Sánchez, R. (1983). *Chicano discourse: Socio-historic perspectives.* Rowley, MA: Newberry House Publishers.

van Dijk, T. A. (1995). Discourse semantics and ideology. *Discourse & Society*, 6(2), 243–289.

Young, V. A. (2004). Your average nigga. *College Composition and Communication*, 55(4), 693–715.

5

CULTIVATING CITIZENS
IN THE MAKING

I sometimes wonder how my life would have played out in terms of my commitment to and engagement in social justice issues associated with the communities of belonging I have allied myself with over the years if I had stayed in south Texas instead of moving to Chicago to live with my sister in the summer of 1967 where I attended my last year of high school. Because I worked the second shift (4 pm to midnight) at Admiral Corporation (a television factory that produced cathode ray tubes) in the company of Puerto Rican and African American working-class men twice my age during my senior year at Carl Schurz High School, I had little time to consider much less become involved in political activity of any kind. Although demonstrations at the Democratic convention raged downtown during the summer of 1968 right after I graduated from high school, I remember paying little attention to the ruckus beyond reading about it in the newspapers or seeing it on the evening news. All that changed when at the end of that summer I enrolled at the University of Illinois at Chicago Circle (UICC) and immediately became involved in the growing anti-war movement on campus. For the first time in my life, I began to ponder what it meant to be an active citizen, to worry less about myself and more about others, and to imagine ways in which what I was learning in the classroom could be put to productive use in historically underserved communities of color beyond the academy.

After I graduated with a B.A. in English and got a job as a basic writing teacher in UICC's educational opportunity program,[1] I suddenly found myself firmly committed to *la lucha* as my colleagues in the program and I fought to expand the educational opportunities many of us working in the program were providing to an ever increasing number of African American and Latino/Latina students graduating from public schools in Chicago's inner city neighborhoods and working-class suburbs. Among the students who enrolled in my classes, I came to know a cadre of young Puerto Rican men and women who were profoundly dedicated to their homeland's independence. In and out of the classroom, I found myself immersed in conversations with them about their efforts to educate others through dialog and in an array of leaflets, reports and other written documents they shared with me about the United States' colonization of Puerto Rico. Eddie Cortés, who enrolled in my first-year introductory and research writing classes,[2] made it his goal to talk with me and share information about the struggle for Puerto Rican independence every chance he got. Although I did not know it at the time, Eddie was a member of *Fuerzas Armadas de Liberación Nacional*, an underground military arm of the struggle for Puerto Rican independence. Like everyone else, I only learned about his affiliation with the group after he and several other members were arrested in April 1980 in Evanston, a suburb north of Chicago, and charged with seditious conspiracy against the United States. Sentenced to 35 years in prison, he and several of his compatriots were released in 1999 after President Bill Clinton granted them amnesty.

In addition to my marginal participation in the political activities of Puerto Rican *independentistas*, I became involved at the local level in efforts to improve the education of Latino children in Chicago's public schools and at the national level with Rodolfo "Corky" Gonzáles, the Director of the Crusade for Justice in Denver, Colorado. The author of the epic poem, *I Am Joaquín/Yo Soy Joaquín* (1972), Corky was widely regarded as one of the founders of the Chicano move-ment. A number of us involved in campus and community activism established a relationship with Corky and traveled back and forth between Chicago and Den-ver to participate in and support one another's efforts in community organizing. Most of our work, however, was done locally. Because I wanted to participate in a collective effort to gain community control of a public high school about to be built that would serve students in Pilsen and Little Village, the histori-cally Mexican immigrant communities in the near southwest side of Chicago, I became a member of *El Comité de Educación del Barrio*. *El Comité* consisted of a group of progressive Chicano/Chicana and Latino/Latina activists who met regularly at *Casa Aztlán*, a cultural and social service center located in one of the oldest settlement houses in Chicago. On *el cinco de mayo* in 1976, in solidarity with several other like-minded organizations, *El Comité* led a student walk-out of more than 600 students from middle schools in Pilsen and Little Village to gain greater community control of the decision-making process in the establish-ment of the new high school being built in Pilsen that eventually came to be called *Benito Juarez*.

Although the forms of community involvement I just described fit in nicely with what many of us imagine as possible long-term outcomes of classroom activities related to service learning and civic engagement, Wan's groundbreak-ing work in *Producing Good Citizens* (2014) suggests that using "citizenship" as shorthand to describe these and similar goals related to literacy learning "obscures the distinctions among them because it assumes citizenship is synonymous with the most overt of these civic activities" (p. 21). In the course of reflecting on the experiences that I just described regarding my involvement in community activism, and the work I have been doing in the college classroom for more than 40 years to encourage my students to become more involved in social justice issues, I have become more convinced than ever that it is time for theorists, researchers and educators in composition and literacy studies to move beyond what Wan (2014) calls an "ambient awareness" of citizenship. The concept, Wan tells us, describes "both the frequency and the surface nature of dealings with citizenship in writing instruction," but it simultaneously acknowledges "the cumulative impact of these small bits of civic activity to form a more complicated understanding of citizenship" (p. 22).

What that means for me, in the context of the ideas I have been presenting in this book, is that what we think of as citizenship must be seen as a direct consequence of the different ways in which language and culture are implicated in the production of a particular kind of identity, one that is fluid and multi-faceted but simultaneously acknowledges and responds to the ever-present linguistic, social, cultural and political opportunities and constraints that govern our lives. In keeping with Wan's argument that the "role of the teacher-citizen is not one in which the teacher awards or judges the citizenship of students, but rather a more delicate one in which the teacher recognizes his or her role, both implicit and explicit, in a larger process of citizenship production" (2014, p. 176), I want to describe my own sense of how we can best work toward that goal.

This chapter builds on the ideas I presented in the preceding three chapters in the course of arguing that the different ways in which language (Chapter 2) and culture (Chapter 3) are implicated in the production of identity (Chapter 4) influence the form that citizenship is likely to take. It begins with a discussion of the historical evolution of citizenship as the acquisition of civil, political and social rights that Marshall (1950) argues were gained by members of nation states in their centuries-long struggle to gain agency and authority over their personal and public lives. The chapter next disrupts and extends Marshall's liberal conception of citizenship by suggesting that the introduction of cultural rights by scholars in recent years overcomes the limitations of his analysis by adding a perspective that acknowledges the role of difference in ways that Marshall's historical model elided. In introducing the notion of cultural citizenship into the mix, I argue that the translingual and transcultural forces that produce the kinds of emergent identities students perform in college classrooms and other communities of belonging could potentially contribute to the formation of dispositions that prepare the ground for a form of citizenship that is not just preconceived as a legal right or an achieved status (Wan, 2014, p. 26), but beyond that as an emergent process best described by the phrase *citizens in the making*.

Because I am persuaded by Wan's argument that we need to "create spaces where our citizen-making through the teaching of literacy is a more deliberate activity, one that enlivens the concept of citizenship by connecting classroom practices to other instances of citizenship production that happen outside of the classroom" (2014, p. 178), I then frame Dryzek's (2000) discussion of discursive democracy as a rhetorical and discursive space that citizens in the making must necessarily navigate and negotiate as they attempt to locate themselves in the context of what he calls the "contestation of discourses," a process that involves the deliberation of difference in a wide range of linguistic, civic, social, cultural and political arenas. I conclude by describing the concept of citizens in the making as the pedagogical product of an ever evolving relationship that members of particular communities of belonging have with one another as they come together to address individual and collective goals. In so doing, I reinforce Wan's contention that the practice of cultivating citizens in the making requires "a shift in scale: rather than only trying to amplify those citizenship habits that seem most obvious, we should also consider the multiple ways that habits of citizenship are encouraged through literacy learning" (2014, p. 33).

Evolving Conceptions of Citizenship

Anyone who has reviewed the literature in citizenship studies cannot help but conclude that the concept of citizenship is highly contested. Scholars have been compelled to formulate a rich array of suggestive terms for their theoretical formulations: republican citizenship, liberal citizenship, multicultural citizenship, situated citizenship, differentiated citizenship, cosmopolitan citizenship, and so on. Not surprisingly, each of these reflects a particular strain of thought, a companion ideology about how best members of a deliberative or discursive democracy can participate generically or substantively—depending on the particular view of citizenship being discussed—to bring about meaningful change in their lives and the lives of others. In his useful but problematic argument, Marshall (1950) delineates a historical description of how members of western societies (based on his case study of citizenship and class in England) were granted rights through the grace of enlightened others, or as was more often true according to his critics, through the indefatigable response, always radical and revolutionary, of commoners to those in power.

In Marshall's view, the first period in the historical evolution of citizenship occurred between the seventeenth and the mid-nineteenth centuries as new citizens acquired an array of *civil rights* that permitted them to "engage in a range of social and economic activities, from the freedoms to own property and exchange goods, services, and labor required by a functioning market, to the freedom of religion and the right to express dissent" (Bellamy, 2008, p. 47). The second period from the end of the eighteenth century to the start of the twentieth ended with the gaining of *political rights*, that is, the right "to vote and stand for election, first by all property owners, then all adult males, and finally women as well" (pp. 47–48). In citizenship's third iteration, which Marshall (1950) suggests took place from the end of the nineteenth to the mid-twentieth century, *social rights* emerged as members of western cultures won the right to economic welfare and security in the form of "social insurance against unemployment or debilitating illness," as well as rights to education, health care and pensions (Bellamy, 2008, p. 49). Despite their many problematic qualities, there is general agreement that the various phases in Marshall's conception of citizenship reflect the hard won rights of citizens vis-à-vis an all-powerful state.

Increasingly, however, a growing number of scholars in citizenship studies have critiqued what they consider Marshall's limited conception of citizenship. Isin and Wood (1999), for example, identify three critical shortcomings in Marshall's analysis that at least in part reflect the era in which he was writing. Although it is true that citizenship at the time tempered class conflict by persuading a broader number of people that they were more fully empowered than their economic circumstances dictated, in Isin and Wood's view, Marshall downplays the role that class struggle played in the achievement of the rights that he outlined. In their view, citizenship restructured class as much as class conditioned citizenship (1999, p. 10). Second, they challenge Marshall's narrative of progress as too simplistic and linear, arguing instead that citizenship emerged in a much more recursive and circuitous fashion. Third, and most important because of the position I am taking here, they criticize Marshall for assuming that class was the only pattern of inequality worth examining. After all, Isin and Wood remind us, gender, race and ethnic inequalities—which Marshall did not mention at all—have played as important a role in the evolution of citizenship as class has and therefore deserve our critical attention.

In the context of Isin and Wood's analysis, Marshall's conception of citizenship has been most forcefully challenged and complicated by proponents of what Rosaldo (1994) first referred to in the late 1980s as cultural citizenship in the course of examining "Latino civic participation in the voicing, claiming, and negotiating of cultural space" (cited in Del Castillo, n.d., n.p.). In Rosaldo's view, cultural citizenship embodies "the right to be different (in terms of race, ethnicity, or native language) with respect to the norms of the dominant national community, without compromising one's right to belong, in the sense of participating in the nation-state's democratic processes" (1994, p. 57). While there are various strands of cultural citizenship, each emphasizing the particular ideological grounding of its promoters, proponents as a whole see it as "a critique of the liberal concept of the citizen as the bearer of abstract rights" reflected in "the neoliberal idea of the individual as a consumer and older liberal notion of citizenship as a formal status" (Delanty, 2003, p. 1). In line with this logic, Pakulski (1997) has noted that *cultural rights*—which more often than not come in the form of negotiated claims rather than institutionalized legal entitlements— "include rights to unhindered and dignified representation, as well as to the maintenance and propagation of distinct cultural identities and lifestyles." In his view, however, claims for cultural citizenship are not limited to a tolerance for diverse identities; also included at an increasing pace are claims "to dignifying representation, normative accommodation, and active cultivation of these identities and their symbolic correlates" (p. 77). It is for this reason that Vega and van Hensbroek (2010) have described cultural citizenship as "a tool for addressing issues of cultural and social dominance rather than lack of rights" (p. 249).

While I align myself with this particular critique of Marshall's delineation of citizenship and appreciate the extent to which it moves us beyond a constricted view of citizenship as an achieved status or a set of rights granted to individuals by the state (Wan, 2014) and toward a view of citizenship as a negotiated relationship between the state and individuals, as well the social or cultural groups to which they belong, I am concerned by what I see as an absence of the role that language plays in and the reification of the notion of culture that informs this particular manifestation of citizenship. Although reference is often made to the cultivation of a multiplicity of identities in discussions of cultural citizenship, these are often represented as distinct and unique to particular groups rather than the consequence of what Ortiz (1947) first described as transculturation and other scholars have more recently described as translanguaging (Canagarajah, 2011; García, 2009; García & Wei, 2014) or translingualism (Canagarajah, 2013; Horner, NeCamp & Donahue, 2011; Horner, Lu, Royster & Trimbur, 2011; Lu & Horner, 2013). Part of this correlation is an outgrowth of the concept's formulation by Rosaldo (1994) to represent characteristics closely identified with Latinos as a cultural or ethnic group. I certainly do not mean to suggest that one's linguistic or cultural identity with a particular group or the legal rights that have been accumulated over the years are no longer important. Because scholarly work has successfully challenged the idea that individuals possess single identities closely correlated with a particular set of cultural characteristics, I propose a reconceptualization of cultural citizenship as an orientation that acknowledges this important awareness: Each of us not only possesses a multiplicity of linguistically and culturally-accented identities; we also invoke hybrid, or what I prefer to call translingual/transcultural, identities[3] as we move across the varied communities of belonging that we occupy at any given moment and that are themselves continuously changing.

As productive as the concept of cultural citizenship has been in serving our theoretical, curricular and pedagogical needs, I want to argue that a notion of translingual/transcultural citizenship—grounded in what I have described in the past as the critical practice of transcultural repositioning (Guerra, 2000, 2004a, 2004b, 2007)—represents a more dynamic conception of what I refer to here as citizens in the making, which not only acknowledges but makes productive use of the flux and fluidity of language, culture and identity in everyday life. As I have also argued in the past, disenfranchised students, more than mainstream ones, often develop and enact this particular set of dispositions, not as a consequence of formal instruction in schools, but out of a specific and felt everyday need to navigate and negotiate the "diasporic movements and transnational circuits of culture" (Gutiérrez-Jones, 2004, p. 1) at the core of their postmodern experience as border crossers who, when they are also residents of the borderlands, inhabit an even more complicated and shifting identity as *transfronterizos* (i.e., frontier or borderland dwellers)[4] (de la Piedra & Guerra, 2012, p. 627). The concept of translingual/transcultural citizenship—as reflected in the less onerous notion of citizens in the making that I will use for the most part from here on out—also bears greater explanatory power than either cultural or global citizenship because it offers a critique of traditional conceptions of language and culture, reflects the local and the global simultaneously, and provides a frame of reference for understanding citizenship as an on-going process of development that complicates notions of citizenship as simply a legal right or an achieved status.

The first part of this conceptual notion (translingual) urges us to see "difference *as* the norm, to be found not only in utterances that dominant ideology has marked as different but also in utterances that dominant definitions of language, language relations, and language users would identify as 'standard'" (Lu & Horner, 2013, p. 585, emphasis in original). In this context, citizenship is not constrained by a particular set of language practices that exclusively reflect assimilation into a dominant group in our society; instead, it highlights the capacity of citizens in the making to use every language or dialect at their disposal to achieve their individual and collective ends. The second part (transcultural) reminds us that culture is "a relational phenomenon constituted by acts of appropriation, not an entity that merely participates in appropriation" (Rogers, 2006, p. 474). Unlike the range of other acts of appropriation available to us that posit a "distinctive, singular, clearly bounded, sovereign culture . . . easily conflated with the nation state," transcultural appropriation involves "cultural elements created from and/or by multiple cultures, such that identification of a single originating culture is problematic" (p. 477).[5] In keeping with Wan's (2011) critique of citizenship as an achieved status, we need to keep in mind that "the relationships among citizens '*is* [what constitutes] citizenship'" (pp. 45–46, emphasis in original). As Wan (2014) is careful to remind us, citizenship is not "charity to be doled out by sponsors, but rather a collective practice, one that [not only] relies on the relationships among citizens" (p. 177), but simultaneously requires the presence of a cache of rhetorical and discursive tools that citizens can use to navigate and negotiate the ever-changing linguistic, social, cultural and political frontiers they share with others at any given moment.

Discursive Democracy as Crucible

The literature I have just described on the evolution of citizenship contributes immensely to our understanding of how we can best go about creating conditions in the college classroom and other communities of belonging that will contribute to the transformation of our students into citizens in the making. At the heart of this approach is a commitment to developing in students an attitude, an orientation or a set of dispositions that they can use tactically and strategically to navigate and negotiate the range of social spaces they are likely to inhabit in their college classrooms and other communities of belonging beyond the academy. If reading, writing and rhetoric are among the most powerful tools we have to make a difference in our own lives and the lives of others, it behooves us to learn how to deploy them individually and collectively to bring about the kind of change that honors our commitment to equity, inclusion and social justice. But this we cannot do unless we know how to engage one another deliberatively in personal and public spheres,[6] unless we learn how to declare our positions, listen to the positions of others, then negotiate our differences in ways that acknowledge our collective respect for the process, if not our mutual respect for one another. This is clearly not an easy task in a world where so many of us hold diametrically opposing views and seem unwilling to give an inch, especially to those we perceive as our enemies. So, how can we go about conceiving of these personal and public spheres as generative contexts where our students can acquire and utilize the linguistic, cultural and semiotic resources they need to make a difference? How can we best conceptualize a notion of democracy that is both local and global enough to serve as a crucible for the cultivation of citizens in the making?

According to Dryzek (2000), a momentous shift occurred in the 1990s that signaled a willingness among theorists, researchers and educators to imagine a frame of reference that could potentially generate the kinds of social spaces where differences could be worked out. A decade and a half after its inception, the term *deliberative democracy*—coined by Bessette (1980) and given impetus by various other theorists (Cohen, 1989; Manin, 1987)—was thrust into the mainstream when Rawls (1993) and Habermas (1996) "lent their prestige to the deliberative turn by publishing major works in which they identified themselves as deliberative democrats" (Dryzek, 2000, p. 2). Although the terms *deliberative democracy* and *discursive democracy* are used interchangeably, Dryzek prefers the latter term for several reasons. Deliberation can be construed as "a personal decision process" rather than "a collective social process"; it has "connotations of calm, reasoned argument" and fails to include the more expansive kind of communication, including unruly and contentious communication from the margins, that a discursive process connotes; and the term discourse draws attention to the Foucauldian and Habermassian traditions of political theory that Dryzek believes "are central when it comes to making sense of deliberation" (p. vi). Although I generally agree with Dryzek's critique of deliberation, I want to suggest that it can and should be construed as a personal and collective social process. To limit deliberative acts to the public sphere alone is to deny their power in our everyday lives.

For our purposes here, it is important to note that in *Deliberative Democracy and Beyond: Liberals, Critics, Contestations*, Dryzek (2000) outlines three theories of democracy then contrasts them with one another. Besides his own theory of discursive democracy, which I will discuss in a moment, Dryzek describes two competing accounts of democratic theory that he contends lack the rigor and comprehensiveness of his own position: minimal democracy (or social choice theory) and difference democracy. Because social choice theory is not relevant to the current discussion, let me describe it quickly and simply. Where individuals participating in the process of discursive democracy "are amenable to changing their minds and their preferences as a result of the reflection induced by deliberation," individuals who favor social choice theory pursue goals and interests strategically and compete for advantage (p. 31). In other words, "an actor's preferences, utility function, or goals are not changed in the course of [the] social and political interaction" (p. 32) that takes place when social choice theory is enacted.

In Dryzek's view, difference democrats—and I would count myself and almost every scholar I have cited in this book among them—share "a stress on the variety of oppressions and so subject-positions, leading them to oppose ostensibly neutral rationalistic practices that exclude or silence particular kinds of oppressed subjects" (p. 58). Beyond that, not all difference democrats take the same position. Some (Laclau & Mouffe, 1985; McClure, 1992; Mouffe, 1996) contend that "the politics of identity and difference are played out not just in the unconstrained open-ended interaction of a variety of selves, their identities and their others, but rather in a conflict" with the liberal capitalist order (Dryzek, 2000, p. 59). Those in this group who are more poststructuralist in orientation are particularly suspicious of any dominant discourses, including the discourse of democracy itself, because "they believe that discourses are the taken-for-granted assumptions that constitute subjects and so subjugate them to power" (p. 63). Others (Guinier, 1994; Phillips, 1995; Young, 1990) believe that the liberal capitalist order "can be reformed from within to better accommodate difference." As Dryzek describes them, proponents of this particular perspective support a "politics of presence" as opposed to a "politics of ideas," one in which "efforts are made to ensure the presence of members of disadvantaged groups in the institutions of liberal democracy" (2000, p. 61).

Although he leaves little doubt that difference democracy and discursive democracy differ in principle on a variety of fronts, Dryzek (2000) leaves the door open for some degree of reconciliation between the two. The question for difference democrats is whether there are enough points of contact between the two perspectives to consider the possibility that discursive democracy potentially offers the better option among the range of political theories of democracy available to us for understanding the ways in which the English Language Arts classroom in K-12 settings, as well as first-year college writing and writing across the curriculum programs, can provide an institutional framework for enacting the critical practice of transcultural repositioning and for cultivating citizens in the making. I would argue that they do. As Dryzek notes, "[s]upport for difference does not have to entail hostility to deliberation" (p. 62). Contrary to the claim posed by some difference democrats, discursive democracy is not solely based on the assumption that rational argument is the only valid or viable form of discourse permitted. Such varied discourses as testimony, story-telling, greeting, and rhetoric are readily admissible, if they—as is true of rational argument itself—pass two tests: "First, any communication that involves coercion or the threat of coercion should be excluded. Second, any communication that cannot connect the particular to the general"—i.e., that cannot link "the particular experience of an individual or group with some more general point or principle" (Mendonça, 2008, p. 6)—"should [also] be excluded" (Dryzek, p. 68). Dryzek, concludes—and I agree with him—that "deliberative democracy can cope with issues of difference by conditionally admitting a variety of forms of communication, as well as being attuned to plurality in subject positions and associated ways of life" (pp. 71–72).

Discursive democracy provides a powerful frame of reference for students who are learning how to enact the critical practice of transcultural repositioning *and* translingual/transcultural citizenship in our classrooms, in their everyday lives and in the personal and public spheres where they inevitably engage an assortment of others with opposing perspectives. To demonstrate how this might happen, I want to highlight some of discursive democracy's key features and suggest that the positions of difference democrats and discursive democrats are potentially reconcilable.

A key element at the heart of Dryzek's formulation is a conception of discourse that I believe difference democrats can readily support:

> A discourse is a shared means of making sense of the world embedded in language. Any discourse will always be grounded in assumptions, judgments, contentions, dispositions, and capabilities. These shared terms of reference enable those who subscribe to a particular discourse to perceive and compile bits of sensory information into coherent stories or accounts that can be communicated in intersubjectively meaningful ways. Thus a discourse will generally revolve around a central storyline, containing opinions about both facts and values.
>
> *2000, p. 18*

In Mendonça's view, discourses are not construed by Dryzek as ideas "floating in some kind of semantic sphere." Discourses actually affect how people behave and manifest themselves "through individuals' actions and words." As Mendonça describes them, they are "frames that organize the world [by] providing ways to interpret reality and act upon it" (2008, p. 5). Discourses are also simultaneously enabling and constraining. Although they restrict a subject's options by providing certain boundaries that make interpretations possible (Mendonça, p. 5), discourses also make it feasible for individuals "to compile the bits of information they receive into coherent accounts organized around storylines that can be shared" (Dryzek, 2000, p. 1).

A second critical element that distinguishes Dryzek's conception of discursive democracy from all other forms of deliberative democracy is what he refers to as the "contestation of discourses." Dryzek contends that "[d]eliberation across difference is best conceptualized in terms of the contestation of discourses rather than the (post-modern) play of identity and difference" (p. 5). According to Dryzek,

> [O]ne cannot abolish prejudice, racism, sectarianism, and rational egoism by forbidding their proponents from public speaking. A model of deliberative democracy that stresses the contestation of discourses in the public sphere allows for challenge of sectarian positions, as it allows for challenge of all kinds of oppressive discourses. Indeed, if there were no such oppressive discourses to challenge, a vital democratic life in the public sphere would be hard to imagine. . . . Rather than attach preconditions for entry into deliberation, we should rely as far as possible on mechanisms endogenous to deliberation itself to change views and beliefs in a benign direction.
>
> *pp. 168–169*

To highlight this notion's relevance to the college classroom, I will describe in the next section how the contestation of discourses has been made relevant in the context of recent scholarship in composition and literacy studies that continues to influence our current pedagogical practices.

The final key element of Dryzek's formulation, and the one I find most problematic, is a concept of civil society, or the public sphere, that has much in common with the more Habermassian public sphere proposed by various difference democrats that I have cited thus far. Dryzek's formulation of the public sphere, however, differs in ways that highlight what he considers a more critical take on it. For one thing, Dryzek's public sphere is not construed as a specific physical space or place. In the view of discursive democrats, "deliberation cannot be thought of as situated in specific forums. If understood as an amplified process, deliberation happens in several intersecting public spheres, which make the clash of discourses possible. The connections among these spheres create constellations of discourse that form the public sphere" (Mendonça, 2008, p. 6). I would add that we need to conceive of the elements in the constellations of discourse Mendonça describes as also including the less formal and less public rhetorical and discursive actions—what Wan (2014) describes as habits of citizenship—that we engage in over the course of our everyday lives and inevitably inform the positions we take in the public sphere. If proponents of discursive democracy fail to include these smaller acts that occur in more personal contexts but still manage to influence and inform deliberations that occur in more public ones, the contestation of discourses becomes a form of deliberation problematically disconnected from our everyday lives. If that happens, we invariably end up going where Wan (2014) argues we simply cannot go: Citizenship becomes "a kind of shorthand with an unspoken and assumed meaning that conceals other ways of being a citizen" (p. 22).

Pedagogy and Citizenship

In the more than forty years I have been teaching first-year writing and related courses in various university settings, I have witnessed up close many of the most salient changes that have taken place in how we conceptualize our notions of the teaching and learning of reading, writing and rhetoric. Because a well-grounded understanding of what it means to engage our students in sophisticated conversations about writing in particular was only beginning to emerge at the time, early in my career I believed that it was possible for us to develop a master curriculum and pedagogy that would solve every writing problem we would ever encounter as teachers and prepare our students for engaging the world at large as active citizens. My essay, "Putting Literacy in its Place" (Guerra, 2004b), traces this naïve assumption on my part and simultaneously illustrates my willingness to buy into the idea that, even if a master approach could not be formulated, every development along the way was still a building block in the narrative of progress (Harris, 1997, p. 55) that informed our work. I know better now. Having lived through many of the heated battles that we have had in the field of rhetoric and composition studies in particular—among them, whether or not we should even be teaching first-year writing, and now whether it is possible to cultivate a set of predispositions that will transform students into citizens in the making—has provided me with a dose of vulgar reality, enough certainly to realize that what we endeavor to do as educators is more complex than what any of us could have ever imagined.

Certainly, much of what I have been proposing in this book—especially in curricular and pedagogical terms—is not new. Few scholars have captured the realization that we cannot prepare students for active participation in the personal and public spheres of their lives if we do not take into consideration what they bring with them to the classroom better than Bizzell (2009). In the course of critiquing Fish's (2008) diatribe on why he believes "teachers cannot . . . fashion moral character, or inculcate respect for others, or produce citizens of a certain temper" (p. 26) without proselytizing, Bizzell (2009) demonstrates a willingness to change her own mind that effectively reflects an orientation for the kind of active citizenship she promulgates: "Students as well as colleagues," she affirms, "*can* lead me to see things differently" (p. 186, emphasis added). To illustrate just such a change in her thinking, Bizzell recalls how earlier in her career she argued for the importance of "understanding the diverse discourse communities from which our students were coming, so that we could better tailor our initiation activities, that is, better devise pedagogies that eased their transition into traditional academic ways of thinking and writing" (p. 178). In time, however, it became apparent to her (and the rest of us) that "a process that worked all one way, changing all comers into little clones of the traditional, skeptical, agonistic, gender- and race-neutral academic" was not enough (p. 178). Teachers and students alike, Bizzell reminds us, discovered

> that what was needed was not a one-way acculturation process, but a two-way, indeed a multidirectional, process of collaboration and change whereby new forms of discourse were incorporated into academic ways of doing things, and new types of intellectual work were thereby enabled. The academy was enriched and the students experienced more success as they moved through it.
>
> *p. 178*

At the same time, we learned that it is not enough to disrupt academic ways of doing things by inviting students to bring their alternative forms of discourse into the classroom; we also realized that it was important to have students leave the academy and explore the contestation of these discourses in their other communities of belonging.

In *Community Literacy and the Rhetoric of Public Engagement*, Flower (2008) introduced us to a literacy project designed to train students to do just that, and in so doing, captured the level of commitment that citizens in the making must demonstrate as they move beyond the academy to enact what she calls the rhetoric of engagement. In her view, "once one steps beyond academic analysis and critique, perhaps the most significant aspiration and dilemma is how to relate to others—especially to marginalized or culturally diverse 'Others'—across chasms of difference" (p. 2). This important shift requires students to move beyond the kinds of rhetorical awareness that most college and university writing courses typically encourage students to develop and toward what is often missing in classrooms: the rhetorical action and agency that make a difference in one's life and in the lives of others (pp. 205–206). Long (2008) effectively complements Flower's view by offering a range of pedagogical practices that we can call on as we support students in their efforts to go public, that is, to leave the college or university and enter community sites where they can use alternative and vernacular discourses "to support strategic border crossing, at once linguistic, symbolic, literal, and political" (p. 41). Long's recommendations for enacting these varied discourses are by no means a recital of best practices that she has identified in her work; instead, strong conflicts and contradictions exist among the pedagogical practices she discusses (p. 154). Although elements of all five clusters of pedagogical practices that she describes reflect the classroom work that teachers need to do to cultivate citizens in the making, for our purposes, I believe the inquiry-driven pedagogies are the most directly applicable because they "support discursive spaces where students work with intercultural partners to inquire into and deliberate about pressing social problems, working toward both personal and public change" (p. 175).

As citizens in the making, our students must first develop the critical language and cultural awareness that comes from knowing that discourse operates in very different ways across the varied communities to which they belong. Unfortunately, too many of them—especially those who bring alternative genres and discourses into our classrooms with them—are already alienated from the learning that takes place in our public schools and institutions of higher learning. For them, academic discourse is not just a foreign language; it is a way with words that distances them from the tones and rhythms of the multiple discourse tracks that make up their lives. The horror of it all is that the alienation they feel begins very early in their education. By the third or fourth grade—despite the current shift from No Child Left Behind to Common Core State Standards[7]—too many of our students are already feeling put off by the distinct values reflected in the official discourses reshaping their identities in what many of them perceive as very dangerous and potentially harmful ways. We all know this, which is why so many of us engage in pedagogical tactics and strategies that value our students' linguistic and cultural practices, and make use of them to anticipate the kinds of learning we want them to experience and the kinds of identities they prefer to embrace. We are also more likely to keep students engaged long enough for them to discover the consequences of becoming agents willing and able to participate in deliberative or discursive practices that reflect the sociopolitical values and beliefs we all profess to honor.

Among the many other efforts to reconstitute curricular and pedagogical practices in the field of composition and literacy studies, one that continues to exert a formidable degree of influence is reflected in the important work the New London Group (NLG) developed to explain what they call the "what" and the "how" of a pedagogy designed to address many of the concerns I have raised here. Their description of the "how" is useful in helping us understand the important roles that multimodalities and multiliteracies play in preparing students to engage the richly texted and textured world of "local diversity and global connectedness" (1996, p. 69) that has emerged in the early years of the twenty-first century. The meta-language that the NLG developed—which uses the concepts of available designs, designing and the redesigned to frame its analysis of how teachers can be seen "as designers of learning processes and environments," as individuals engaged in "studying how different curricular, pedagogical, and classroom designs motivate and achieve different sorts of learning" (p. 73; see also Cope & Kalantzis, 2000)—is indispensable to the project at hand. In the context of the NLG's goals, teachers are expected to motivate students to take available designs (available conventions and resources), engage in designing new configurations (transforming available resources and conventions), and in the process create the redesigned (conventions and resources that are simultaneously reproduced and transformed). As the NLG notes, linguistic design in particular is not

> the basis for detached critique or reflection; [r]ather, the Design notion emphasizes the productive and innovative potential of language as a

meaning-making system. This is an action, a generative description of language as a means of representation. . . . [S]uch an orientation to society and text will be an essential requirement of the economies and societies of the present and the future. It will also be essential for the production of particular kinds of democratic and participatory subjectivity.

1996, p. 79

Equally important for our purposes is the meta-language that the NLG developed to describe the "how" of a pedagogy of multiliteracies. In many ways, this language provides the contextual cues missing from earlier pedagogical formulations that focused on what students need to engage in contact zones and to learn the conflicts. In their earlier iterations of conflict- or contestation-based progressive pedagogies, Pratt (1991) and Graff (1993) successfully described the social arenas within which students are expected to work, but constrained their analyses by not explicitly providing the kind of comprehensive view of "mind, society, and learning" (New London Group, 1996, p. 82) that the NLG outlines in great detail. The NLG begins by highlighting the importance of having students engage in situated practice, that is, in having them use their "previous and current experiences, as well as their extra-school communities and discourses, as an integral part of the learning experience" (p. 85). In so doing, the NLG acknowledges the importance of considering "the affective and sociocultural needs and identities of all learners," while affirming the need of learners to feel "secure in taking risks and trusting the guidance of others" (p. 85). The NLG then emphasizes the important role of overt instruction, that is, of "all those active interventions on the part of the teacher and other experts that scaffold learning activities" by focusing the learner on the important features of their experiences and activities within the community of learners. This kind of work is collaborative in orientation and marked by the teacher's use of the kind of meta-language I described in Chapters 2 and 3 that encourages students to "come to conscious awareness of the teacher's representation and interpretation" of the tasks at hand and their relationship to other salient aspects of their learning (p. 86).

In helping students build on the linguistic, cultural and semiotic resources they enact in their other communities of belonging by integrating them into what teachers provide in the classroom, the NLG proposes a third factor that needs to come into play: critical framing. Because students typically integrate the experiences they bring with them and what they learn in the classroom in ways that tend to naturalize both, critical framing must be introduced by the teacher to help learners "denaturalize and make strange again what they have learned and mastered" (p. 86). This is an important step in the process if we ever hope to ensure that our students do not over commit themselves to particular readings of the world. As the NLG notes, learners must "gain the necessary personal and theoretical distance from what they have learned, constructively critique it, account for its cultural location, creatively extend and apply it, and eventually innovate on their own, within old communities and new ones" (p. 87). Finally, it is not enough for students to articulate or critique what they have learned and now understand, that is, it is not enough for them to become aware in a self-reflective manner of their newly acquired knowledge; they must also be able to engage in transformed practice: Teachers need to give students actionable opportunities "to demonstrate how they can design and carry out, in a reflective manner, new practices embedded in their own goals and values." In other words, they must extend what they have learned in the course of integrating their lived experience with their classroom experience and put it "to work in other contexts or cultural sites" (pp. 87–88).

In the final chapter of this book, I present a case study of a new kind of Writing Across the Curriculum program, dubbed Writing Across Communities, that Kells (2007) and her colleagues have been developing at the University of New Mexico (UNM), with some theoretical support from me, over the course of the last 12 years. Kells, her colleagues and I certainly do not want to claim that we have somehow discovered the holy grail, that the mere implementation of our collective ideas is going to revolutionize the work we do as reading, writing and rhetoric teachers. The teaching and learning of these subjects has become much too complex for any single model or approach to encompass in a meaningful way. On the other hand, I am convinced that what the UNM has to offer may provide the kind of institutional opportunity we need to take the next step beyond a traditional Writing Across the Curriculum approach, one that will lead us out into the larger world but will still keep us anchored in the academic one that none of us is prepared to leave behind. Somehow, we all need to find a way to build on the crucial connections between the writing classroom, the university and the broader public sphere. As Harris (1997) argued some years ago, we need

> to imagine a different sort of social space where people have *reason* to come into contact with each other because they have claims and interests that extend beyond the borders of their own safe houses, neighborhoods, disciplines, or communities. . . . We need, that is, to find ways of urging writers not simply to defend the cultures into which they were born but to imagine new public spheres which they'd like to have a hand in making.
>
> *p. 124*

As much as many of us want to extend ourselves into the larger world outside of the academy, we must keep in mind that college classrooms—like personal and public spheres in all communities of belonging—are potential sites for the contestation of discourses. Every interaction we have with our students is an opportunity for us to engage in conversations about their and our place in the world. Some of our colleagues will misconstrue our goals and accuse us of proselytizing, as Fish (2008) has done, or of preaching a particular ideological view with which they disagree, and that's fine. After all, that is what the contestation of discourses is all about. In the end, each of us must do what we can, all of us must work together as best we can, to create conditions in our college classrooms and other communities of belonging that will give our students an opportunity to empower themselves and, at the same time, acknowledge their obligations and responsibilities to the world we are creating together and are committed to changing. Whether or not they take us up on the offer is up to them. But if they do, we will have contributed our share by having done what we could under the prevailing circumstances to address the burgeoning challenges that we all continue to face in the early years of the twenty-first century.

Spanish to English Glossary

la lucha [the struggle]
Fuerzas Armadas de Liberación Nacional [Armed Forces for National Liberation]
independentistas [supporters of independence]
El Comité de Educación del Barrio [The Committee for the Education of the Barrio]
el cinco de mayo [the fifth of May]
El Comité [The Committee]
mestizaje [miscegenation]

Notes

1. In 1968, the University of Illinois at Chicago Circle (renamed the University of Illinois at Chicago in 1982) established the Educational Assistance Program (EAP) as part of a nationwide effort to increase the recruitment and retention of underrepresented minority students. When I first started working at EAP in 1973, the program had an administrative unit of three, 20 academic advisors, three specialists in reading and mathematics, and 12 lecturers in composition who taught basic writing outside of but in affiliation with the English Department. I served as a lecturer in the program until 1988.
2. Because of the influence Eddie and other activist students at UICC had on me, I developed an English 102 research course in the mid-1970s titled "Revolution in America" where the students and I read, discussed and pondered the possibility of a second revolution in the United States. Almost every student enrolled in the course was affiliated in one way or another with the Chicano, Black Nationalist or Puerto Rican independence movements.
3. After considering the progressive replacement of transculturation by other paradigms, among them *mestizaje*, heterogeneity and hybridity, Trigo (2000) "makes a critical distinction in the current use of hybrid and transcultural." In his analysis, he argues that there is not adequate reason "to discard the hermeneutic tools offered by transculturation, a concept that if properly brought up to date . . . would productively harness the undeniably processual nature of current cultural phenomenon" (p. 102).
4. In discussing the difference between borders and frontiers, Trigo (2000) makes this critical observation: "Borders, converted into migrant habitats, become a frontier: more a space than a line, more a highway than a signpost, more a liminality than a limit, the frontier is the inscription of multiple and blurred paths upon a place deterritorialized by contraband and transmigration. Frontiers imply a transitoriness,

a transitivity, a translocality, nurturing perhaps the perspectivism of exile in which Rama perceived a new transcultural productivity" (p. 104).

5. Rogers' (2006) incisive discussion of what he describes as 4 types of cultural appropriation (cultural exchange, cultural dominance, cultural exploitation and transculturation) provides us with a frame of reference for understanding how transculturation functions in comparison to other forms of appropriation (pp. 476–477).

6. Because I concur with Wan's (2014) argument that we should not limit our notions of citizenship to overt acts of civic engagement, but must also include the habits of citizenship "located in everyday activities" (p. 33), I make an effort here to expand the notion of participation in public spheres (the global) to include the habits of citizenship we enact in our personal, everyday lives (the local).

7. Despite a shift currently in progress from No Child Left Behind (NCLB) to Common Core State Standards (CCSS), critiques by educators who are expected to institute "test-based incentive programs" based on "high stakes standardized testing" have not diminished (Hawkins, 2014). Although CCSS claims that it focuses on "developing critical learning skills instead of mastering fragmented bits of knowledge" through "more progressive, student-centered [efforts] with strong elements of collaborative and reflective learning," its implementation is still being challenged by many parents and educators who continue to see little difference between the two aforementioned programs (Au et al., 2013, n.p.).

References

Au, W. et al. (2013). The trouble with the common core. *Rethinking Schools*, 27(4), n.p. Retrieved from www.rethinkingschools.org/archive/27_04/edit274.shtml

Bellamy, R. (2008). *Citizenship: A very short introduction.* Oxford, UK: Oxford University Press.

Bessette, J. (1980). Deliberative democracy: The majoritarian principle in republican government. In R. A. Goldwin & W. A. Shambra (Eds.), *How democratic is the constitution?* (pp. 102–116). Washington, DC: American Enterprise Institute.

Bizzell, P. (2009). Composition studies saves the world. *College English*, 72(2), 174–187.

Canagarajah, S. (2011). Codemeshing in academic writing: Identifying teachable strategies of translanguaging. *Modern Language Journal*, 95(iii), 401–417.

Canagarajah, S. (2013). *Translingual practice: Global Englishes and cosmopolitan relations.* New York, NY: Routledge.

Cohen, J. (1989). Deliberation and democratic legitimacy. In A. Hamlin & P. Pettit (Eds.), *The good polity: Normative analysis of the state* (pp. 17–34). Oxford, UK: Basil Blackwell.

Cope, B. & Kalantzis, M. (Eds.). (2000). *Multiliteracies: Literacy learning and the design of social futures.* New York, NY: Routledge.

Delanty, G. (2003). Citizenship as a learning process: Disciplinary citizenship versus cultural citizenship. Retrieved from www.eurozine.com/articles/2007–06–30-delanty-en.html

de la Piedra, M. T. & Guerra, J. C. (2012). The literacy practices of *Transfronterizos* in a multilingual world. *International Journal of Bilingual Education and Bilingualism*, 15(6), 627–634.

Del Castillo, A. (n.d.). Cultural citizenship. *New Dictionary of the History of Ideas.* Retrieved from www.encyclopedia.com/doc/1G2–3424300116.html

Dryzek, J. S. (2000). *Deliberative democracy and beyond: Liberals, critics, contestations.* New York, NY: Oxford University Press.

Fish, S. (2008). *Save the world on your own time.* New York, NY: Oxford University Press.

Flower, L. (2008). *Community literacy and the rhetoric of public engagement.* Carbondale, IL: Southern Illinois University Press.

García, O. (2009). Education, multilingualism and translanguaging in the 21st century. In T. Skutnabb-Kangas, R. Phillipson, A. K. Mohanty & M. Panda (Eds.), *Multilingual education for social justice: Globalising the local* (pp. 140–158). New York, NY: Multilingual Matters.

García, O. & Wei, L. (2014). *Translanguaging: Language, bilingualism and education.* New York, NY: Palgrave Macmillan.

Gonzáles, R. (1972). *I am Joaquín/Yo soy Joaquín.* New York, NY: Bantam Books.

Graff, G. (1993). *Beyond the culture wars: How teaching the conflicts can revitalize American education.* New York, NY: W. W. Norton.

Guerra, J. C. (2000). *The practice of transcultural repositioning: A possible alternative in education to assimilation and accommodation.* Peabody College, Department of Teaching and Learning, Vanderbilt University.

Guerra, J. C. (2004a). Emerging representations, situated literacies, and the practice of transcultural repositioning. In M. Hall Kells, V. Balester & V. Villanueva (Eds.), *Latina/o discourses: On language, identity, and literacy education* (pp. 7–23). Portsmouth, NH: Boynton/Cook.

Guerra, J. C. (2004b). Putting literacy in its place: Nomadic consciousness and the practice of transcultural repositioning. In C. Gutiérrez-Jones (Ed.), *Rebellious readings: The dynamics of Chicana/o literacy* (pp. 19–37). Center for Chicana/o Studies: UC Santa Barbara.

Guerra, J. C. (2007). Out of the valley: Transcultural repositioning as a rhetorical practice in ethnographic research and other aspects of everyday life. In C. Lewis, P. Enciso & E. B. Moje (Eds.), *Reframing sociocultural research on literacy: Identity, agency, and power* (pp. 137–162). Mahwah, NJ: Erlbaum.

Guinier, L. (1994). *The tyranny of the majority.* New York, NY: Free Press.

Gutiérrez-Jones, C. (2004). Introduction. In C. Gutiérrez-Jones (Ed.), *Rebellious reading: The dynamics of Chicana/o literacy* (pp. 1–15). Santa Barbara, CA: University of California.

Habermas, J. (1996). *Between facts and norms: Contributions to a discourse theory of law and democracy.* Cambridge, MA: MIT Press.

Harris, J. (1997). *A teaching subject.* Upper Saddle River, NJ: Prentice Hall.

Hawkins, P. (2014). A brief history on NCLB and common core. Retrieved from www.huffingtonpost.com/pauline-hawkins/nclb-and-common-core_b_5236016.html

Horner, B., Lu, M.-Z., Royster, J. J. & Trimbur J. (2011). Language difference in writing: Toward a translingual approach. *College English, 73*(3), 303–321.

Horner, B., NeCamp, S. & Donahue, C. (2011). Toward a multilingual composition scholarship: From English only to a translingual norm. *College Composition and Communication, 63*(2), 269–300.

Isin, E. F. & Wood, P. K. (1999). *Citizenship and identity.* Thousand Oaks, CA: Sage.

Kells, M. H. (2007). Writing across communities: Deliberation and the discursive possibilities of WAC. *Reflections, 6*(1), 87–108.

Laclau, E. & Mouffe, C. (1985). *Hegemony and socialist strategy: Towards a radical democratic politics.* London, UK: Verso.

Long, E. (2008). *Community literacy and the rhetoric of local publics.* West Lafayette, IA: Parlor Press.

Lu, M.-Z. & Horner, B. (2013). Translingual literacy, language difference, and matters of agency. *College English, 75*(6), 582–607.

Manin, B. (1987). On legitimacy and political deliberation. *Political Theory,* 15, 338–368.

Marshall, T. H. (1950). *Citizenship and social class and other essays.* Cambridge, UK: Cambridge University Press.

McClure, K. (1992). On the subject of rights: Pluralism, plurality, and political identity. In C. Mouffe (Ed.), *Dimensions of radical democracy* (pp. 108–127). London, UK: Verso.

Mendonça, R. F. (2008). Why discursive democracy? Australian National University. Retrieved from http://deliberativedemocracy.anu.edu.au/documents/MendoncaDiscursiveDemocracy 2008.pdf

Mouffe, C. (1996). Democracy, power, and the "political." In S. Benhabib (Ed.), *Democracy and difference: Contesting the boundaries of the political* (pp. 245–256). Princeton, NJ: Princeton University Press.

New London Group. (1996). A pedagogy of multiliteracies: Designing social futures. *Harvard Educational Review,* 66(1), 60–92.

Ortiz, F. (1947). *Cuban counterpoint: Tobacco and sugar.* (H. de Onis, Trans.). New York, NY: Alfred A. Knopf.

Pakulski, J. (1997). Cultural citizenship. *Citizenship Studies,* 1, 73–86.

Phillips, A. (1995). *The politics of presence.* Oxford, UK: Oxford University Press.

Pratt, M. L. (1991). Arts of the contact zone. *Profession,* 91, 33–40.

Rawls, J. (1993). *Political liberalism.* New York, NY: Columbia University Press.

Rogers, R. (2006). From cultural exchange to transculturation: A review and reconceptualization of cultural appropriation. *Communication Theory,* 16, 474–503.

Rosaldo, R. (1994). Cultural citizenship in San Jose, California. *POLAR: Political and Legal Anthropology Review,* 17(2), 57–64.

Trigo, A. (2000). Shifting paradigms: From transcultural to hybridity: A theoretical critique. In R. de Grandis & Z. Bernd (Eds.), *Unforseeable Americas: Questioning cultural hybridity in the Americas* (pp. 85–111). Amsterdam/Talanta: Rodopi.

Vega, J. & van Hensbroek, P. B. (2010). The agendas of cultural citizenship: A political-theoretical exercise. *Citizenship Studies,* 14(3), 245–257.

Wan, A. (2011). In the name of citizenship: The writing classroom and the promise of citizenship. *College English,* 74(1), 28–49.

Wan, A. (2014). *Producing good citizens.* Pittsburgh, PA: University of Pittsburgh Press.

Young, I. M. (1990). *Justice and the politics of difference.* Princeton, NJ: Princeton University Press.

PART II

Putting Theory into Play

6

VOICES FROM THE FRONT LINE

Over the course of my more than forty years as a lecturer in basic writing at the University of Illinois at Chicago (UIC) and as a tenure-track faculty member at the University of Washington (UW) in Seattle, I have regularly solicited information from my students about the history of their language and literacy experiences—especially as it relates to the range of languages and dialects they bring to the classroom—first, to make them aware of the dispositions (Bourdieu, 1977) and discursive resources (Lu, 2004) they have at their disposal; second, to help me better understand the extent to which what they bring informs what we have been charged to teach them in our writing classes; and finally, to encourage them to add new dispositions and discursive resources to their repertoires of practice that will help them navigate and negotiate the varied social spaces they are likely to inhabit in their everyday lives in and out of school. Not surprisingly, the degree of compatibility between what they bring with them and what we have to offer typically varies on the basis of their race, ethnicity, class, age, gender, ability, sexual orientation, lifestyle and citizenship status, especially as these axes of differentiation (Braidotti, 1994) are marked and rendered visible in the ecological context of the factors I discussed in Chapters 2–4: language, culture and identity. This was particularly true during my early years at UIC when almost every student in each of the three writing classes I taught every quarter was either poor or working class and a person of color.

When I moved to Seattle in 1990 to take a tenure-track job after earning my Ph.D. at UIC, I suddenly found myself standing in front of a very different group of students whose axes of differentiation were marked and rendered visible in very different ways. Most of my UW students were white and from the suburbs or urban middle-class neighborhoods of Seattle; very few came from the inner city. Unlike my UIC students, who had come to my classes with what we used to refer to as limited or remedial literacy skills, the overwhelming majority of my UW students had not only been exposed in their high school English classes to the five-paragraph essay and other conventional genres, but knew how to deploy them. As a consequence, they came to class armed with basic tools they could build on. From the moment I stepped into my first classroom on the UW campus in Seattle, I reasonably concluded that my students were more privileged—especially by their race, ethnicity, place of residence, class membership and upbringing—than the students I had worked with at UIC. As I got to know more of my students as individuals, however, I came to understand that my first reading of them had been distorted by the biases I had brought with me from my previous teaching experiences. About two years after I started teaching at the UW, I began to notice the significant degrees of difference among my students—mainly because these differences were no longer hidden among the overwhelming majority of them under the surface of what I had perceived as their shared whiteness.

In comparing these two very different groups of students that I have worked with over a 40 plus year teaching career (16 at UIC and 25 at the UW), what emerges as most salient for me—even beyond the obviously significant matters of race, ethnicity, class, place of residence, prior language experience and lifestyle—is the degree to which an overwhelming majority of the students in both groups have bought into the rigid ideologies of monolingualism and monoculturalism that inform any college classroom (outside of foreign language classes, of course) in which a significant amount of writing is expected. They have good reason to hold tightly to these ideological beliefs, considering the never-ending propaganda they are exposed to every day of their lives (by us in the professoriate, especially) regarding the relationship between language, culture and identity. As the literature in composition and literacy studies that I have cited in this book to substantiate my position has consistently demonstrated, despite its acknowledgement of how important the linguistic and cultural practices students bring to the academy have been, especially as they continue to inform their identity, too many of the students in our college writing classrooms are dismissing them and privileging the hegemonic power of the rhetorical and discursive practices we have convinced them they come to the university specifically to acquire.

In this chapter, I want to examine the written work and spoken words produced by a group of students enrolled in an advanced writing class[1] that I taught during Winter Quarter 2012 at the UW titled "Language Variation and Language Policy in North America." After I describe the writing activities I assigned and the reasons I assigned them, I examine some of the written work they produced for the class, as well as information I gathered during a series of interviews I conducted with half of them, in the course of exploring the place of language, culture and identity[2] in their lives. Along the way, I highlight the contradiction between what I see as the students' critical awareness of language and culture and their general willingness to argue that they as students should be required to abide by and deploy the more constraining practices reflected in an ideology that informs their collective goal of achieving competency in Standard Written American English. My primary objective in this chapter is to describe and explain what I see in most, but not all, of my students as the dramatic but understandable disjuncture between the varied nature of their and their families' day-to-day lived experiences with language and culture and the restrictive identity they are encouraged to embrace in the typical college writing classroom. In the process, I argue that our goal as their teachers is to help them cultivate a rhetorical and discursive sensibility that equips them with the tools they need to respond to the disjuncture by calling on their prior knowledge in ways that acknowledge shifts in context, purpose and audience.

Engaging Language, Culture and Identity

To provide greater coherence across the ample set of readings on language variation and language policy that I had students read in preparation for our classroom discussions, on the first day of class, I framed the journal articles and book chapters we would be reading during the quarter in the context of Horner, Lu, Royster and Trimbur's (2011) groundbreaking essay titled "Language Difference in Writing: Toward a Translingual Approach." We also reviewed two handouts I passed out on the first day of class. The first one offered a vocabulary of critical terms and a frame of reference for the three approaches to language and cultural difference similar to those listed in Table 1.1 in the first chapter; the second handout provided guidelines for posing discussion questions and a brief description of Therborn's (1980) conception of ideology.[3] Throughout the quarter, I urged students to use these materials to anchor and guide our classroom discussions as we collectively analyzed and interpreted the ideological tendencies reflected in the assigned readings. As I will indicate throughout my discussion of the written work they produced, our discussion of these materials on the first day of class also helped students think about their positions vis-à-vis the standardization of the English language in the writing classroom.

Before I describe the writing prompts I gave my students, I want to briefly describe how they engaged the assigned readings to demonstrate the extent to which I provided them with opportunities to interact with one another on a regular basis. Although there were 34 students in the class, I decided to have them discuss all of the assigned readings in workshop fashion. Based on a questionnaire I used to elicit information about their language use and some family history, I divided the students into six groups of 5 to 6 students so that each group represented as diverse a set of voices and views as possible on the basis of the information I had gathered. After I provided them with oral instructions on how the groups would operate, I reminded them in writing that "the primary goal of each group is not to reach consensus, but to present a multiplicity of well-argued positions that support or counter the essay under discussion." I also told students that each group would be expected to report and lead a discussion for 1/6 of the assigned readings in a round robin fashion over the course of the quarter. Because the amount of reading I had assigned would have proved overwhelming if I had asked everyone in class to read it all, I had the first three of the six groups read half of the readings and the second three groups read the other half. This of course also meant that not everyone (although some chose to do so) would read all of the assigned material and would have to depend on each group's reports and our class discussions to develop a comprehensive understanding of all the assigned readings.

Because there is a tendency for the readings in this kind of class to encourage students to automatically "other" members of the disenfranchised groups they are reading about on the basis of their language and cultural practices, I purposefully had students first write two short self-reflective essays[4] where they explicitly focused on their own language and cultural practices and more implicitly reflected on how these two dimensions contributed to their identity formation. My hope was that this would push them to "other" themselves in the context of how individuals in their other communities of belonging engage one another linguistically and culturally and in so doing gain some insight into what it feels like to be "othered." The first assignment asked them to reflect on the registers, styles, dialects or languages they spoke, their origins and characteristics and whether these were socially favored. It also asked them to consider their attitudes toward the registers, styles, dialects or languages of others. The second assignment—which shifted the focus from their individual experience with language and culture to their experience as members of particular groups—asked them to reflect on how their languages, dialects or styles were influenced by their social network(s) (neighborhood, community, or town; family, peers, or coworkers, etc.), keeping in mind as well the varied influences of their race, ethnicity, social class, place of residence, age, gender or lifestyle.

In contrast to the focus on their individual and collective linguistic histories and experiences in the two self-reflective essays, the midterm and final essays asked them either to continue writing about themselves (using their self-reflective essays as a starting point) or to address language issues that were not only more distant from their individual experiences but more likely to require them to deploy a more academically-oriented form of discourse. Despite my best efforts to encourage them to disrupt the academic register in which they were prone to write these more "formal" essays by inviting them to engage in code-meshing[5] as they understood it after our discussions in class, except in the context of providing examples, students overwhelmingly chose not to include registers, dialects or languages from other facets of their lived experience.[6] As I will argue later, these choices on their part were governed by their rhetorical understanding and interpretation of the implied expectations they assume inform their writing in college classroom settings. Finally, despite my best efforts to persuade them that the language and cultural practices deployed in the various communities to which they belong outside the UW are as legitimate as those used in the academy, almost every one of them (even those who spoke in favor of translingual practices) clung to the belief (understandably so) that the monolingual and monocultural practices instituted in college writing classrooms are more legitimate and should always guide one's writing in an academic context.

For their midterm essay, I gave them an opportunity to reread their two self-reflective essays critically to understand how the theoretical or methodological lenses we use to examine data often shape our interpretations of those data. I also wanted to see if and how they would engage in code-meshing in a context that called for academically-oriented discourse. Here are the two options I provided them:

1. Argue in favor of or against the position Horner et al. take in their opinion piece, and explain why you think your position provides the more reasonable or appropriate take on how best to utilize language difference in writing. If you like, use the material you generated for your two self-reflective essays—in addition to any new information you may want to add about your language and cultural practices—as data for your analysis and interpretation. Think about the ways that you described your various dialects, registers, and styles, as well as the social forces that influenced their development, then, examine them through one or more of the theoretical lenses Horner et al. or I provided.

2. Based on the material we read for this class (including the chapters from Wolfram and Schilling-Estes' *American English*), find ways to highlight the place of language and culture in your own life. In preparation, you may want to think about how you would answer some of the following questions: How do the language and cultural practices you describe in your two self-reflective essays translate into writing in the classroom, if at all? How would *you* like them to translate? In other words, to what degree would *you* like your teachers to honor and encourage your varied language and cultural practices in the classroom? How would you deploy them if your teachers granted you that opportunity?

Of the 24 students who selected the first option, 13 took a stance against Horner et al.'s argument for a translingual approach and 11 supported it, although most in the latter group qualified their stance by describing the translingual approach as too difficult to implement in an actual college writing classroom. The 10 who selected the second option took such varied positions that it was difficult to identify patterns in their responses. Because the topics the students chose for their final papers were generally beyond the scope of the issues I am interested in addressing here, I do not include them in my discussion and analysis.

As I hope this section makes clear, the class provided me with an opportunity first to examine the perspectives of a group of undergraduate and graduate students on a number of the more divisive language and cultural issues of the day among scholars in our field and lay people in the society at large, second to see how language and culture manifest themselves in their lives, and third to extrapolate how their experiences with language and culture influence their identity formation. As will become clear shortly, my analysis in this chapter is designed to complicate theoretical discussions by scholars who argue for particular approaches to language and cultural difference in the writing classroom (Canagarajah, 2006; Horner et al., 2011; Tardy, 2011; Young, 2009; Young & Martínez, 2011) by positing the perspectives of undergraduate and graduate students on these issues. The rest of this chapter delves more deeply and more broadly into how language and culture continue to play an active role in the identity formation of our students and puts the theoretical ideas I presented in the first four chapters of the book into play.

The Influence of Affluence

As much as we belabor the challenges our students encounter in our college classrooms because of the difficulties they have negotiating our expectation that they produce Standard American English (SAE) in their writing, we do well to remind ourselves that many of our students (the percentage no doubt varies from one class to the next) bring with them a well-grounded ability to use the English language in ways that sometimes dazzle those of us who teach writing. As we appreciate how effectively such students are able to write within the assumed constraints of SAE, we are also impressed by how fresh and lively their writing is. In other words, they not only know how to operate within the constraints of standard academic discourse; they also know how to break the rules in such subtle ways that most of us do not even notice it. In ways more powerful than Lu and Horner's discussion of the standardized but stilted writing produced by the student who wrote the "White Shoes" essay (2013, p. 590) popularized by Bartholomae (1986), these students make a mockery of the assumption that writers who follow what we often think of as prescriptive grammatical and syntactical rules are simply mimicking or repeating what has been done before.

What I have just described of course becomes even more apparent when the students in our college classrooms are graduate students who have not only had an opportunity to develop their writing skills above and beyond what many undergraduate students can do, but often demonstrate a profound allegiance to the prescriptive rules of writing in academic discourse because many of them, especially in composition and literacy studies, are also first- and second-language teachers in the making who are more aware than most that producing a particular kind of writing presents a particular set of challenges for all student writers, but especially for second language learners in their classrooms. David Evans and Jessica Larsen (all names used in this chapter are pseudonyms selected by the students), the two graduate students whose self-reflective writing I want to present first, epitomize that perspective in ways that I think will enlighten and instruct us, especially as we delve into the descriptions and explanations they provide about the successes and the challenges each of them has experienced as speakers and writers of English, as well as of other languages later in life. Above all, David and Jessica embody the contradictions that mainstream, monolingual students are more prone to encounter today than ever before as a consequence of the effects of globalization. While we can still assume that learning a standard form of any language is necessary, it is clearly insufficient in the imagined worlds (Appadurai, 1996) that we all now occupy.

In his first self-reflective essay, David immediately invites us to understand how his identity has been shaped by the monolingual and monocultural practices that have defined his linguistic and cultural upbringing in a relatively affluent family and community of belonging: "I was raised in the Seattle area (Issaquah) and I went to high quality public schools (at least, from my perspective) where I was surrounded by other middle-class, relatively affluent, predominantly white English speakers." Because he is aware of his privileged upbringing in a particular household and community of belonging, as well as his education at a select university that is essentially monolingual in its practices, David understands firsthand the cultural predilections reflected in the pragmatics of our linguistic practices and the ways they contribute to our identity:

> My parents' English has marked my understanding of pragmatics (something I believe is so fundamental); I see my sensibilities in their speech and mannerisms. I believe that both being raised in the Northwest and my education in this period (up to age 25), culminating in an undergraduate degree from the UW, further cemented this. . . . The English I used at the UW was an extension of the English I used in high school; I do not believe I was aware that there were other Englishes being spoken and used around me, or being used in the U.S. as a whole.

Interestingly, in our interview, David revises the linear representation of the upbringing he described in his writing: "My growing up was the process of my parents becoming more and more financially secure, as I got older, and so I think when I was younger, I saw a lot more working class and I learned a lot more working-class English. As I reached middle school and high school . . . I think I became a little more isolated" (Interview).[7] David also understandably qualifies the highly standardized representation of his language use in his written work: "[In my self-reflective essays] I painted too homogenous a picture of my language use. I think there's a lot more variety within my own use than what I acknowledged there" (Interview). In so doing, he reminds us all that what we often characterize as strictly monolingual or monocultural is always so much more complicated than it seems at first glance.

As educators, we would all do well to remember that when we teach writing, as difficult as they are to master in a short period of time, grammar and syntax simply provide the infrastructure for our language use. What every student finds equally or often more challenging, especially if they grew up speaking or writing a different language in a different culture, is the parallel challenge that we all face in trying to make them aware of and learn how to use the more subtle tools that make someone capable of doing language, and in the context of this book's subject matter, of passing as a native speaker or writer of SAE if they are going to be successful in the academy (or so, unfortunately, the thinking among too many of us still goes). David's description of the factors that influence his language use is instructive in that regard:

> Much more profoundly than lexis, phonology or grammar, I believe my understanding of English pragmatics marks me as a middle-class European American, and more specifically, as someone from the Seattle area. . . . The lexis may change, the grammar may even change—but this pragmatic awareness, like a beacon, remains fixed.

Significantly, many of our students learn best how pragmatics works in the classroom when they choose (if they are privileged) or are required (if they are marginalized) to use a language other than the one they learned while growing up. In David's case, this opportunity emerged when he moved to Austria, married an Austrian, studied and learned German, then decided to live there for seven years before returning to the states to learn how to teach English as a second language. For the first time in his life, he became aware in Austria of the multiple variations in any given language beyond the standard:

> While I clearly use English much more flexibly and "naturally" (as noted in class, a difficult term), my life in German has profoundly affected my understanding of language and, remarkably, my understanding and use of English. . . . My use of German is much more rudimentary and I admit this causes me a great deal of consternation as a speaker and user of that language. My lexis, phonology and grammar all mark me quite distinctly as a foreigner, a feeling I have grown to hate.

The anxiety David feels is further complicated by how members of his wife's family respond to his efforts to engage them in the same way he perceives them engaging him:

> My in-laws, for example, think that I'm getting really angry at them, and I'm just trying to, like, react at the same level of intensity that I feel I'm receiving from them. And then all of a sudden I'll get this reaction, like, "Why is he so—what's happening with him?" And I don't—I feel like

everyone's been yelling for the last ten minutes in the conversation and I'm just amping up, so, that's the difficult part.

Interview

David's linguistic experience in Austria was further dramatized when he began to realize "that what I spoke and wrote [in English] did not always match the norms other teachers around me espoused." The most obvious distinction for him involved British English, which in his view most of the ESL teachers in Austria (and Europe generally) speak. "The net effect," he reports, "was that my language use began to be proscriptively shaped." Here, David gets at one of the more subtle issues that we sometimes ignore when we question the imposition of rules in standard language training. Equally problematic, as anyone who has taught writing knows, is our tendency to prohibit, denounce or condemn particular forms of language as inappropriate, to engage—as David put it—in proscription. After considering the social, economic and cultural influences on his language use over the course of his upbringing and development as a professional, David—who is now in his mid-thirties—comes to a conclusion that he probably would not have arrived at if he had never left the safety of his family and principal community of belonging:

> Living in Austria, teaching English to other Europeans, teaching to a culture which is older and prouder than my own, I did not perceive how crushing and proscriptive "Edited American English" is. Now, back in Seattle, I see things differently. Our culture, our lives and our campus are intensely stratified by language use. Had I grown up in another part of Seattle, with different parents, I could just as easily be taking the courses I teach. I could still be a "Northwesterner," just not the right one.

Unlike David, Jessica migrated to the Northwest from California when she decided to attend college in the state of Washington, first in Walla Walla, then in Seattle. While she brings a different set of values nurtured in her own family and in a principal community of belonging with partial roots in Australia, her perspective on language and culture and the role they play in identity formation parallels David's in ways that signal a shared but slightly divergent set of experiences. One of the key signatures in both of their lives is the self-identified affluence that has had a dramatic impact on their language development. Here is how she frames her relationship with English:

> Informal Standard English, according to Wolfram and Shilling-Estes (12–13), can be defined as language that is consistently not stigmatized by other American English speakers. This essentially describes my English. I cannot recall having a teacher or other American English speaker label any of my utterances as "bad" English (although I have been mocked by Britons).

In her interview, Jessica expounded further on the complexity of her actual language use, which was clearly influenced by students from other communities of belonging at her school: "There was a large African American community in the area, and so my high school, I would say, was probably more African American than any other ethnic group, and so I was exposed to a lot of African American English" (Interview). Because she grew up in the San Francisco Bay Area, she also noted that she was exposed to "lots of Spanish, lots of Chicano English, I guess. So even though I don't speak Spanish, I always kind of think of it as the language—a language of the area where I grew up" (Interview). Exposure of course does not automatically lead to practice in every case, so it is not surprising that she "would feel uncomfortable using [Spanish, Chicano English or African American English] because I don't feel like I identify with—those aren't communities that I belong to" (Interview).

After a brief discussion of the early influence of her Australian heritage on "my openness to, you know, an interest in other varieties of English and other languages," as well as her growing up "in a community like the Bay area that is actually pretty multilingual" (Interview), unlike David who reflects on his first-language development in some depth, Jessica switches quickly and dramatically in her second self-reflective essay to her own experience studying Mandarin Chinese and teaching English as a second language in China:

> Teaching in China, and studying Mandarin Chinese, also changed my language both in specific contexts and overall. In the fairly isolated campus language community of teachers who all spoke varying amounts of English and Chinese, we spoke a form of English peppered with Chinese phrases and vocabulary that would be quite confusing to those outside of our speech community. For example, we might say, "let's chi some fan" for "let's eat." We would use favorite phrases like "xiao xin" (careful) and "wo e le" (I'm hungry) to the exclusion of their English counterparts.

Here, for the first time in this chapter, we encounter the kind of code-meshing—to use Young's (2004) preferred term—that is currently all the rage in the teaching of writing. Notably, these practices take place in relaxed and informal contexts away from the classroom. Not surprisingly, Jessica's approach to language and culture, as well as to her identity, shifts dramatically and necessarily to more self-conscious dialects and registers (especially as they are informed by pragmatics) when she is in class:

> As a teacher I also speak very specific varieties of English in my classrooms. With lower-level students I speak more slowly, pause often, use fewer contractions, hyper-articulate harder words and repeat myself. With higher-level students I speak more as I would as a student in a classroom or with co-workers, which is to say still quickly but with less in-group vocabulary.

In all classroom settings I ask more questions than I would normally, and I try to pause longer at points where students can interject.

Not surprisingly, Jessica, now in her late twenties, uses language in the classroom strategically to respond to what she perceives as her students' communicative needs. She is probably most attuned to her language practices in classroom settings because as a second-language teacher she feels a greater sense of responsibility for how language operates in these moments than at any other time in her everyday life. Here is how she describes it:

> [My] approach to giving feedback is just one of the ways I conform to the expectations of a classroom community, while also shaping my identity as a teacher for my students. The encouraged practice, which I generally follow, is not to tell students the answer directly, but to lead them towards the answer with questions.

What I find most interesting in Jessica's self-reflective writing is the degree to which she seems compelled to invoke the important role of standards in teaching and learning at the same time that she disrupts this practice depending always on the immediate circumstances. As she put it in our interview, "Identity is something you always kind of co-construct with environment—you can't really separate it from that." Finally, her attention to detail and her ability to rationalize her teaching practices in productive terms reflects the on-going concerns that anyone who teaches college-level writing, but especially colleagues who work exclusively with second language learners, must consider in the process of doing what she describes above: We do what we can to create conditions in the classroom that produce opportunities for students to empower themselves.

What, then, do David and Jessica's perspectives teach those of us who continually struggle with the ideoscapes (Appadurai, 1996) that inform our approach to language and cultural difference in the writing classroom? As I tried to make clear in this section, for my purposes in this chapter, David and Jessica serve as a baseline that identifies the shared but simultaneously divergent perspectives of students whose affluent upbringing has shaped their experiences with language and culture, and in the process, has produced a particular range of identities. There is no surprise, of course, in the realization that students who have been granted the opportunity to exploit the linguistic and cultural capital with which they have been blessed as an accident of their births often make the most of it. Increasingly, as a more diverse range of students come into our college classrooms, many of them often find themselves in a more conflicted position because students also bring a cache of linguistic and cultural capital from their other communities of belonging that is less directly synchronized with what they will need to learn from and with us. In an effort to understand the changes this kind of shift brings about, in the next section I turn to three undergraduate students who, even while they may now share certain aspects of the affluence David and Jessica have experienced, had their lives informed by language and cultural histories that produced identities many of us are still trying to integrate into the work we do in the college writing classroom.

Convention and Innovation

In describing his response to the challenges that he faced in performing German in conversations with members of his wife's family and other individuals in Austria, David lamented how his more rudimentary skills in German caused him a great deal of consternation as a speaker and user of that language: "[My] lexis, phonology and grammar all mark me quite distinctly as a foreigner, a feeling I have grown to hate." To his credit, he also acknowledges how the experience has made him "more aware now of how difficult it is to be a foreign English speaker, or to be perceived as a speaker of a foreign or different English." The three undergraduate, Asian American women[8] whose self-reflective writing I examine in this section share this feeling to different degrees, especially as all of them were first exposed to their immigrant parents' native languages and only later learned English. It is important to note that the exposure to languages and dialects other than Standard American English that each of them experienced plays out in a number of different ways. One key difference that emerges in my analysis of their writing is reflected in the different degrees to which they are weighed down by a sense of consternation and obligation, inherent in the more conventional Standard American English practices that surround them at school, and are yet able to enact an innovative playfulness that mimics the use of code-switching or code-meshing in the languages and dialects that surround them at home and in their other communities of belonging.[9] As a consequence, each of them positions and repositions herself—as the rhetorical situation changes along a continuum with a code-segregating set of practices at one end, a code-switching set in the middle and a code-meshing set at the other end—in ways that highlight her shifting relationship with the full range of languages and dialects at her disposal.

Not surprisingly, many of the students in the class who shared their written work with me located themselves toward the monolingual, conventional, code-segregating end of the continuum that I just described and reported varying degrees of discomfort in the course of learning English and the various languages that their immigrant parents and other members of their communities of belonging practice. At the heart of their ambivalence is the same pressure that any student in a college classroom who is made to feel inadequate as a writer experiences when they assume that the main purpose of the course will be to standardize their use of the English language. Emma Lau, a junior in Linguistics and a tutor at the UW's Writing Center, presents an interesting first case. She was brought up by a father who emigrated from Cambodia and a mother who emigrated from China. Over the course of his life, Emma's father—whose first language was Cambodian—was exposed to a variety of other languages by the time he arrived in the United States because his Vietnamese-born Chinese parents spoke Vietnamese, as well as Mandarin, Cantonese, French and a bit of Japanese. When he first came to the U.S., Emma's father took some ESL courses, so he now "knows enough English to get by, but not more than what he needs" (Interview). Emma's mother also took ESL classes when she first came to the U.S., then later went to a technical college to study accounting where she received more training in English. A further defining characteristic of Emma's language development was the fact that her grandparents on her mother's side started living with the family from the moment she was born, so she was expected to learn Cantonese and began studying it formally at the age of six at a weekend Chinese school.

As many of the scholars I have cited in this book have noticed in recent years, the inclination to engage in code-switching and code-meshing is rampant and inevitable in the homes of immigrants where children are often exposed to the family's native language(s), as well as to the English(es) that begin(s) to seep in as a consequence of the media and the children's enrollment in school. There is a difference, however, between how immigrant children communicate with their parents and their siblings. In the course of reflecting on her language use, for example, Emma invoked Amy Tan's work to describe her own linguistic relationship with her parents:

> In Amy Tan's "Mother Tongue," Tan uses the term "simple" (278) to describe the English she spoke to her mother. I might describe my own English that I speak to my parents in the same way. I don't use as varied a vocabulary as I might in academic settings, but I don't think I need to. When speaking to my parents, I sometimes feel that there is a lot more guesswork involved. For example, when talking to my mom, she might say in Cantonese, "Bring the something to that place." If I'm not paying attention, I will have no idea what she is talking about. However, if I know what's going on, I'd realize that we're cleaning the bathroom and she wants me to bring the laundry basket downstairs to the laundry room.

On the other hand, when she speaks with her siblings, Emma has noticed that the languages at her disposal manifest themselves differently and allow her to engage in a kind of innovative playfulness:

> There's less of a Cantonese or Mandarin influence since [my siblings and I] mostly speak English with each other, but we still use Cantonese terms, especially when referring to food. I've also noticed that I'm more creative with my language use when I speak to my siblings because I have the freedom to make cross-language puns that they'll understand. For example, the word for "rice noodles" in Cantonese sounds like "fun," so I can ask,

"Who wants to have some fun?" I've also noticed that more overlap occurs when I'm talking to my siblings than when I'm talking to anyone else.

As challenging as English may have been for her early on, Emma has mastered it well enough to have served as a peer tutor at the university's Writing Center since her freshman year. Ironically, the challenges that learning informal standard Chinese has produced have on different occasions made her feel inadequate in terms of her sense of identity:

> When I was in Hong Kong, even though the classes were taught in English, the students often spoke Cantonese to one another. And then it was, like, quite obvious, if they talked to me, my Cantonese wasn't, like, native speaker level. And so every time that happened, I was reminded again that I'm not a native Cantonese speaker. I'm an exchange student. And I'm American.
>
> *Interview*

Things were not much different closer to home where she often experienced embarrassment and disappointment, especially when it comes to being judged by relatives outside of her immediate family:

> "You've been studying Chinese for this long," my irritated uncle scolded in Cantonese, "and you still can't speak it?! How can you call yourself Chinese?" I've gotten this response from countless other relatives and family friends—if not in words, then in head-shakes of disappointment. But they're right. My parents and grandparents have spoken Cantonese to me since I was a baby, but while Cantonese may have been literally the "first language" I spoke, it is by no means my mother tongue or the language I speak best.

Fortunately, her mother has occasionally intervened to defend her. "The excuse that my mom gives to those relatives and family friends is always the same," Emma writes, "—that I was born and raised in Federal Way, Washington, where there aren't a whole lot of Chinese speakers. 'It's the environment we live in,' she would go on to say." Here, Emma's mother is of course expressing her awareness of how language use is influenced by the social spaces that we occupy, as well as by their rhetorical demands.

While her mother's efforts may have been partially successful in persuading her relatives, they did little to assuage Emma's guilt:

> As my mother made this justification to my relatives and her friends, I didn't buy it. For one thing, I'm only second generation. I've had plenty of opportunity to learn Chinese, as my grandparents emigrated from China and moved in with us shortly after I was born. . . . Those sentences my

mother spoke in my defense never seemed to tell the whole story. It is not necessarily true that the environment I grew up in didn't allow for Chinese language acquisition. The truth is I didn't take full advantage of my situation. I didn't see what great opportunity I had, and thus missed, to become bilingual.

Weighed down by a sense of obligation, Emma continues to work at studying her Chinese even though she knows that she will never achieve the kind of fluency she would like:

> Finding ways of using the little Chinese I knew was, and still is, both difficult and frustrating. I made little games with my sisters to make it fun. We'd compete in daily conversations with each other to see who could last the longest using only Cantonese or only Mandarin. While we seldom play these games any longer, I still try to use Chinese in my daily speech at home. . . . This can be both mentally exhausting and frustrating. It still takes a conscious effort, but this is a decision I choose to make.

Despite the consternation she often feels and the occasional bumps she experiences along the way, Emma generally trusts her ability to make her way across a range of language situations in her day-to-day life: "In most situations I flow from one position to another pretty smoothly, but, like, there's still some times I feel like I'm very conscious of being Asian American" (Interview).

Tilycrisa "Tily" Yokota, who left Guam at the age of 14—she is now in her early 20s, a junior in Business Administration and a member of the ROTC—more often than not occupies the midrange between Emma and Mina Nokeo, the third student whose writing I will examine in a moment. She does, however, tend to lean more in Mina's direction on the continuum between convention and innovation because she has experience with a similar range of languages and dialects. In addition to her exposure to such languages and dialects as Chamorro, Chaud, Chuukese and Filipino in Guam, Tily has immersed herself in various U.S. dialects, including Ebonics and Hawaiian pidgin, over the course of her youth. In our interview, she recalled how she didn't think she spoke differently when she was in Guam. "I just thought I was speaking English," she said, "I didn't speak Chamorro, that's for sure." Once she moved to Las Vegas, she started speaking differently: "I didn't notice until I'd call back home and my cousins would be like, 'Why do you sound so black?' And I'm like, 'What?' Or, I guess it depends on who I was talking to: 'Why do you sound white?' And I'm like, 'What?'" (Interview). Upon further reflection, Tily realized that her language use was influenced by the fact that "my neighborhood was the ghetto, and then we were zoned for an upper class white school. . . . We had the valley girl, we had the Cholas and the African Americans, and whenever I was around a certain group, I'd speak just like them" (Interview). In many ways, Tily illustrates the plasticity of language use among students who gain access to a range of communities of belonging in a highly mixed community, something that, as you may recall, Jessica was not prone to do.

Tily also had an opportunity to hear pidgin in high school for the first time after befriending a young Filipina born and raised in Hawai'i, as well as a young man who became her boyfriend and later her husband and also spoke pidgin fluently. Not surprisingly, over the course of her immersion in her boyfriend/husband's linguistic and cultural environment, Tily "adapted and started to speak pidgin whenever I'm in Hawai'i or around local Hawaiians." In the most vivid example she provided in her first self-reflective essay of how the innovative playfulness of language can be used to connect with others and achieve one's goals, Tily told the story of how pidgin provided the family behind-the-scenes admission to the family meet-and-greet of the San Francisco 49ers a couple of months earlier:

> We bought tickets to the game against the Arizona Cardinals and when the game was done, my mother-in-law noticed #77's mom (islanders can spot islanders like an oasis in the desert). All she had to do was say, "Eh Aunty (we weren't related, never met her before), your son Iupati, #77 yea? Wow ah, he's my favorite one! Today's my son's birthday, try check if we can see him lidat, all we want is one autograph, can?" That translated to "Hi Aunty. Is your son #77, Iupati? He's my favorite. Today is my son's birthday and we would love to get your son's autograph. Is that possible?" Once we got through security my mother-in-law said giggling, "Kay now Aunty, no forget now, we family lidat." I remember telling [my husband] in amazement, after we took pictures with the players, and got autographs from the quarterback that only Hawaiians can do that. Not my Chaud accent nor Chamorro language (if I spoke it) could ever get us backstage to any celebrity or pro-athlete event.

Despite Tily's suggestion that pidgin-speaking Hawaiians do not have any rules for syntax when they speak, they do as anyone who speaks a language does, but her point is well taken: We always think anyone who uses language differently from us (unless it is a widely acclaimed standard form) has fewer rules governing its use. Moreover, as playful as pidgin sounds to the unfamiliar ear of an English dominant speaker, as Tily and most of us are, it is certainly more readily available to a broader population than, say, the very private and invented language that I will describe later when I discuss Mina's experience with a language she and her brother invented. On the other hand, as was true in this case, what made pidgin so effective was that her mother-in-law knew that the humor embedded in her expression was also a critical factor in having her fulfill her rhetorical end goal.

When it came to the language forms available to members of the Guam community in which she grew up, the challenges that Tily had to deal with brought into sharp relief the difficulties that anyone who speaks a disenfranchised language or dialect must inevitably confront. In her case, the price she would have paid was so great in her eyes that she self-consciously decided to focus her energies on learning English. This is how she describes the conundrum members of her generation face:

> Unfortunately my generation doesn't speak our native tongue; only my father does in my family. It was the generations before them who spoke the language fluently and tried, without success, to pass on the heritage. I grew up relishing in the fact that I didn't "sound" Chaud when I spoke English, but I also didn't care about learning my native language. When my grandfather barked out orders in Chamorro, I would simply ignore him and pretend I didn't hear. My cousins and I opted out of learning the language because it was not enforced at school. For all we knew, those who spoke Chamorro sounded chaud, and those who sounded chaud were made fun of. We did not want to be outcasts at school so we chose to speak English only.

Once her family settled in Las Vegas, Tily realized what she had lost, but she was no longer in any position to learn her family's language. As someone "brown skinned in a sea of white people," Tily suddenly felt colorless and decided that her exposure to other languages and dialects would provide her with an opportunity to change it:

> All at once, I was inundated with a plethora of languages, dialects, and styles of speech that I'd never heard before. I realized how empty my palette was and that watercolor English would not get me very far in a melting pot city like Las Vegas. . . . I couldn't understand these new dialects, and they couldn't understand me; therefore, I knew I'd have to adjust my speech pattern, or switch my palette in order to converse with other ethnicities. . . . I picked up more slang, changed the way I pronounced words, and changed the pragmatics of my speech; in essence, I was adding to my English dialect palette without knowing it.

From that point on, Tily became an accomplished code-switcher (as I describe it in Chapter 2) across the various slang dialects that she experienced at a critical moment in her life. It proved to be a partial victory in that she found a way to add color to her pale English palette, but it also failed to connect her with the language of her original community of belonging.

Toward the innovative, code-meshing end of the continuum, we find Mina Nokeo, a woman in her early twenties born and raised in Tacoma, Washington who planned to complete her degree in Linguistics at the end of the current quarter, then travel to Guatemala afterwards (something she actually ended up doing) to teach English. Possibly because of her parents' distinct linguistic practices (her mother is White and speaks only English, but her father is Laotian and speaks Lao, French, Chinese and English), Mina's language development as a child was dominated by English and the various ways in which it was mixed in a code-meshing sense with a range of languages and dialects that cut across her family and her communities of belonging. No doubt because everyone in her family was very comfortable with the blending of tongues, Mina describes herself as having always been enthralled with the playful forms that language use can take, especially in its wicked disruption of grammatical, syntactic and pragmatic rules of standardization. Here is how she describes a series of typical events in her household:

> It's Sunday morning and my family is getting ready for church. There's only one bathroom in the house so a few of us are waiting just outside the door for my dad to finish shaving. "Why are we all having what the audience?" he calls out. Another day he's getting ready to go down to DuPont [a small town 10 miles away] to visit my uncle and he says to me, "I was wondering if you want to go see if Dennis has a baby, see baby's Dennis, Dennis' baby!!" Yet another day he is working on our car with one of my brothers and they're having trouble getting some of the nuts out. Finally, when they start to come loose, he exclaims, "Now we're speaking!" I've grown up hearing all sorts of things from my dad's mouth that don't quite sound right, and I've spent quite a few conversations translating his English to "Standard English" for people who don't quite get what he's trying to say.

What we begin to sense immediately as readers is an appreciation of the remarkable linguistic dexterity that plays itself out in Mina's home. At the root of it all, she suggests, is the multiplicity of languages in her father's repertoire:

> Whether it's changing the syntax, replacing words with synonyms that don't quite work in the figure of speech, inserting extra words, pronouncing words with odd emphasis, or just not really making any sense at all, I've heard them all from my dad. English is my dad's fourth language, although he now only speaks three. He grew up in Laos when it was a French colony, so he learned Lao at home and French in school, then studied Chinese in a French University, and then he came to the United States and learned English. Thus, even though I've spent the majority of my life in western Washington I still find myself saying things like, "Watch your footing!" when my brother has stepped on some food I dropped on the kitchen floor.

During our interview, Mina explained that she and her brother became intrigued by their father's language use and "would start to kind of like, not make fun of him, but kind of point them out. And then we would start to say them, just to be funny, and then they kind of worked their way into our own vocabulary, and then we just built new ones off of that."

As if this were not enough for those of us who delight in code-meshing, Mina and her older brother have taken this innovative playfulness to a new level in their daily interactions as they both immerse themselves in the fecundity of languages in motion all around them:

> My brother and I have created a sort of hybrid-English in which we incorporate words from French, Lao and/or Thai, Hebrew, Russian, Spanish, and Arabic. We also hum some words or phrases that we often say with a particular timing and pitch so the humming mirrors our speech. Our mom thinks it's amazing that we can talk to each other without actually talking, and our other two brothers have started to pick up on it a little, but they're not quite as practiced as we are.

When I asked her how the various languages got folded into their language play, Mina explained that she "learned some Lao from my dad, and French. And also from living in France [for six months]. And then Hebrew from my brother, who's studying it. Oh, and Russian. A friend of mine, she was learning Russian, and so I was practicing with her, and she was teaching me some" (Interview). In addition, because she was majoring in linguistics and wanted to be able to communicate with her grandparents and the rest of her extended family, she studied Thai, which in her view is mutually intelligible with Lao. As if that were not enough, Mina traveled to Guatemala and simultaneously taught English and studied Spanish, in addition to Mam, one of the indigenous languages in the area that someone taught her a little bit of the last time she traveled there (Interview). Of all the students in this group of three undergraduates, Mina easily had the broadest exposure to the widest range of languages and dialects and found a good way to make use of them at home with her siblings.

Despite the rich texture of her language use, if someone were to ask her what dialect of English she speaks, like David, she "would probably say the Pacific Northwest dialect" because she "primarily [uses] PNW vocabulary and pronunciations." As she put it, "[i]n a formal context, yes, I'd say I'm a typical Pacific Northwesterner, but at any other given time I'm all over the place." Not surprisingly, Mina is exceedingly self-aware of what she does with language and why she does it: "Maybe changing how I speak in all of these different contexts could be seen as inconsistency on my part, but I think that each way of speaking shows a different aspect of who I am." As I will demonstrate in the next section, Mina is still driven by her desire to be successful in the world, to perform language in standardized forms that will meet the expectations of others, and for that reason joined a majority of students in the class who took a position against instituting a translingual approach in the classroom, but Mina clearly still values the code-meshing qualities that inform her use of language at home:

> The way that I speak around my family is my favorite way of speaking. I don't have to think through what I want to say before I say it to make sure it's free of "errors" or "sounds smart." I can just say what's in my head and if I can't think of a word I make one up or use a sound effect or gesture in its place.

In listening to the voices of the students whose stories I just shared, we come to understand how and why most of them are persuaded that learning what they perceive and describe as a standard language (in English and otherwise) continues to be a goal worth pursuing. A translingual approach, half of them say, is a wonderful idea but it remains too idealistic, a little too far beyond the limits of comprehension. Many of them argue that we should not be so easily repulsed by the human desire to fix language or seduced by the fluidity and flexibility of languages in motion. That, they argue, is a fool's paradise. Instead, as they told me over and over again, we should do everything in our power to use language rhetorically in the course of responding to the fixity and fluidity that we encounter. Code-segregation is out; on this, most of them generally agree. Code-switching and code-meshing as I described them in Chapter 2, on the other hand, are both fully viable approaches to difference because they allow us to navigate the broad linguistic and cultural terrain that we traverse every day of our lives as we engage in the difficult task of identity formation.

In the next section, I shift my discussion and analysis away from how students in my class recall doing language in their everyday lives and consider the various positions several students took in relation to the three prominent curricular and pedagogical approaches to language and cultural difference that I discussed in Chapters 1, 2 and 3. This more formal discussion should provide yet another take on the varied perspectives students in my class chose to take in the course of experiencing a jarring shift in focus (or not) from the sense of solidarity they bring from their other communities of belonging to the college writing classroom. As many of them acknowledged, students are rewarded or punished depending on their adherence to a language—in our case, a monolingual form of Standard American English—perceived as perfect by everyone empowered to sustain the ruse, but challenged by everyone else from first language speakers who now know better and second language speakers who learned it through experience.

Taking a Stance

In the first three chapters of this book, I discussed at length the various approaches to language and cultural difference that have emerged as a consequence of the ideological perspectives that teachers and students must be aware of to more effectively navigate and negotiate the varied social spaces they inhabit in college classrooms and other communities of belonging. Proponents of a translingual (Horner et al., 2011; Lu & Horner, 2013) and transcultural approach (Kostogriz, 2004; Lu, 2009) to language and cultural difference have described three distinct yet simultaneously overlapping ideological approaches—the monolingual/monocultural, the multilingual/multicultural and the translingual/transcultural—that provide us with a frame of reference for understanding the options available to us and our students. In the course of examining these positions in class, students read the Horner et al. (2011) opinion piece I mentioned earlier, discussed the three ideological approaches the authors describe, then argued in favor of one or the other of these positions in response to a prompt in their midterm essay. Of the 24 students in class who took this option, 11 took a position in favor of and 13 a position against a translingual approach. Possibly because of their former shared experiences as second language educators, the graduate students in the class were more forthright in their support or critique of Horner et al.'s position. For that reason, my review of the group's varied takes will focus primarily on the work of the graduate students in the class.

On the surface, the balanced distribution for and against a translingual approach suggests that efforts to persuade students that translingualism is a viable response to language and cultural difference have made some significant inroads. A closer look at the results, however, demonstrates that those of us in the field who are doing everything we can to persuade our students to embrace a position that recognizes flexibility and fluidity in language use still have much work to do. On the positive side, it is encouraging to see that not a single student in the group spoke strongly (one student did acknowledge that such constraints could potentially be used productively in a classroom) in favor of a monolingual approach; that is, students were generally put off by the position's strong argument for a fixed and routine conception of the roles that language and culture play in our lives. As I will demonstrate in a moment, students who spoke firmly against a translingual approach favored what they saw as the more pragmatic code-switching (as I described it in Chapter 2) consequences of a multilingual approach. Based on their experience in school and out of school contexts, many of them valued an individual's ability to read the rhetorical and discursive expectations of a particular audience in a particular setting, then to respond to and accommodate the communicative needs of others as the need arose. While students who supported a translingual approach found much to praise, especially the position's recognition of the role that contingency and emergence play in every linguistic or cultural interaction with others, every one of them qualified their stance by raising concerns about the advisability of enacting a translingual approach in college classrooms and professional settings that continue to be informed by expectations grounded in a monolingual/monocultural stance.

Despite the range of experiences that each of them has had with the complicated roles that language and culture have played in their lives, almost every one of the students—except for Tily Yokota, whose self-reflective writing and interviews I presented in the preceding section, and a couple of other students—took a position against efforts to implement a translingual approach to language and cultural difference in the classroom. Like everyone else in the larger group, Tily also qualified her stance to the point where it weakened her efforts to speak up in its favor. Others, however, spoke out more strongly as proponents of the Horner et al. (2011) position. In her midterm essay, for example, Sandra Fournier, one of the strongest proponents of a translingual approach, recognized a "conscious awareness of language choice" as one of the tenets of Horner et al.'s argument. "An awareness of language options in communication," she argued, "is an invaluable lesson that all students should learn. Language awareness not only means knowledge of how you communicate in different situations and why, but also an awareness of variation in power." In line with Lu and Horner's (2013) argument in a follow up to the Horner et al. (2011) essay, Sandra contended that "language awareness is important for majority monolingual students as well. We must not only empower the disenfranchised, but empower, or inspire, majority members to effect change as well." In so doing, Sandra established the most persuasive element inherent in a translingual approach: the now widely acknowledged realization that educators can best prepare their students for future reading, writing and rhetorical opportunities by cultivating in them the kind of critical self-awareness of language and culture that scholars I discussed in earlier chapters support.

Donna Chang, another advocate, noted that the implementation of a translingual approach would have made a difference in her own life. Two key benefits of the approach for her, she explained, "lie in its emphasis on recognizing that power relationships exist in language use [and] its emphasis on being conscious about what we are doing as teachers and students when we use language." Melody Heston, a student who shared Donna's teaching goals, specifically acknowledged that "altering standards is subject to the criticism that we are *softening* standards, but I stand by translingualism's claim that the current system is 'invoking standards not to improve communication and assist language learners, but to exclude voices and perspectives at odds with those in power' (Horner et al., 2011, p. 305)." Her commitment to pursuing a translingual approach despite the misgivings of some was powerfully demonstrated in her commitment to implement it in her future role as a second-language writing teacher:

> I expect to carry the idea of translingual writing with me into my next teaching appointment and to continue to discover and develop new ways of drawing my students into the conversation around English(es) and legitimacy. I also expect to be met with resistance and strong emotions from those who do not see the "standards" as negotiable. Though my politics may not permeate my community I do have some control over how they permeate my classroom, and I plan to be careful and intentional about the stance I take.

Overall, those who spoke out in favor of a translingual approach emphasized the power and agency that critical language and cultural awareness can provide students who are faced with making difficult choices in the monolingual contexts they are likely to continue encountering in almost every college classroom or other communities of belonging that they inhabit.

Despite their often firm position against implementing a translingual approach in first and second language writing classrooms, the images evoked by the arguments posed by students who spoke firmly against the approach did not seem that different from the positions of the various proponents that I just cited. In the view of students who took a position against the idea of implementing a translingual curriculum in the classroom, what often emerged as the most salient factor was their concern that standardized language continues to be an integral element that informs schooling and professional contexts. In a nutshell, they felt compelled to find ways to teach language standardization to students in college writing classrooms with a concomitant critical self-awareness about the politics of such a move because they were afraid that students might otherwise find themselves shortchanged, or worse discriminated against, for using a non-standard language or dialect. For them, a multilingual approach offered a better way to address student needs because it simultaneously acknowledges the importance of standardization across all language dialects and varieties in schools and communities, and encourages students to make use of their ability to switch from one to the other as the need arises.

In what I found to be one of the most incisive critiques of a translingual approach intentionally taken to the extreme, Jessica Larsen began her midterm essay with the following epigraph:

> My 语言 simultaneously shapes who I am & tells ppl who I am – 教师
> 同学 Californian TESOLer Aussie American ελουλα 朋有 et cetera. Their
> perceptions of me & my projections 常常不是一样的, 所以当然有时我
> 应该 vertere. Aber wie der romishe elegische Poet Propertius hat einmal
> geschrieben: quid mirare meas tot in uno corpore formas?

The epigraph, she argued, "takes an extreme translingual approach, where a writer fully and forcefully claims 'the right to their own language' (Horner et al. 2011, p. 304) to the exclusion of any set of standards. The epigraph also serves neither the reader's desire to understand nor the writer's desire to be understood." Despite the seemingly entrenched view that her epigraph suggests, Jessica was quite aware of, and open to, the inherently changing nature of language, no matter what anyone does to constrain it. As she pointed out in the course of presenting an alternative perspective that refuses to buy into the fixity and rigidity suggested by a monolingual approach or the fluidity and flexibility of a translingual one, "standards are not to be thrown out the window. Rather, they should be valued but interrogated thoroughly. . . . Standards are inherently changeable, and making students aware of that changeability empowers them to eventually become complicit in it."

What I appreciated most about Jessica's position was her ability to explore with some degree of nuance the contradictions inherent in any either/or argument that disallows a position that accepts standardization as an inherent element of language but is simultaneously aware of the ever present need to critique it in the same breath:

> It takes more than one unit or one class to change deeply held views about language, especially when textbooks still promote binaries of right and wrong, but I hold out hope that if students and teachers can realize together the extent to which language change is happening and has always been happening within and around us, then students will feel a greater right to understand, own and eventually bend the standard.

In keeping with my own position that fixity is as inherent a characteristic of language and what individuals do with it as fluidity is, Jessica refused to assume that any particular policy was likely to change how teachers or students decide to conceptualize its characteristics. Standards, she concluded,

> are inevitable, but the orientation of those standards can shift to favor different groups, and as more people with clearly multilingual identities gain powerful positions in relation to and through manipulation of the standards, English standards could well shift in their favor, whether a full policy of translingualism is widely embraced or not.

In other words, because languages are always in motion, there is as strong a chance that what proponents of a translingual approach aim to accomplish will happen of its own accord as individuals with multilingual identities assert their right to enact certain practices in their everyday lives, in and out of school.

Carmen Valenzuela and Sidney Pavlov, two other graduate students in the class, stood firm as well regarding their views of the place of standardization in the first and second language writing classroom. As a Mexican American born in Spain while her father was stationed there during his military service, Carmen described the challenges she encountered as a student and later as a journalist who gave up her first language early in life to accommodate the English standardization that her parents and employers pressed upon her. Instead of feeling bitter about having to adapt to such circumstances, she came to understand the degree of agency and power that her ability to use standard language afforded her. As she put it, "The harsh truth is that Standard American English is still viewed by hundreds of millions of people around the world as the language of prestige and power." As a Mexican American, Carmen notes, she feels compelled to serve as a model, especially for disenfranchised students who are expected to step out of their own language comfort zones and learn SAE:

> I feel it is important that I serve as a role model for other Mexican-Americans or minorities, for those who do not think they can break into the inner circle, or for English language learners who aspire to go to university here in the U.S., or who want to teach English themselves someday. It is with an eye toward all these populations still on the outside that I strive to use a high standard of English, specifically SAE, as a student and a teacher.

This is not to suggest that Carmen sees herself living in some wonderland where knowing SAE will solve everyone's problems. When I pointed out during our interview that the imposition of SAE on disenfranchised students often disempowered them because they were not afforded access to their own rich linguistic and cultural repertoires, Carmen acknowledged the contradiction in her position: "And that's just the harsh reality. Does it mean that I like that reality? No, I don't, because it's—it creates a sense of exclusion, that your culture, your language, your dialect is not legit, but, yeah" (Interview).

Finally, Sidney Pavlov enriched the discussion by locating it in the context of someone who was raised in Russia and speaks English and Russian fluently. After declaring "much of what is stated in the opinion piece by Horner et al. . . . indisputable truisms," Sidney found it difficult to agree with their call "for a blanket acceptance of all written forms of English in an academic setting. While the idea is good and noble, it is not practical." In her view, "it is more realistic to allow for a multiplicity of *spoken* language variations" (italics in original), which she would certainly invite students to use in the classroom, but she would "want them to acquire the 'academic' dialect, especially for writing." Above all, Sidney raised some serious concerns during our interview about the potential disservice that a translingual curriculum would do to students over the course of their lives:

> I think that is, in the end, doing a disservice to the students because not everybody is accepting, and that's the reality. If you just release the students out there and then they do not get a job, are not employed or get fired or something like that because of the inappropriate—what is considered inappropriate use of language by somebody else—then it's doing a disservice.

Despite her misgivings, Sidney acknowledged in her interview that the readings and discussions in class had reinforced a position that she will want to take the next time she is standing in front of her own classroom: "I now understand that my role in the classroom should not be limited to teaching English, but should also include promoting the validity of the students' first language and culture in order to help them preserve their identity."

Although the implementation of a translingual approach is often painted as an inevitable outcome of the tremendous demographic and policy changes taking place in colleges and universities as migrant, immigrant and international students enroll in ever increasing numbers, the work that students produced in my class hints at just how difficult a transition away from a still present monolingual approach in the teaching of writing is likely to be. Over and over again, through their varied experiences at home, in the classroom and in their communities of belonging, my students painted a complex picture that vividly illustrates the degree to which the competing ideologies that inform current approaches to language and cultural difference will continue to complicate our collective efforts to transform the curriculum and institute pedagogical strategies grounded in the undeniable reality that languages are always in motion, cultures are always in transition and identities are always created in practice. I think we can take solace in my students' willingness to engage the competing ideologies in the course of demonstrating their willingness to imagine a world in which code-switching and code-meshing operate simultaneously as we all respond to the everchanging rhetorical and discursive circumstances in which we find ourselves. But as I hope to demonstrate in the next chapter, it is not enough for us to try to intervene in the single college classroom to bring about the kinds of changes that we all wish to see. Eventually, we will need to expand the scope of our involvement beyond the classroom to include the campus and other communities of belonging as we acknowledge the need for institutional change informed by the important roles that language, culture, identity—and citizenship as well—play in our students' lives.

Notes

1. Although this is an upper-division content course, English 479 meets the standards for what at the UW is referred to as a "writing-intensive" (W) class where students are expected to produce "10–15 pages of graded, out-of-class writing, in the form of a longer paper with a required revision of two or more short papers." In my class I expected every student to write a minimum of 14 and a maximum of 20 double-spaced pages over the course of the quarter. While not every student exercised the option, they were each permitted to revise their work and get written feedback from me over the course of the quarter. Only those who also agreed to revise their work received W credit. In an unexpected turn of events, almost half (15) of the 34 students who enrolled in the course that quarter were graduate students enrolled in the English Department's Masters of Arts in the Teaching of English to Speakers of Other Languages (MATESOL) program.
2. Because I taught this class in the midst of formulating my ideas for this book and I had not yet immersed myself adequately in the citizenship literature, I decided not to assign any readings to the class that dealt with that topic. As a consequence, I only focus on language, culture and identity in my discussion and analysis of the written work that students did for the class and the interviews I conducted with a number of them after the quarter was over.
3. According to Therborn (1980), ideology always addresses three specific questions: What exists? What is good? What is possible? The first question focuses on

epistemological concerns: "what exists, and its corollary, what does not exist: that is, who we are, what the world is, what nature, society, men and women are like." The second responds to our need to establish ethical and aesthetic standards: "what is good, right, just, beautiful, attractive, enjoyable, and its opposites. In this way our desires become structured and normalized." Finally, ideology lets us know whether our expectations are reasonable: "what is possible and impossible; our sense of the mutability of our being-in-the-world and the consequences of change are hereby patterned, and our hopes, ambitions, and fears given shape" (p. 18). In order "to become committed to changing something," Therborn argues, "one must first get to know that it exists, then make up one's mind whether it is good that it exists. Before deciding to do something about a bad state of affairs, one must first be convinced that there is some chance of actually changing it" (p. 19).

4. The genre I used to frame these two assignments is typically referred to as a language autobiography or a literacy narrative. I decided, however, to refer to it as a self-reflective essay because I wanted to accent the role that self-reflection necessarily plays in the process.

5. Because I differentiated code-switching and code-meshing for students at the beginning of this class in the ways that I described in Chapter 2, I use code-meshing in this chapter to indicate intra- and inter-sentential shifts across the various languages and dialects that students used in their writing.

6. On second thought, this should not come as much of a surprise. Of the large number of scholars in our field who encourage the use of code-meshing among our students, only Smitherman (1977) and Villanueva (1993) deploy the practice in their work on a regular basis and to any measurable extent. It is, as I am suggesting here, difficult for all of us to work against the monolingual and standardizing ideologies that inform publication venues as much as the college writing classroom.

7. Occasionally, I include material from my interviews with the students whose writing I am presenting here to clarify or expand on what they wrote in their self-reflective essays. I have elected not to cite any of the written material, except to indicate who wrote it. On the other hand, whenever I quote material from my interviews, I cite it by inserting the word "Interview" in parentheses.

8. After reviewing the writing of everyone in the class who granted me permission to use it in this study, in this section I elected to present the writing and interviews that these three Asian American women produced and provided because they most effectively reflected the contestation of ideologies reflected in our current discussions in the field of composition and literacy studies about language difference. Their descriptions of how they used language at home, at school and in their varied and shifting communities of belonging not only struck me as vivid and engaging; it also illustrated the tensions between convention and innovation that I wanted to discuss in this chapter. Finally, their writing and descriptions of their oral language use provided a continuation of, and a contrast with, the writing and descriptions of oral language use that David and Jessica shared in the preceding section.

9. I would be remiss if I did not disrupt the neat and tidy continuum I just described here by pointing out that the role of standardization in native languages used by the families of second-language speakers can also produce consternation and a sense of obligation. I illustrate this later when I describe Emma Lau's experience trying to learn Cantonese in Chinese language school.

References

Appadurai, A. (1996). Disjuncture and difference in the global cultural economy. *Theory, Culture and Society, 7*, 295–310.

Bartholomae, D. (1986). Inventing the university. *Journal of Basic Writing*, 5(1), 4–23.

Bourdieu, P. (1977). *Outline of a theory of practice*. Cambridge, UK: Cambridge University Press.

Braidotti, R. (1994). *Nomadic subjects*. New York, NY: Cambridge University Press.

Canagarajah, A. S. (2006). The place of world Englishes in composition: Pluralization continued. *College Composition and Communication*, 57(4), 586–619.

Horner, B., Lu, M. Z., Royster, J. J. & Trimbur J. (2011). Language difference in writing: Toward a translingual approach. *College English*, 73(3), 303–321.

Kostogriz, A. (2004). Rethinking the spatiality of literacy practices in multicultural conditions. Retrieved from www.aare.edu.au/04pap/kos04610.pdf

Lu, M.-Z. (2004). An essay on the work of composition: Composing English against the order of fast capitalism. *College Composition and Communication*, 56(1), 16–50.

Lu, M.-Z. (2009). Metaphors matter: Transcultural literacy. *Journal of Advanced Composition*, 29(1/2), 285–293.

Lu, M.-Z. & Horner, B. (2013). Translingual literacy, language difference, and matters of agency. *College English*, 75(6), 582–607.

Smitherman, G. (1977). *Talkin' and testifyin': The language of Black America*. Detroit, MI: Wayne State University.

Tardy, C. M. (2011). Enacting and transforming local language policies. *College Composition and Communication*, 62(4), 634–661.

Therborn, G. (1980). *The ideology of power and the power of ideology*. New York, NY: Verso.

Villanueva, V. (1993). *Bootstraps: From an American academic of color*. Urbana, IL: NCTE Press.

Young, V. A. (2004). Your average nigga. *College Composition and Communication*, 55(4), 693–715.

Young, V. A. (2009). Nah, we straight: An argument against code switching. *Journal of Advanced Composition*, 29(1–2), 49–76.

Young, V. A. & Martínez, A. Y. (2011). *Code-meshing as world Englishes: Pedagogy, policy and performance*. Urbana, IL: National Council of Teachers of English.

7

ENACTING AND SUSTAINING INSTITUTIONAL CHANGE

Most First-Year Writing (FYW) and Writing Across the Curriculum (WAC) programs operate under the assumption that our job as college writing teachers is to train our students to produce academic discourse so that they can learn how writing operates in different academic disciplines while we simultaneously prepare them for the kind of parallel writing they will be asked to do later in their majors and future professions. A number of scholars, Downs and Wardle (2007) among them, have rightly criticized the continuing tendency in most FYW programs to "teach, in one or two early courses, 'college writing' as a set of basic, fundamental skills that will apply in other college courses and in business and public spheres after college" (p. 553). Although I empathize with Downs and Wardle's position that writing teachers need to stop acting "as if writing is a basic, universal skill" and instead start acting "as if writing studies is a discipline with content knowledge to which students should be introduced, thereby changing their understandings about writing and thus changing the ways they write" (p. 553), I am concerned that they do not push the envelope far enough.

As I have argued in this book, we need to reconstitute our notions of what it means to teach reading, writing and rhetoric in FYW and WAC programs, as well as in K–12 contexts, so that we can all do a better job of preparing our students for the plethora of linguistic, cultural and semiotic circumstances they are likely to encounter over the course of their studies and beyond. But we also need to make sure that we undertake these efforts in the context of the theoretical and ecological framework I described in Part I of this book, one that draws attention to the central roles that language, culture, identity and citizenship play in the process. For just as every college writing class needs to make sure that students learn about the important role critical language and cultural awareness play in the development of their identities as readers, writers and rhetoricians, faculty and graduate students in FYW and WAC programs need to do more than have students mimic our practices as writing specialists. Instead, we need to equip students with a repertoire of rhetorical and discursive tools that they can deploy in the varied linguistic, cultural and semiotic spaces they are likely to inhabit over the course of their everyday lives. Even more directly and explicitly than the individual classroom I describe in the preceding chapter and Downs and Wardle (2007) illustrate in their critique of current first-year writing practices, FYW and WAC programs need to equip students with the tools of the trade every citizen in the making needs to be a productive member of various communities of belonging at the local, regional, national and international levels, something that I am persuaded will only happen through a campus-wide, ecologically sound approach rather than through any single class.[1] For all these reasons, I contend that the current shift from a Writing Across the Curriculum to a writing across difference approach best illustrated by the Writing Across Communities (hereafter, WAC[2]) program[2] established at the University of New Mexico in January 2005 is the best response currently available to address our collective concerns.

Although there is an understandable tendency in the field to think of programs like WAC[2] as recent innovations with little history behind them, evidence suggests that scholars have been imagining parallel possibilities for some time now. Almost 20 years ago in what many composition and literacy scholars would consider a "harsh"[3] but fruitful critique of WAC, for example, LeCourt (1996) argued that certain aspects of critical pedagogy should be integrated into WAC programs to destabilize "their localized, specific articulations of a more generalized academic discourse" (p. 390). A key concern that she highlighted was the tendency among students in WAC courses "to allow the disciplinary discourses to name their reality for them by internalizing its ways of thinking, accepting them as more authoritative and viable than alternatives" they already possessed (p. 397). Although she supported Bazerman's (1992) recommendation that we encourage students to reflect critically on disciplinary discourses, LeCourt (1996) pushed further and called for "a concomitant focus on the writer's multiple discursive positions as a way of allowing for student difference and alternative literacies to find a space within disciplinary discourses" (p. 399). Over the course of her critique, she put forth an alternative model that she imagined could provide "a way for the personal and disciplinary to interact in a dialectical fashion rather than one in which one voice must be silenced for the other to speak" (p. 400). LeCourt's critical model of WAC redefined "thinking and learning through writing in terms that recognize the viability of the student discourses as much as disciplinary ones" (p. 402).

Since LeCourt (1996) first presented her trenchant critique, a number of other scholars in composition and literacy studies have added their voices to the chorus. Their arguments suggest that limiting the focus to academic discourse in a WAC program disempowers students (Flower, 2008; Goldblatt, 2007; Mathieu, 2005; Parks and Goldblatt, 2000; Weisser, 2002) because it fails to acknowledge the "learning incomes" (Guerra, 2008a, p. 296) and "discursive resources" (Lu, 2004, p. 28; Reiff & Bawarshi, 2011, p. 312) that they bring with them from their various "communities of belonging" (Kells, 2007, p. 88). Before they leave the academy, these scholars insist, our students need to figure out how to become effective readers, writers and rhetoricians in a rich array of personal, professional and civic spaces as well, something that a WAC approach limited to the study of academic discourse cannot help them do. LeCourt and scholars who have taken up her call are also concerned about how we can best "resist the rigidity and homogenization of administrative structures" (LeCourt, 1996, p. 391) that inadvertently paralyze our best efforts to provide all novice writers, but particularly those who have been disenfranchised, with the rhetorical and discursive tools they need as citizens in the making to navigate and negotiate the various linguistic and cultural circumstances they face in their everyday lives on and off campus.

In what follows, I tell the story of the WAC[2] initiative that began at the University of New Mexico (UNM) in January 2005, one that embodies an ecological approach to writing instruction and reflects the kind of radical alternative LeCourt envisioned. The WAC[2] story builds on LeCourt's contention that WAC programs need to respect and make use of the alternative discourses that students bring with them into the classroom, but it goes a step further by providing a model for enacting institutional change that acknowledges the critical role of faculty, graduate and undergraduate students, as well as staff, administrators and community members, in creating changes that begin at the grassroots level rather than from the top down. Along the way, I show how WAC[2] proponents utilize the tactics and strategies that Adler-Kassner (2008) proposes in *The Activist WPA*, as well as critical elements of the theory and methodology proposed by Giddens (1976), Miller (1998) and Porter, Sullivan, Blythe, Grabill and Miles (2000), for undertaking institutional change to support the eventual implementation of the WAC[2] initiative they propose. Because of the role it plays in the process, I add another layer of conversation to the rich stories that Kells—the principal founder of WAC[2] at UNM—has already shared in several publications (2007, 2013) by introducing the insightful voices of some of the graduate students[4] that she mentored over a period of 5 years before my visit in 2013. For anyone in composition and literacy studies weighing the possibility of building a new, or remodeling an existing, WAC program so that it responds more readily and effectively to the diverse needs of all students on a given campus, the WAC[2] story I tell may well serve as a model and a cautionary tale worth considering.

Setting the Stage

In the interest of full disclosure, let me begin by implicating myself and describing my early role in the WAC[2] story. Michelle[5] and I met in 1999 while she was working on a Ph.D. in the Literacy and Discourse Studies Program at Texas

A&M University College Station, and I was at the tail end of my first 10 years as a tenure-track faculty member in the Language and Rhetoric Program at the University of Washington at Seattle. Because of her knack for organizing large groups of people, it came as no surprise when in the fall of 2000, Michelle and Valerie Balester, her faculty advisor, co-organized a symposium at Texas A&M titled "Literacies and Literary Representations: Posing Questions, Framing Conversations about Language and Hispanic Identities." In my keynote address at that event, I introduced the concept of *transcultural repositioning*, a term that speaks directly to LeCourt's call for "a concomitant focus on the writer's multiple discursive positions" (1996, p. 399). Michelle later used the term as a frame of reference in two essays—"Linguistic Contact Zones in the College Writing Classroom: An Examination of Ethnolinguistic Identity and Language Attitudes" (Kells, 2002) and "Understanding the Rhetorical Value of *tejano* Codeswitching" (Kells, 2004)—to study the roles that language and culture play in the formation of identity among historically underserved students in writing classrooms at Texas A&M Kingsville. All these years later, the concept of transcultural repositioning continues to play a role in on-going collective efforts to establish WAC[2] at UNM.

Shortly after her arrival as a tenure-track faculty member at UNM in the fall of 2004, the Chair of the English Department charged Michelle with exploring the possibility of building a WAC program on campus. "When the chair of the department asked me to take on this project in 2004," Michelle wrote recently, "I think he had something else in mind. Certainly, initiating an ongoing conversation of social diversity, civil rights, and cultural-based literacy education was not the WAC model that came immediately to his mind" (Kells, 2013, p. 128). But Michelle had come to this moment equipped with a radical vision shaped by her experience as a graduate student whose dissertation and first book, titled *Héctor P. García: Everyday Rhetoric and Mexican American Civil Rights* (2006a), focused on the role of Mexican Americans in the civil rights movement of the 1950s and 1960s. She also came as a basic writing teacher who had worked extensively with historically underserved students at Texas A&M at Kingsville and College Station (2002, 2004). As a consequence, by the time she set foot at UNM, Michelle knew that

> Social movements evolve out of coordinated rhetorical responses confronting inequitable conditions, seeded by a collective sense that the distribution of social wealth is out of balance. Scarcity—the disparate circulation of resources, privilege, justice, access, opportunity—stirs individuals and communities into action.
>
> *Kells, 2013, p. 119*

In a recent interview, Mark Peceny, Dean of the College of Arts & Sciences at UNM, characterized the work Michelle and other WAC[2] proponents have been doing at UNM over the last 10 years in much the same terms. A former chair of the Department of Political Science at UNM and the author of a book on insurgency and counterinsurgency movements in Latin America titled *Democracy at the Point of Bayonets* (1999), Dean Peceny describes WAC[2]'s work in this way:

> I've taken to characterizing WAC as it has developed at UNM as an insurgent movement. And I've since switched to a social movement. It hasn't been institutionalized in the curriculum, and it hasn't been institutionalized in the bureaucracy of the university. But it has been a movement of people committed to social change. Social change in the way we do business at the university, which we hope will lead to social change in the way the university impacts the world by sending students who are formed in an interesting and new way because of the experience.
>
> *Interview*

This characterization makes sense, especially as proponents of WAC[2] at UNM have called on the tactical and strategic approaches to activist organizing that Adler-Kassner (2008) insists writing program administrators and writing teachers must implement if they "want to build different stories, construct different tropes and narratives and shift frames in ways that balance strategies and ideals" (p. 35). Once Michelle and a core group of graduate students who joined the effort at its inception decided that the elements for a successful WAC[2] program needed to be put in place, they made the strategic decision to use the interest-oriented approach, the most tactical of the three that Adler-Kassner (2008) describes in *The Activist WPA*, and the one most directly associated with the grassroots work of Saul Alinksy (see also Goldblatt, 2005, 2007). The short-term goal of this approach, Adler-Kassner (2008) contends, is action because "action both addresses issues and helps people understand that they have the power to make change" (p. 99). "Actions," she notes later, are also "aimed toward [issues] you can do something about." Its long-term goal, on the other hand, "is to cultivate individual's senses of power and authority to make change within the culture." And that change, Adler-Kassner (2008) makes clear, "is defined by and stems from the specific, short-term interests of individuals who have come together to work for that change" (p. 99). As Michelle observed recently in describing the role that she has played in building a sustainable WAC[2] at UNM:

> My role as [WAC[2]][6] program chair has been primarily as liaison and advocate, connecting the local context to the national conversation. In practice, I have been less an administrator and more of an agitator and intellectual architect. This protean role not only has required organizing social action behind the scenes, but finding new ways to mobilize diverse constituencies toward a collective re-evaluation of how we teach writing across the university.
>
> *Kells, 2013, p. 128*

Again, it is important to acknowledge that the challenging work Michelle and her colleagues at UNM have undertaken to establish a WAC² approach on their campus would not have been possible without the rich legacy on which it builds. While WAC² acknowledges the importance of expecting students in FYW and linked writing courses affiliated with WAC programs to delve into and develop an enhanced understanding of how language, culture and identity operate in the course of their academic careers, they agree with a growing number of colleagues from across the country (Flower, 2008; Goldblatt, 2005, 2007; Long, 2008; Parks & Goldblatt, 2000; Weisser, 2002) who argue that we must also contribute to the cultivation of individuals as writers who need and want to participate as active and engaged citizens in a multiplicity of intersecting communities of belonging. Their sympathies are also clearly aligned with the extensive work that theorists, researchers and educators have undertaken in the last 20 years to develop service-learning activities (Adler-Kassner, Crooks & Watters, 1997; Deans, 2000; Waterman, 1997) that give students opportunities to learn how to deploy their reading, writing and rhetorical skills in extracurricular settings. WAC² proponents also value the work of colleagues who have implemented WAC programs in a variety of college and university settings with the explicit intention of stretching students' reading, writing and rhetorical abilities beyond the curriculum itself. In this sense, WAC² proponents are neither interested in calling for the elimination of WAC programs nor in ignoring the many contributions the programs have made. If anything, they want to encourage the extension and expansion of the work that WAC programs do by suggesting ways in which such programs can more directly and explicitly address the twenty-first-century needs and concerns of students who must be well-equipped as citizens in the making to not only survive, but thrive, in an increasingly challenging world.

In that respect, the WAC² program that Michelle and her colleagues at UNM have been putting in place since January 2005 is a potential prototype for imagining ways to take everything scholars in the field have learned about WAC programs and expand it to include a focus on the forces of translingualism and transculturation as well. As Michelle and I have described its conception in recent presentations (Guerra, 2005, 2008b, 2009; Kells, 2006b, 2009) and publications (Guerra, 2008a; Kells, 2007), the WAC² approach is founded on the basic notion that we must create conditions under which students can learn to expand their already considerable talents as readers, writers and rhetoricians capable of navigating and negotiating difference. In Bawarshi's words, we want "to teach our students how to become more rhetorically astute and agile, how in other words, to . . . become more effective and critical 'readers' of the sites of action [i.e., rhetorical and social scenes] within which writing takes place" (2003, p. 165), especially in larger and more complex social contexts than we have assumed in the past. It is no longer enough for students in our college writing classes to learn the fundamentals of written communication in an effort to address the immediate expectations of their teachers and the many disciplinary contexts that they represent. Our students must also cultivate the sensibilities they will need to take on reading, writing and rhetorical tasks that call on their histories of participation (Rogers & Fuller, 2007, p. 75) in a multiplicity of intersecting communities of belonging inside and outside of the academy, especially as those histories relate to their involvement in social justice issues. They must also know how to activate their critical language and cultural awareness in the course of performing the multiplicity of identities in practice that they will have to invoke as active and engaged citizens in the making.

In "Writing Across Communities: Deliberation and the Discursive Possibilities of WAC," Michelle describes how the UNM launched the WAC^2 initiative in the course of engaging in a series of campus-wide discussions of the connections between cultural diversity and academic, professional, and civic literacies (Kells, 2007, p. 89). In keeping with their interest in situating literacy practices in the lived experiences of students attending the university, Michelle and her colleagues focus their concerns on student diversity—something that makes sense because UNM is "the only R1 Hispanic-serving, open-admissions institution that also serves one of the largest Native American student populations in the nation" (p. 90)—and the overall cultural ecology of their regional environment. As such, the WAC^2 initiative focuses as much on "learning incomes—i.e., what students bring with them when they come to school" (Guerra, 2008a, p. 296)— as it does on the learning outcomes that writing programs have increasingly highlighted in recent years (Yancey, 2001).

The WAC^2 approach is also in keeping with recent calls by community literacy advocates to rethink the work that we do in the teaching of reading, writing and rhetoric. Much of the work Michelle and I have been doing together has been in direct response to Parks and Goldblatt's invitation that WAC programs "integrate a multiplicity of writing and reading modes with a conception of literacy instruction not limited to serving the needs of established disciplines" (2000, p. 585). Their argument, Parks and Goldblatt (2000) are careful to note,

> is not that WAC needs to abandon its traditional support for writing in the disciplines, but that we should imagine our project as one that combines discipline-based instruction with a range of other literacy experiences that will help students and faculty see writing and reading in a wider social and intellectual context than the college curriculum.
>
> *pp. 585–586*

More recently, in *Because We Live Here: Sponsoring Literacy Beyond the College Curriculum*, Goldblatt (2007) amplifies this position by providing detailed descriptions of important partnerships that he and his colleagues at Temple University established with local high schools, community colleges, and community organizations in their collective effort to institute "a highly activist and multidimensional conception of writing beyond the curriculum" (p. 14).

WAC^2 is also a direct response to a call by Flower (2008) who has extended our collective interest in moving beyond the curriculum into what she refers to as public engagement. In many ways, a WAC^2 approach parallels Flower's interest in a "rhetoric of engagement [that] moves us out of closed academic conversations, classroom conventions, or service-learning 'assignments' and into the unruly dynamics of a live public sphere" (p. 4). Flower is correct in arguing that it is not enough that the dominant discourses of engagement in composition have taught us and our students how to *speak up* as an expressive practice, and how to *speak against* something with the techniques of discourse analysis and critique." Our pedagogical practices, she declares, must also "teach us how to *speak with* others or to *speak for* our commitments in a nonfoundational way" (p. 2, emphasis in original). I would argue—and Flower would no doubt agree—that our students, the disenfranchised among them in particular, must also continue to *speak up for themselves* in the academy. As more nontraditional and historically underrepresented students make their way into our colleges and universities, we must find ways to help them develop the critical practice of transcultural repositioning so that they can more effectively share the varied perspectives of the life worlds they bring with them into our classrooms.

One concern that cannot be avoided at this juncture in my description of WAC^2 is our seemingly naturalized use of the word "writing" in our conception of this alternative approach to WAC. If truth be told, this has remained a thorn in our sides because too many of us in the field continue to use writing to represent the act of putting words on a page rather than as a trope or a figurative stand-in—as "text" became in literary studies and "literacy" became in literacy studies—for the broader range of reading, writing and rhetorical modalities our students use in their daily lives. Just as Freire argued for the importance of "reading the word and the world," I would like to suggest that we need to argue for the importance of "writing the word and the world." As Selfe (2009) noted in her recent essay on aurality that I have alluded to several times already because of the critical role that her perspective plays in my work, students "need a full quiver of semiotic modes from which to select" as they work to address the "wickedly complex communicative tasks" that we all face in an increasingly "challenging and difficult world" (p. 645). While I have sometimes been compelled to use terms like modalities, semiotics, communicative practices and transcultural rhetorics in place of writing in the conceptual lens that Michelle has proposed (i.e., Writing Across Communities), I prefer that we rehabilitate our use of the word writing despite what I see as the greater accuracy of the various terms I listed because I am not convinced that provosts and presidents would be as likely to fund a Semiotics Across Communities (SAC) or a Transcultural Rhetorics Across Communities (TRAC) initiative as readily as they would a Writing Across Communities (WAC^2) one.

In a nutshell, then, a WAC^2 initiative argues that teachers and contexts play a critical role in alerting students to the importance of integrating the knowledge and experiences that they regularly enact in their various communities of belonging into any new social or cultural setting that they happen to inhabit (Guerra, 2008a, p. 298). Moreover, as Michelle has asserted, work by Parks and Goldblatt (2000), Flower (2008) and Long (2008), among others, is providing "a vision of WAC from the point of view of students as citizens of multiple spheres. Models that fail to connect the dimensions of human interaction with local and global environments obscure the interdependence and interrelationships integral to community development and survival" (Kells, 2007, p. 97). Although the WAC^2 approach as I have outlined its theoretical possibilities here provides an institutional framework that rationalizes our expansion of more traditional WAC approaches out into the larger public world, the challenges that proponents at UNM face in their effort to institutionalize it are, not surprisingly, difficult and multifaceted. Over the time that Michelle and her associates have worked to establish a WAC^2 program at UNM, the internal political situation they have had to contend with, as is true at any other college or university in the U.S., has been fraught with complications informed by a general resistance to change what is already in place without some guarantee that the proposed modifications will bring about lasting effect. How WAC^2 proponents at UNM have responded to this challenge is the topic of the next section.

Laying the Groundwork

According to Adler-Kassner (2008), "Change starts with individual principles— from an individual's anger, passions, and . . . *emotions*. It's about understanding one's self, and then connecting with others around one's own interests" (p. 23, italics in original). This is the same perspective that has driven Michelle from the moment she arrived on the UNM campus in the fall of 2004. Because of her prior experience organizing colloquia and symposia as a Ph.D. student at Texas A&M, Michelle knew that proponents of a WAC^2 initiative would first need to create a social space where faculty, students, staff, administrators and community members could get together and develop a set of working principles. To do so, WAC^2 proponents needed to ask each other the following three questions: "What do we want to do? Who are our allies? How can we reach out to them?" (Adler-Kassner, 2008, p. 124). As a first step, WAC^2 supporters at UNM sponsored a three-semester colloquium series designed to build a grassroots, campus-wide conversation to engage individuals from UNM and the surrounding community committed to the development of critical literacy and civic engagement with a focus on issues of ethnolinguistic diversity. After the English Department established a Ph.D. program in Writing and Rhetoric a couple of years later, new graduate students who had heard through the grapevine about the excitement brewing at UNM found their way there and immersed themselves in what everyone I have spoken with has described as an unprecedented opportunity to intervene meaningfully and productively in the reading, writing and rhetorical lives of all students, but especially what I refer to as the disenfranchised and Kells calls "the historically underserved" (2007, p. 93).

To ensure that it would have lasting power, WAC² proponents buffered their work on the ground with a set of theoretical and methodological ideas designed to help them build a provisional blueprint for engaging in institutional change. At the heart of their approach was an understanding voiced by Giddens (1976) in his theory of structuration that far from being opposed, human agency and structure presuppose each other (cited in Sewell, 1992, p. 4). As Giddens (1976) put it, institutional "structures must not be conceptualized as simply placing constraints on human agency, but as enabling" (p. 161). To bolster their approach, WAC² proponents took very seriously Sewell's discussion of the role of agency in Giddens' analytical framework. "Agency," Sewell (1992) argues, must not be seen "as opposed to, but as constituent of, structure. To be an agent," he declares, "means to be capable of exerting some degree of control over social relations in which one is enmeshed, which in turn implies the ability to transform those social relations to some degree" (p. 20).

Although neither considers their work to be directly influenced by Giddens, Miller (1998) and Porter et al. (2000) add critical elements to the frame of reference that informed the early work of WAC² proponents. On the one hand, Miller (1998) reminds us that agency must be "understood as learning how to work within extant constraints, as an activity that simultaneously preserves and creates the sense of self-worth that comes from participating in the social world." Such a perspective, he contends, provides "a sufficiently nuanced understanding of how power is disseminated in a bureaucracy to see that *constraining* conditions are not *paralyzing* conditions" (p. 211, italics in original). On the other hand, Porter et al. (2000) provide a methodology for engaging in institutional critique, which maintains that "institutions, as unchangeable as they may seem (and, indeed, often are), do contain spaces for reflection, resistance, revision, and productive action. This method insists that sometimes individuals (writing teachers, researchers, writers, students, citizens) can rewrite institutions through *rhetorical action*" (p. 613, emphasis added). As the WAC² narrative being constructed by proponents in their collective effort to establish an alternative to the traditional WAC approach unfolded, these theoretical and methodological frames of reference guided their efforts to bring about institutional change.

The WAC² story, however, is not complete without first looking back to the last time the UNM made an effort to establish a WAC program on campus. As part of the Ford Foundation's "Literacy and the Liberal Arts Program," designed "to assist institutions of higher education in developing undergraduate curricula in which the teaching of writing was integrated with the content of curricula in general" (Townsend, 1991, p. 1), the College of Arts & Sciences at UNM received funding in the fall of 1987 to establish what came to be called the Arts and Sciences Participatory Seminars (ASPS) Project. The hope was that the ASPS Project would in time mushroom into a campus-wide WAC program that would provide the kind of support all students, but especially those "students whose degree of literacy preparedness is insufficient" (p. 4), would need to thrive academically at UNM. Couched in language that likened the ASPS Project's format "to a specialized writing across the curriculum scheme" (p. 142), proposal writers at UNM outlined two short-term objectives: a focus on faculty development and the implementation of thinking-writing seminars. Their expectations were that the ASPS Project in time would increase the number of seminars offered, integrate the seminars into the core curriculum and improve students' ability to read and think critically and to write and speak cogently (p. 142). Although the outcomes as reported by faculty and students who participated were positive, the ASPS Project encountered serious challenges that led to its final demise in 1990.[7] In addition to limited buy-in from faculty and departments, a lack of publicity and inadequate information hindered student recruitment at the program's outset; that in turn led to lower than anticipated enrollment in the courses. Faculty also reported that the course had somehow "acquired the stigma that accompanies remedial preparation" (p. 150).

In contrast to the top-down efforts and the external funding that guided and supported the development of the ASPS Project, WAC[2] proponents selfconsciously established a grassroots organization and supported it through donations solicited from stakeholders on campus and in the surrounding community.[8] This tactic ensured that WAC[2] would operate independently and reflect the participation of a wide array of representatives from both on and off campus units and organizations. In their eyes, WAC[2] was also informed by a critical perspective that addressed "issues of ethnolinguistic diversity, community engagement, and teaching writing" (Kells, 2013, p. 121). This is how one of the documents readily available on their original and current UNM websites[9] describes WAC[2]'s mission:

> Writing Across Communities at the University of New Mexico supports, connects, and enhances the intellectual life of students and faculty engaged in the academic mission of creating and circulating knowledge. [WAC[2]] asserts that literacy education is both a civil right and civic responsibility. [WAC[2]] promotes student-faculty engagement through writing for the benefit of diverse disciplinary, civic, and professional communities.
>
> *Kells, 2012, n.p.*

In a talk that she gave at the 2006 International Conference on WAC at Clemson University, Michelle dug deeper into the underlying assumptions that inform the WAC[2] initiative:

- Our students arrive already embedded in complex discourse communities;
- Membership in different discourse communities is a dynamic (ever expanding and receding) process as students shift between the communities to which they already belong and those to which they seek to belong;

- Each student brings his or her idiolect and sociolect that is subject to change with contact;
- Agency in language does not begin or end in the college classroom;
- Teachers . . . serve an important role as cultural mediators between the academy, students and their home as well as their target discourse communities (n.p.).

To have a plan is one thing, to figure out a way to carry it out deliberately is a different story, but that is exactly what WAC^2 proponents at UNM have managed to do over the last 10 years.

After they outlined the parameters of their alternative to a traditional WAC program at UNM, Michelle and the graduate students that she was mentoring worked together to build a critical mass of interest in the project. To that end, WAC^2 proponents organized and promoted a colloquium series and invited faculty, graduate and undergraduate students, staff and administrators, as well as community members, to join in the process of beginning to imagine the possibilities for a twenty-first-century version of WAC. The colloquium series provided them with an opportunity to share information about where UNM students come from, what UNM can offer them in the classroom, and what students need to succeed after they complete their studies. In spring 2005, WAC^2 proponents sponsored their first colloquium, titled "Knowing Our Students," which was carefully designed to answer the following questions: What are the characteristics of the discourse communities—personal, civic, and academic—that our students bring to the university? How diverse are these practices, and how does that diversity affect curriculum and teaching? As their inaugural keynote speaker, I was charged with setting the tone for the campus-wide conversations that took place over two days of workshops and panel sessions that explored how WAC^2 could best create pathways for UNM students that would prepare them for academic work and beyond by building on what UNM faculty, staff and administrators know or can learn about them.

The second colloquium in the fall of 2005—titled "Inviting Our Students to Academic Literacies"—highlighted keynotes by Susan McLeod and Barbara Johnstone that addressed the following questions: How do disciplinary discourses at the university build on what students learn in writing courses? How can we bridge academic and community discourses to help our students enter the disciplinary communities they seek to join? McLeod's and Johnstone's talks inspired WAC^2 organizers, as well as the campus and community members who attended the various sessions, to think about the kind of WAC program the UNM would need because of its diverse student population[10] and the challenges facing the larger community. The final colloquium in the spring of 2006—titled "Preparing Paths to Professional Literacies"—looked toward the future and addressed the following questions: How can we prepare all our students for access to and success in the professional and workplace discourse communities they will enter after graduation? Two leading scholars in the field, Michael Palmquist and John Bean, were invited to engage members of the UNM community in conversations about curricular issues and the range of professional opportunities available to UNM students. In the process of building on the ideas that had emerged from the two preceding colloquia, participants in the final symposium also had an opportunity to imagine the kinds of changes that instituting a WAC^2 approach at UNM would produce. By all measures, the colloquia were a great success and generated interest across the UNM campus that persuaded many of those present to continue working together to address the personal, academic, civic and professional needs of all, but especially historically underserved students, by building on the language and cultural practices that inform their varied communities of belonging.

Propelled by the energy produced by their intimate involvement in the colloquium series and with Michelle as their faculty advisor, a core group of graduate students in the department took it a step further over the next several months and chartered a graduate student organization called the Writing Across Communities Alliance to provide a UNM recognized forum for their planning. The WAC Alliance, their abbreviation for it, became a crucible where members could share their ideas about the kinds of events and projects they thought would bring people together and push the conversation forward. Through its efforts in nurturing the well-grounded relationships and projects that members had established with stakeholders across campus and in the community-at-large, the WAC Alliance grew into a formidable graduate student organization well-equipped to provide the kind of leadership essential to sustaining WAC^2's efforts both on and off campus. In addition to establishing committees and chairs responsible for each among the array of campus-wide activities that I will describe shortly, the WAC Alliance forged relationships with various groups and units across the campus and in the wider community. In their own words, the WAC Alliance offered its members and their affiliates "a forum for conversations regarding writing, [as well as] a think tank of and for the UNM learning community" (Kells, Interview).

In their mission statement, we also find a description of the vision shared by all members of the WAC Alliance:

> We advocate active, engaged writing-to-learn processes across disciplines through innovative teaching in order to cultivate a culture of writing and inquiry. Our goal is to engage the campus in dialogue regarding writing to learn and writing to communicate while addressing accommodation of the changing needs of the student body to ensure academic as well as professional success at all levels.
>
> *WAC Alliance, n.d.b, n.p.*

Their goals are then set forth in their constitution and by-laws:

> The three main components of Writing Across Communities include civic, academic, and professional communities. The WAC Alliance seeks to

> bridge these communities and maintain communication between the various entities on and off campus while cultivating discussion and pedagogical support for diverse literacy practices across UNM discourse communities.
>
> *WAC Alliance, n.d.b, n.p.*

Because of her respect for the work that graduate students have done as members of the WAC Alliance, Michelle situates their work at the very center of WAC²'s collective enterprise: "I really see the WAC Alliance as being the soul of the conversation," she told me when we spoke. "Let a lot of this policy be appropriated, become part of the dominant structure, get a WAC office, get a WAC director. We can be vanilla flavored WAC if you will," she noted with a smile, "but you always have a counter discourse, a space for a counter discourse to evolve like a flash mob when conditions call for it. And that's what the graduate students see as their legacy" (Interview).

Since their inception, WAC² and the WAC Alliance have sponsored a plethora of events and projects on three fronts—the classroom, campus and community—to foster conditions under which an enhanced WAC program informed by their shared principles could emerge. Just as their organizational efforts are informed by the theoretical principles that I outlined in the preceding section, the products of their labor—the range of events and activities to which I will turn in a moment—are informed by their shared commitment to ensuring that language, culture and identity are always at the forefront of their efforts with the specific intention of calling on those dimensions as they are reflected among the students at UNM and as they work to cultivate in students a set of dispositions that will inform their engagement on campus and beyond as citizens in the making. Because there is not enough space and time available to do justice to all of the work WAC² and the WAC Alliance have done, in the next section, I use the words of several current graduate students that I interviewed in 2013, along with Michelle's reflections in her scholarly work, to describe the key events and activities they have sponsored over the last 10 years. Against all odds, WAC² proponents have laid the groundwork for the potential institutionalization of an enhanced approach to WAC that takes into consideration the diverse needs of students on campus and provides a network of support designed to make a difference.

Taking Action, Fomenting Change

Dan Cryer, a graduate student who arrived at UNM in the fall of 2007, was attracted by the English Department's MA program because it "was much less focused on training people to be academics and much more focused on training people to be professional writers in industry" (Interview). But after taking a graduate course with Michelle on contemporary rhetorical theory and finding out more about the WAC² initiative, Dan applied for and received a graduate assistantship available at the time for anyone interested in serving as the WAC²

Events Coordinator on a half-time basis. In that capacity, Dan—like events coordinators before and after him—was responsible for organizing one of the four civil rights symposia that WAC² sponsored between 2007 and 2011. The first symposium, titled "40 Years of Community Activism, 1967–2007," included a keynote presentation by Jacqueline Jones Royster, a highly acclaimed scholar and activist in composition and literacy studies. In her address, "Literacy and Civic Engagement: The Role of the University in Promoting Social Justice," Royster carefully unpacked and defined the three key terms in her title—literacy, civic and engagement—to provide listeners with a sense of the terms' histories and their cross relationships. In one of many telling passages pertinent to the current discussion, Royster reminded audience members that "what we know in the field of rhetoric, composition, and literacy is the inextricable linkages between literacy and social action and our obligations, therefore, to make those linkages conscious, deliberate, visible, and usable with consequence" (p. 15). Because I served as a respondent for Royster's keynote and attended the entire symposium, I was in a position to witness a very well attended series of events. I also witnessed the rich and vibrant conversations that galvanized interest in WAC²'s goals and demonstrated how much campus-wide events of this kind can contribute to bringing about authentic institutional change over the long term.

The second symposium, the one Dan put together during his term as events coordinator, extended the theme of the first one to great effect. "Civic Literacy Across Communities: A Public Forum" featured a riveting keynote address by Keith Gilyard where he laid out "a partial agenda for doing the work of needed analysis. This activity," he stressed, "involves a basic or at least beginning examination of the American political vocabulary and, in the spirit of this symposium, related examination of some of King's ideas and their continuing relevance with respect to the unfinished business of civil rights" (p. 3). In a moving tribute to the civil rights movement titled "Hate Acts, Public Rhetoric & Civil Rights Activism: 40 Years Since Dr. Martin Luther King, Jr.," Gilyard (2008) reminded members of the audience that the connection between language and public deliberation "has in a sense been the key connection of my career as I have been greatly absorbed with the project of how best to interpret language in the public sphere, how to examine its effects relative to educational and social equity, how to produce it, how to help students wield language skillfully both in production terms and in hermeneutic terms" (p. 1). The final two civil rights symposia— "Significant Voices: Women on Equal Rights and Sexual Justice" and "Mental Health and the Community: Conversations about Civic Literacy and Social Justice"—were less directly related to composition and literacy studies, but each in its own way vividly demonstrated WAC²'s commitment to social justice issues that continue to play a critical role in the local, regional, national and international experiences of UNM students.

During our interview, Dan told me that WAC² events like the civil rights symposia bolstered his commitment to addressing social justice issues. The values embodied in WAC², he declared toward the end of our conversation, "are not just on my radar now; they're becoming part of my identity as a teacher, as a scholar, as a citizen, and just generally as a human being in my everyday life" (Interview). Dan's leadership role in WAC² has also led to his involvement in critical projects sponsored by the Office of the Dean of the College of Arts & Sciences. These institutionally-sanctioned projects may well serve as the groundwork for WAC²'s transformation from what Dan described as "a scrappy organization" made up of individuals who fancied themselves "iconoclasts" to an institutionally-recognized and university-funded program at UNM (Interview).

Because it was clear to WAC² proponents that they needed to organize additional events that would bring together faculty, students, staff, administrators and community members to discuss various aspects of their plans to institute a locally-informed WAC initiative, WAC² proponents also organized campus-wide events where the immediate needs of first-year students as readers, writers and rhetoricians could be addressed. In the fall of 2005 as part of what they came to call WAC Week, for example, WAC² proponents launched the *Write On! Workshop* (or *WOW!*). In Michelle's words:

> The idea was to jump start a writing center without walls. So in collaboration with staff from the tutoring center on campus, we invited all the Core Writing students who were getting ready for their portfolios at the end of the semester to drop in at the Student Union Building (SUB) and get some feedback on their work. That day we had more than 200 undergraduate students lining up and down through the SUB for this drop-in lab in a small space with pizza boxes everywhere. And we invited the local slam poets to come and entertain the students in line while they waited to meet with TAs, faculty, and guest speakers available to sit down and chat with them.
>
> *Interview*

Because WAC² and the WAC Alliance have sponsored the Write On! Workshop event every year since then, they have provided mentoring support for and have greatly enhanced the attitudes toward writing of thousands of UNM students in a very short time. The Write On! Workshop event has also provided WAC² and the WAC Alliance with name recognition and the opportunity to engage the UNM community in work that will no doubt benefit the eventual institutionalization of WAC² on the UNM campus.

The *Celebration of Student Writing*, another first-year student-oriented event initiated at UNM in the fall of 2009 by members of the WAC Alliance to kick off Freshmen Week, has annually attracted between 600 and 900 students. Interestingly, the Celebration of Student Writing came about when Linda Adler-Kassner—who visited the UNM to give a keynote address as part of the Writing Assessment Colloquium sponsored by the WAC Alliance in April 2009—mentioned how successful a similar event had been on her previous campus at Eastern Michigan University. According to Genesea Carter, the WAC Alliance member who originally proposed that UNM sponsor a similar event, then worked hard to make it a reality, "the event encourages participants to use skills acquired beyond the classroom by giving them the option to write through art, music, video and interactive art installations" (quoted in Gray, 2011, n.p.). A blog kept by the WAC Alliance describes the event in this way:

> While many resources are directed toward upper-class and graduate students, the *Celebration* sends a message to first-year and beginning students that their voices, ideas, and research will be valued *throughout* their time at UNM. In addition, *Celebration* promotes civic literacy shared among communities. It seeks to create public spaces in which conversation, debate, and learning is encouraged, and it helps to create opportunities for conversation that defies institutional and disciplinary boundaries between students, instructors, and administrators.
>
> *WAC Alliance, n.d.a, n.p., italics in original*

The range of activities that Carter describes engages students in multimodal experiences that give them an opportunity to showcase and highlight the varied ways in which language and culture inform the range of identities they perform through their work. The activities also encourage students to engage members of real audiences as citizens in the making outside the safety of their classrooms and in the more volatile public spaces provided for them in the SUB.

The efforts of WAC[2] proponents in the classroom have also addressed the needs of first-year students in ways that reinforce the kinds of linguistic, cultural and semiotic reshaping that campus-wide events have attempted to create. Much of it has happened in an array of graduate seminars that Michelle has offered in response to issues that have emerged in the course of WAC[2]'s work. Over the last 10 years, for example, Michelle has designed graduate seminars on writing program administration, environmental rhetoric, ideologies of literacy and tutoring college writing that have served as think tanks where graduate students, but especially WAC Alliance members, could learn and test new ideas. In the environmental rhetoric course, for example, Michelle and her students teased out the principles that inform a writing across communities approach as well as the role that a cultural ecology model plays in that process. The seminar on tutoring college writing, on the other hand, helped them seed the eventual formation of a writing and language center as part of UNM's tutoring center. Michelle has described it as one of a handful of writing centers[11] in the country right now "that actually tutors in languages other than English, among them Navaho, Danai, Spanish and Portuguese" (Interview). Together, Michelle and WAC Alliance members have also enhanced an alternative version of the first-year writing course offered in the English Department's Core Writing Program by adding a WAC[2] orientation to it.

One of the more interesting endeavors taking place now is reflected in the work of two WAC Alliance members, Brian Hendrickson and Genevieve García de Mueller, who have developed an intermediate expository writing class on civic engagement that bridges the classroom and the community in very productive ways. From the moment they both arrived at UNM in the fall of 2010, Brian and Genevieve have been interested in teaching a course that combines "community-based research and community-based assessment in one class" (García de Mueller, Interview). As Genevieve describes it, the course they are developing is designed to serve as a practicum to teach students "the kinds of things we expect them to do in the community, a way to approach the community, a way to interact with the community, before they venture out to establish a service learning connection" (Interview). It is also designed to train students to assess their own work as writers in a community setting by having them

> think about what they value about writing, about the kinds of past experiences they bring to their writing that makes them value certain things in a particular way. We also want students to reflect consistently about why they're thinking the way they're thinking in terms of writing, in terms of composition. We also think that may help them learn to transfer those skills to other areas of their lives.
>
> *García de Mueller, Interview*

Brian and Genevieve are also exploring the possibility of using the course to prepare students to serve as tutors at the Albuquerque Community Writing Center (ACWC), another project that several WAC Alliance members have pursued.

From the time he arrived at UNM in the fall of 2010 to pursue a Ph.D. in Writing and Rhetoric, Brian had a second idea in mind: "I was thinking, wouldn't it be cool if the University could have a writing center that's open to the public and is actually somewhere off-campus? And maybe it's even mobile. Maybe you go places, you work with other organizations" (Interview). When he shared his idea with Erin Penner Gallegos, a member of the WAC Alliance at the time, Brian learned that Michelle had already taught a graduate seminar focused on establishing a community writing center and the group had already drafted a plan for one. As a consequence, Brian reported, "We started an advisory board that fall and got a pilot project going that spring. Over the summer it got launched" (Interview).

After earning a master's degree in Literature, Film and Theatre Studies at the University of Essex, Genevieve decided to return home to Albuquerque's South Valley to teach at her former high school. She remembers the idea of the writing center as something that grew partially out of her effort to "push for some sort of student engagement in the community." Initially, Genevieve told me, "we thought about having our undergraduate students volunteer at the ACWC, so we thought about creating a course" that would prepare them to do just that. Instead, WAC[2] proponents chose to set that idea aside momentarily and worked to "put together an advisory board to think about what the community needs. We invited community members, we also talked to representatives of the library system in Albuquerque" (García de Mueller, Interview). In the end, members of the advisory board decided that for now they would continue to have graduate students in the WAC Alliance serve as writing tutors at the ACWC, a practice that has been reduced considerably in the last year while they look for ways to reinvigorate the project and provide students in intermediate writing classes an opportunity to work there as well.

At the heart of the work that WAC^2 proponents have been doing on campus, in the classroom and in the community is their fundamental belief that protecting our civil rights requires us to become civically engaged. Their approach to civic engagement, however, is a bit more complicated and contested than the one-way direction apparent in many service-learning programs. For them, civic engagement is not simply defined as something one goes out to do for others or does to gain insight into one's self. In reflecting Wan's (2014) call for a form of citizenship that is not limited to service-learning practices, they conceptualize it as an everyday part of life as well: "You don't want to devalue the kinds of things that students are already doing," Genevieve notes. "They're civically engaged every day. They might not be doing the kinds of things that we think of as civic engagement, but they are civically engaged at home talking about politics, talking about issues, trying to get their families to do certain things" (Interview). Civic engagement is also something that students don't have to leave campus to experience. For example, Genevieve pointed out,

> the Celebration of Student Writing? That's engaging with a certain community, that's engaging with freshmen and teaching them how to engage the campus community and talk about their own writing and literacy practices. That's a form of civic engagement because we're asking them to do certain kinds of things which could be seen as political things because they're taking a stance on writing.
>
> *Interview*

At every level of the work they do together, members of the WAC Alliance continue to build on many of the ideas that I shared in the first part of this book. Their ultimate goal is always to find ways to contribute to the cultivation of students as citizens in the making by integrating the language and cultural practices they regularly call on in their communities of belonging and the tools they acquire in the writing classroom each time they engage the challenges of everyday living. Above all, WAC^2 aims to provide all students at UNM, but especially the disenfranchised among them, with opportunities to connect their experiences in the classroom and the campus to their other communities of belonging through various reading, writing and rhetorical activities they undertake in the personal and public spheres that inform their lives.

Beyond the Arts of Appropriation and Cooptation

Arguably the biggest challenge WAC^2 proponents face at this juncture is deciding whether to sustain their insurgency/social movement indefinitely, or make
a push to institutionalize WAC^2 and integrate it into UNM's very DNA. No
matter what happens eventually, they all see a continuing need to maintain an
insurgency/social movement perspective in one form or another. Christine García, who arrived at UNM in the fall of 2009 after earning a master's degree at
Angelo State University in west Texas, sees great value in the tactical nature of
the work the WAC Alliance has been doing and laments its potential loss:

> Graduate students will lose their think tank and their connection to the
> community and the events that we help to organize and host. And people
> who have a lot more power than we do will be making the decisions.
> Right now, we're making the decisions. It's a graduate student chartered
> organization, and it's ours.
>
> *Interview*

In Brian's view,

> it's more possible now [to establish a WAC program] than it's been before
> because we have a new [university] president who's really into connec-
> tions between student engagement and student success and retention. I
> think there's an opportunity for institutional buy-in, for changing policy
> on campus writing.
>
> *Interview*

At the same time, Brian thinks that

> there is always going to be a need for the WAC Alliance or the Writing
> Across Communities initiative, or something else. There will always be a
> need for somebody who will continue to trouble those waters, continue to
> advocate for a more radical perspective. I don't see *that* becoming institu-
> tionalized anytime soon.
>
> *Interview*

After 10 years of what Michelle described in our conversation as "all of the
vicissitudes of four complete administrative turnovers from president to dean and
chair, four times, that's every two years since I've been here" (Interview), definite
signs have emerged that some form of WAC is now on the brink of becoming
institutionalized. Whether it will be a traditional WAC, or the more capacious
WAC^2 initiative that its proponents have envisioned, is not yet clear. There are,
however, plenty of signs that WAC^2 proponents can point to that suggest the

latter trajectory. To begin with, two of their annual events—*Write On! Workshops* and the *Celebration of Student Writing*—have been incorporated into the Core Writing Program in the English Department that oversees all first-year writing classes. "They're taking our events and institutionalizing them," Christine reported telling WAC Alliance members at a meeting in the spring of 2013 while she was serving as Events Chair. "That means that our events have been successful. Since we don't have to fund them or organize them anymore, our fall and spring are wide open, so let's go for it. Let's go further into the community. Let's keep envisioning new things" (Interview). No matter what happens, Brian realized, "we're still going to have a particular kind of student population. Because of where we are in terms of socioeconomic, political, and racial issues, these are conversations that are going to continue to happen regardless. And they're going to continue to push up against the institution and demand that it take these kinds of conversations seriously" (Interview). Michelle's remarks on this issue parallel Christine's and Brian's:

> We should let a lot of this policy be appropriated, become part of the dominant structure, get a WAC office, get a WAC director. We can be vanilla flavored WAC, if you will, but we must always have a counter discourse, a space for a counter discourse to evolve like a flash mob when conditions call for it.
>
> *Interview*

Another sign that a WAC program is now a strong possibility is reflected in the fact that a number of WAC[2] proponents have participated in formal campus-wide and top-level administration-driven efforts related to first-year students enrolled in writing and content classes across the disciplines. Six years ago, for example, New Mexico State Secretary of Higher Education Peter White appointed Michelle "to chair a task force for the purpose of discussing the strengths and weaknesses of the University of New Mexico core curriculum" (UNM's Core Curriculum Task Force, 2010, n.p.). As Dan noted in our conversation, "Michelle's involvement with Writing Across Communities, I think, was one of the big reasons that Peter White tapped her. He could've asked anyone at the university but he asked her, and I think that's a big reason why" (Interview). Comprised of more than two dozen faculty, staff, administrators and students from across the UNM campus, the Task Force established 5 subcommittees that did research on and talked about educational values, educational models, student learning outcomes, transfer students and Writing Across the Curriculum. As important as the report it produced proved to be in addressing immediate concerns, the Task Force also made a lasting contribution to other efforts at UNM initiated by current President Robert Frank and Provost Chaouki Abdallah, among them the Foundations of Excellence (FoE) self-study of the first year experience at UNM sponsored by the John Gardner Institute. Although the FoE report is not available for public release, a description of the self-study on the Provost's website highlights many of the same issues that WAC[2] proponents have been promulgating:

> The primary outcome of this project was an evidence-based action plan for institutional change and improvement that will be implemented in order to increase the quality of the first-year education experience. We expect this to produce improved retention rates for our freshman class, place students on a solid trajectory toward graduation, and demonstrate national leadership in the area of student academic success.
>
> *John N. Gardiner Institute, n.d., n.p.*

Closer to home, Michelle, Dan and several other WAC Alliance members also participated in a pilot project called Writing Intensive Learning Communities (WILCs) in 2012–2013 administered by the Department of English, the College of Arts & Sciences and University College, the latter a unit on the UNM campus that functions as "the port of entry for almost every beginning student at the University of New Mexico and is committed to helping students engage in academic life and succeed in attaining admission to a college, an undergraduate education, and a degree" (University of New Mexico, n.d., n.p.). Together, these units have been working to develop a range of course pairings "in which both courses are focused on teaching the habits of mind and writing conventions of a specific field" (Cryer, 2013, p. 4). Typically, a WILCs pairing brings together an English 102 research course taught by a Writing Fellow—during the pilot project, all of the Fellows were WAC Alliance members—and a 100- or 200-level course that introduces a particular discipline. Their short-term goal, informed "by a belief that a wide-ranging and sustained conversation about the communication practices and habits of mind in and across majors can markedly improve our teaching and our students' learning," is to establish WILCs within the regular menu of Learning Communities offered to students at UNM. Their official long-term goal is to "deliberately and thoughtfully plan approaches to the teaching and assessment of writing across disciplines, as well as offer support to faculty who must produce written scholarship to earn tenure" (Cryer, 2013, p. 4). Unofficially, as Dan noted in demonstrating the influence of WAC[2] on WILCs,

> there is a push at UNM from Writing Across Communities and other places to include diversity outcomes as part of the curriculum. . . . We want our classes to be our learning communities, to be one of the places on campus where students get different points of view and acknowledge them as different points of view. But not just different disciplinary points of view, although that is part of it, but acknowledging the power differentials in different points of view, what LEAP[12] scholarship calls difficult

difference—those things that are difficult to talk about like racial, gender and socioeconomic differences.

Interview

As Miller (1998) notes in *As if Learning Mattered: Reforming Higher Education*, scholars in the academy have repeatedly made the mistake of assuming that because it is an institution, the university is not only resistant to change but automatically coopts every progressive effort to institute a particular kind of change that it may find troubling. Instead, he argues, we should see "every educational program as being the product of a series of complex, contradictory, compromised, and contingent solutions whose permanence is never assured" (p. 8). This approach, Miller contends,

> reveals that any bureaucratic decision about who should receive an education, in what form, at what cost, and to what end is susceptible, over time, to considerable—if slow-moving—revision. Indeed, by attending to the play between the policy statements and the enacted pedagogical practices of the administrators, curricular planners, teachers, and students, one finds a place where individuals acting alone and collectively have an opportunity to express their agency, albeit in the highly restricted realm of relative freedom.

p. 8

My reading of the story that WAC^2 proponents have shaped over the course of the last 10 years suggests that they are intimately aware of how slowly the academy as an institution moves to acknowledge the value of their work and how important it is to keep pressing forward knowing that when the institution finally decides to integrate the practices they have been advocating into its very fabric, these practices will be transformed yet again. At the same time that they are willing to grant the institution the opportunity to absorb their work and integrate it into its existing practices, WAC^2 proponents hope to sustain what Michelle earlier referred to as "a counter discourse, a space for a counter discourse to evolve like a flash mob when conditions call for it" (Interview). Interestingly, the overall work of WAC^2 proponents also represents a simultaneous acceptance of and challenge to the role played by what Miller (1998) describes as the *intellectual-bureaucrat*—a hybrid persona that he argues will in turn "produce an academic environment that rewards versatility as well as specialization, teaching as well as research, public service as well as investment in the self" (p. 212).

Whether or not literacy insurgents at UNM, who have battled to establish a WAC^2 initiative at UNM, eventually morph into Miller's intellectual-bureaucrat is not as important as the work they continue to do. In this regard, as Adler-Kassner (2008) reminds us repeatedly in *The Activist WPA*, anyone engaged in writing program administration must inevitably address three critical questions: "How are students' literacies defined when they enter our classes? What literacies should be developed in those classes? How should those literacies be assessed when students leave our classes?" (pp. 26–27). The work that WAC² proponents have undertaken over the last 10 years at UNM reflects an effort on their part to address these very questions. At the heart of their response to the first question is an undeniable respect for their students' language and cultural practices: a desire to create conditions in the classroom, campus and affiliated communities that will provide students with opportunities to shape identities of their choosing, and a commitment to participate in the critical cultivation of citizens in the making. Early on, Michelle noted, WAC² proponents obtained a small seed grant from the International Writing Centers Association to conduct research "on the language varieties and attitudes of first year students at UNM." Armed with that information, Michelle and her colleagues set out to change the "deficiency narrative that existed when [she came to UNM] into a sufficiency narrative" (Interview). WAC² proponents also agreed that limiting the focus to academic discourse would not provide students with the repertoire of rhetorical and discursive practices they would need to function successfully outside of the academy in personal, professional and civic contexts. The literacies taught in class, then, would have to prepare them for civic and other forms of engagement in and beyond the academy as well. Brian and Genevieve's work on training students to assess themselves is clearly one of several efforts designed to ensure that students understand the way in which what they are learning can transfer to other contexts.

In the midst of the new academic year that began after my April 2013 interviews of the various individuals I cite in this chapter, all signs point to a strong commitment shared by top-level administrators that the time to establish a new WAC program at UNM has arrived. But a number of challenges still remain. Above all are the jurisdictional issues that have to be addressed in a highly-decentralized institution like UNM. As Dean Peceny noted:

> Dealing with these thorny issues of inequity and citizenship and building ties across communities, these are all the things that the Writing Across Communities model as opposed to the Writing Across the Curriculum model [is] struggling with in trying to figure out how to build that into our curriculum. So I find that compelling because it's exactly what we need to do as an institution and across all dimensions of the scholarship we engage in and the way we teach our students. Although the vision is compelling, it's really complicated to figure out how to implement the vision. And the part that's been especially difficult for me is the old-fashioned jurisdictional questions.

Interview

Like Michelle and other WAC² proponents, Dean Peceny has come face to face with the limits of his own authority when the goal is to establish a campus-wide initiative. Still, he is committed to doing what he can to make it a reality:

> I see our challenge being how do we take Writing Across Communities which has been a social movement or an insurgency trying to change the way we think about our business as an institution and institutionalize that, make that a part of the standard operating procedures of bureaucracy and budget lines at the university. That probably needs to happen at the Provost level, but I'll figure out everything I can to use the resources of the College of Arts & Sciences to help make that possible.
>
> *Interview*

In developing a methodology that action researchers can use to engage elements of their institutions of higher education in a concerted effort to bring about the kind of change that will make a difference for both the students that writing programs serve and the broader community, Porter et al. (2000) sum up the work of institutional critique in the following manner:

- Institutional critique examines structures from a spatial, visual, and organizational perspective.
- Institutional critique looks for gaps or fissures, places where resistance and change are possible.
- Institutional critique undermines the binary between theory and empirical research by engaging in situated theorizing and relating that theorizing through stories of change and attempted change (pp. 630–631).

Although WAC² proponents have not self-consciously engaged in institutional critique using the methodology Porter et al. (2000) describe, there is no question that they make implicit use of the various strategies Porter et al. argue must be implemented. Over the course of their work they have undertaken at UNM, for example, WAC² proponents have made tactical and strategic use of Michelle's graduate seminar classes and the WAC Alliance's think tank to undertake research-based activities in their collective search "for gaps or fissures, places where resistance and change are possible." They have also made every effort to disrupt "the binary between theory and empirical research" by using the data produced through these projects to create a series of powerful stories that reflect their effort to intervene meaningfully and productively in the institutional apparatus that informs their everyday rhetorical and discursive practices in the academy and beyond. Above all, they have used their critique to challenge the structure of traditional WAC programs in making their case that UNM can only achieve its stated goals by instituting a WAC² initiative.

Although there are still a number of tasks to be done, among them, identifying someone to serve as the director of a WAC program and establishing a campus-wide Writing Advisory Council, the mold has now been set. As Michelle put it at the end of our conversation, "We've been waiting for the Messiah for [almost 10] years now. According to Marty Townsend, it takes about 7 years after you have the infrastructure in place to get WAC going. In that respect our clock hasn't even started yet because we still don't have a director" (Interview). For those of us looking in from the outside, it certainly appears that the work WAC² proponents have undertaken at UNM has set the stage for the establishment of a writing initiative that will not only build on what LeCourt (1996) and other scholars have been arguing for years; it will transform the local institutional landscape in ways that not even the most optimistic among them could have ever imagined.

Notes

1. Although the preceding chapter focused specifically on the ways in which language, culture and identity can be addressed in the single writing classroom, this chapter shifts the focus to the challenges of institutionalizing and sustaining a campus-wide program that would not only house a series of such courses but would also provide students with broader opportunities to participate in personal and public spheres on campus and beyond designed to cultivate their development as citizens in the making. The story that this chapter tells highlights the ongoing challenge of establishing such a program when most of the dimensions I discussed in Part I—language, culture, identity and citizenship—lie dormant in most institutions and need to be activated by enacting and sustaining the kinds of institutional change suggested in this chapter.
2. In an effort to make a distinction between Writing Across the Curriculum and Writing Across Communities, both of which employ the same acronym, proponents of Writing Across Communities have used several shorthand identifiers, among them WAC 2.0, WACommunities, and WAC² (i.e., WAC to the second power). Because it seems the least clumsy and intrusive of the options available, I have decided to use WAC²—a version Marty Townsend popularized during a visit to UNM in 2013—as the acronym of choice for Writing Across Communities in this essay. When I am citing an official document or one of the participants in the case study, however, I use whichever term they used in speech or print. Like everyone else in the field, I continue to employ WAC as an acronym for Writing Across the Curriculum.
3. Actually, Mahala (1991) gives an even harsher critique of WAC when he argues the following: "By deflecting attention from consideration of the social effects of curricula and pedagogy, from positivist attitudes that denigrate student language and knowledge, from the full diversity of discursive practices that constitute the work of the academy, WAC theory has circumvented conflict, but also mitigated its potency as an agent for change" (p. 786). Because McLeod and Maimon (2000) alluded to the value reflected in LeCourt's critique and chastised Mahala for what they considered an overly critical perspective of how ideology has negatively influenced WAC, Mahala's critique never picked up much traction in the way that LeCourt's did. Villanueva (2001) also offers a piercing critique, pointing out that "WAC . . . . has tended to be assimilationist, assimilation being a political state of mind more repressive than mere accommodation" (p. 166). More recently, Anson (2012) describes the general absence of the subject of racial and ethnic diversity in the historical context

of WAC's focus on student development as puzzling (p. 17). The literature spanning three decades of WAC history, he notes, gives "little or no voice to the complexities inherent in addressing the diversity of students in the classrooms and programs where WAC is implemented and how their diverse backgrounds and experiences affect teaching, learning and assessment" (p. 19).

4. In the course of gathering data for this case study, I interviewed more than a dozen faculty, graduate students and administrators at UNM affiliated with efforts to establish WAC^2 on campus. There are, of course, a significant number of other graduate students—some of whom are still affiliated with WAC^2 and many who have left UNM—that have played key roles in the writing initiative's development over the years but who for obvious reasons were not interviewed and will not be named in this work. For that reason, this work—like everything else done to advance the WAC^2 cause—is dedicated to their commitment to making a difference in the lives of historically underserved students at UNM.

5. After I introduce Michelle Hall Kells, Dan Cryer, Christine García, Brian Hendrickson and Genevieve García de Mueller the first time around as participants in this case study, I use their first names only to signal the intellectual intimacy that they continue to share to this day as members of WAC^2. Because he officially stands outside of WAC^2, I use Mark Peceny's title as Dean of the College of Arts & Sciences to signal the institutional formality of his relationship to the aforementioned. All the names I use, by the way, are real rather than pseudonyms.

6. During my interviews, Michelle and her colleagues generally used the acronym WAC even when they were referring to Writing Across Communities because they had not yet settled on an acronym that would differentiate it from Writing Across the Curriculum. Whenever the context suggests that they are referring to Writing Across Communities during the interviews, I will insert the acronym WAC^2 in brackets to remind readers that they are referring to Writing Across Communities rather than Writing Across the Curriculum.

7. Although it is beyond the scope of the present discussion to ponder the details of this failed project, work on the demise or reconstitution of writing programs by Severino (1996), Fleming (2011) and Lamos (2011) describes in detail the institutional challenges that writing programs have faced over decades as their proponents battled against a range of challenges that I suspect played a role in the failure of the ASPS Project and continue to inform the difficulties that WAC^2 proponents have had in implementing their program over the last 10 years as well. It bears mentioning that as a basic writing teacher for 15 years in the Educational Assistance Program at the University of Illinois at Chicago that Severino (1996) describes in her essay, I was centrally involved in fighting against the institutional forces that eventually led to the program's demise.

8. One of WAC^2's greatest strengths has been its ability to raise funds through grants from campus units to the tune of almost $100,000 over the last 8 years to support public events. In addition to the four civil rights symposia that I describe here, WAC^2 also sponsored a "Writing the World Symposium: A Regional, Interdisciplinary Conversation on Literacy, Ecology, and Social Justice" twice (2012–2013) and student-oriented events that have attracted hundreds of students, among them the Write On! Workshops (a writing center without walls that attracts hundreds of students in first-year writing courses to the Student Union Building to get feedback on their work) and the Celebration of Student Writing (which gives hundreds of first-year students an opportunity to showcase their writing in the SUB through a visual representation of their work). I describe these later in this section. There have also been several other events that space does not permit me to describe.

9. If you would like to review any of the WAC^2 documents cited in this section, you can access them through the Writing Across Communities website available at the following UNM link: www.unm.edu/~wac/History-Legacy/background.htm

10. According to the UNM's Office of Institutional Analytics (2013), student enrollment at the main campus of the University of New Mexico at Albuquerque during the 2012–2013 academic year consisted of 41% White, 38.1% Hispanic, 5.7% American Indian, 3.2% Asian, 2.5% African American, 3.6% International, 2.5% two or more, 0.2% Native Hawaiian/Pacific Islander and 3.2% no response (p. 2).

11. In keeping with the growing awareness that the writing needs of multilingual students who create texts in languages other than English must be addressed, more and more colleges and universities are expanding their resources at writing centers to provide support. Among them are the Institute for Writing and Rhetoric at Dartmouth College (http://dartmouth.edu/writing-speech/multilingual-support), the Multilingual Writing Center at Dickinson College (www.dickinson.edu/academics/resources/writing-program/content/Multilingual-Writing-Center) and the University Center for Writing-based Learning at DePaul University (http://condor.depaul.edu/writing/what/Writing%20Center/wc.html).

12. The Association of American Colleges and Universities' LEAP (Liberal Education and America's Promise) Outcomes are: (1) Knowledge of Human Cultures and the Physical and Natural World; (2) Intellectual and Practical Skills; (3) Personal and Social Responsibility; and (4) Integrative and Applied Learning. According to Dan, because UNM has responded effectively to the first three, the focus of their recent work has been on finding more effective approaches to integrative and applied learning.

References

Adler-Kassner, L. (2008). *The activist WPA: Changing stories about writing and writers.* Logan, UT: Utah State University Press.

Adler-Kassner, L., Crooks, R. & Watters, A. (Eds.). (1997). *Writing the community: Concepts and models for service-learning in composition (vol. 1).* Washington, DC: American Association for Higher Education.

Anson, C. M. (2012). Black holes: Writing across the curriculum, assessment, and the gravitational invisibility of race. In A. B. Inoue & M. Poe (Eds.), *Race and writing assessment* (pp. 15–28). New York, NY: Peter Lang.

Bawarshi, A. (2003). *Genre and the invention of the writer: Reconsidering the place of invention in composition.* Logan, UT: Utah State University Press.

Bazerman, C. (1992). From cultural criticism to disciplinary participation: Living with powerful words. In A. Herrington & C. Moran (Eds.), *Writing, teaching, and learning in the disciplines* (pp. 61–68). New York, NY: Modern Language Association.

Cryer, D. (2013). Report on the writing intensive learning communities pilot project for fall 2012. Retrieved from www.unm.edu/~wac/files/ReportOnWILCs_Dec2012_FebUpdate.pdf

Deans, T. (2000). *Writing partnerships: Service-learning in composition.* Urbana, IL: NCTE.

Downs, D. & Wardle, E. (2007). Teaching about writing, righting misconceptions: (Re)envisioning "First-year composition" as "Introduction to writing studies." *College Composition and Communication, 58*(4), 552–584.

Fleming, D. (2011). *From form to meaning: Freshman composition and the long sixties, 1957–1974.* Pittsburgh, PA: University of Pittsburgh Press.

Flower, L. (2008). *Community literacy and the rhetoric of public engagement.* Carbondale, IL: Southern Illinois University Press.

Giddens, A. (1976). *New rules of sociological method: A positive critique of interpretive sociologies.* London, UK: Hutchinson.

Gilyard, K. (2008). *Composition and Cornel West: Notes toward a deep democracy.* Carbondale, IL: Southern Illinois University Press.

Goldblatt. (2005). Alinsky's reveille: A community-organizing model for neighborhood based literacy projects. *College English*, 67(3), 274–295.

Goldblatt, E. (2007). *Because we live here: Sponsoring literacy beyond the college curriculum.* Cresskill, NJ: Hampton Press.

Gray, A. (2011). Beginning writers make words jump off page. Daily Lobo.com. Retrieved from www.dailylobo.com/index.php/article/2011/10/beginning_writers_make_words_jump_off_page

Guerra, J.C. (2005, April). Creating pathways to academic literacy and beyond: Situating the personal, professional, and political. Keynote presented at the Writing Across Communities: Literacy and Diversity Symposium, University of New Mexico, Albuquerque.

Guerra, J.C. (2008a). Cultivating transcultural citizenship: A writing across communities model. *Language Arts*, 85(4), 296–304.

Guerra, J.C. (2008b, Feb.) Excerpts from the dark side: Rethinking our terms of engagement in classroom and community settings. Keynote presented at the National Council of Teachers of English Assembly for Research Mid-Winter Conference, Indiana University, Bloomington, IN.

Guerra, J.C. (2009, March). Cultivating transcultural citizenship: A call to self-dissension. Paper presented at the Conference on College Composition and Communication, San Francisco, CA.

John N. Gardner Institute for Excellence in Undergraduate Education. (n.d.). Foundations of excellence final report. Retrieved from http://provost.unm.edu/academic-planning/foundations-of-excellence.html

Kells, M.H. (2002). Linguistic contact zones in the college writing classroom: An examination of ethnolinguistic identity and language attitudes. *Written Communication*, 19(1), 5–43.

Kells, M.H. (2004). Understanding the rhetorical value of *Tejano* codeswitching. In M.H. Kells, V. Balester & V. Villanueva (Eds.), *Latino/a Discourses: On language, identity and literacy education* (pp. 24–39). Portsmouth, NH: Boynton/Cook.

Kells, M.H. (2006a). *Héctor P. García: Everyday rhetoric and Mexican American civil rights.* Carbondale, IL: Southern Illinois University Press.

Kells, M.H. (2006b, March). Writing across communities: Diversity, deliberation and the discursive possibilities of WAC. Paper presented at the meeting of the Conference on College Composition and Communication, Chicago, IL.

Kells, M.H. (2007). Writing across communities: Deliberation and the discursive possibilities of WAC. *Reflections*, 6(1), 87–108.

Kells, M.H. (2009, March). Discursive democracy, civic literacy, and the unfinished work of the civil rights movement. Paper presented at the meeting of the Conference on College Composition and Communication, San Francisco, CA.

Kells, M.H. (2012.) National consortium of writing across communities. Retrieved from www.unm.edu/~wac/files/2012-NCWAC-Summit_Program_Final.pdf

Kells, M.H. (2013). Out of WAC: Democratizing higher education and questions of scarcity and social justice. In C. Wilkey & N. Mauriello (Eds.), *Texts of consequence: Composing social activism for the classroom and community* (pp. 117–156). New York, NY: Hampton Press.

Lamos, S. (2011). *Interests and opportunities: Race, racism and university writing instruction in the post-civil rights era.* Pittsburgh, PA: University of Pittsburgh Press.

LeCourt, D. (1996). WAC as critical pedagogy: The third stage? *Journal of Advanced Composition*, 16(3), 389–405.

Long, E. (2008). *Community literacy and the rhetoric of local publics.* West Lafayette, IA: Parlor Press.

Lu, M.-Z. (2004). An essay on the work of composition: Composing English against the order of fast capitalism. *College Composition and Communication*, 56(1), 16–50.

Mahala, D. (1991). Writing utopias: Writing across the curriculum and the promise of reform. *College English*, 53(7), 773–789.

Mathieu, P. (2005). *Tactics of hope: The public turn in English composition*. Portsmouth, NH: Boynton/Cook.

McLeod, S.H. & Maimon, E. (2000). Clearing the air: WAC myths and realities. *College English*, 62(5), 573–583.

Miller, R.E. (1998). *As if learning mattered: Reforming higher education*. Ithaca, NY: Cornell University Press.

Office of Institutional Analytics. (2013). UNM Fact Book. Retrieved from http://oia.unm.edu/documents/factbook_docs/2012fb_updated.pdf

Parks, S. & Goldblatt, E. (2000). Writing beyond the curriculum: Fostering new collaborations in literacy. *College English*, 62(5), 584–606.

Peceny, M. (1999). *Democracy at the point of bayonets*. University Park, PA: Pennsylvania State University Press.

Porter, J.E., Sullivan, P., Blythe, S., Grabill, J.T. & Miles, L. (2000). Institutional critique: A rhetorical methodology for change. *College Composition and Communication*, 51(4), 610–642.

Reiff, M.J. & Bawarshi, A. (2011). Tracing discursive resources: How students use prior genre knowledge to negotiate new writing contexts in first-year composition. *Written Communication*, 28(3), 312–337.

Rogers, R. & Fuller, C. (2007). "As if you heard it from your momma': Redesigning histories of participation with literacy education in an adult education class. In C. Lewis, P. Enciso & E.B. Moje (Eds.), *Reframing sociocultural research on literacy: Identity, agency, and power* (pp. 75–113). Mahwah, NJ: Erlbaum.

Selfe, C.L. (2009). The movement of air, the breath of meaning: Aurality and multimodal composing. *College Composition and Communication*, 60(4), 616–663.

Severino, C. (1996). An urban university and its academic support program: Teaching basic writing in the context of an "urban mission." *Journal of Basic Writing*, 15(1), 39–56.

Sewell, Jr., W.H. (1992). A theory of structure: Duality, agency and transformation. *American Journal of Sociology*, 98(1), 1–29.

Townsend, M.A. (1991). Instituting changes in curriculum and teaching style in liberal arts programs: A study of nineteen Ford foundation projects. Unpublished doctoral dissertation, Arizona State University.

University of New Mexico. (n.d.). About university college. Retrieved from http://ucollege.unm.edu/about.html

UNM's Core Curriculum Task Force. (2010). Final report. Retrieved from www.unm.edu/~wac/CCFT/Core2010/CCTF_FinalReport_5–15–10.pdf

Villanueva, V. (2001). The politics of literacy across the curriculum. In S. McLeod, E. Miraglia, M. Soven & C. Thaiss (Eds.), *WAC for the new millennium: Strategies for continuing writing-across-the-curriculum programs* (pp. 165–178). Urbana, IL: NCTE.

WAC Alliance. (n.d.a). Welcome to the University of New Mexico's celebration of student writing. Retrieved from http://celebrationunm.wordpress.com/

WAC Alliance. (n.d.b). Writing across communities (WAC) alliance constitution and by-laws. Retrieved from www.unm.edu/~wac/old_site/alliance/bylaws.htm

Wan, A. (2014). *Producing good citizens*. Pittsburgh, PA: University of Pittsburgh Press.

Waterman, A.S., (Ed.). (1997). *Service learning: Applications from the research*. Mahwah, NJ: Erlbaum.

Weisser, C. (2002). *Moving beyond academic discourse: Composition studies and the public sphere*. Carbondale, IL: Southern Illinois University Press.

Yancey, K.B. (2001). WPA outcomes statement for first-year composition. *College English*, 63(3), 321–325.

INDEX

Note: Entries in **bold** refer to tables.

CPSIA information can be obtained
at www.ICGtesting.com
Printed in the USA
FFHW011858091118
49329096-53601FF